ONE MAN'S LIFE—
PACKED WITH ENOUGH
DANGER TO FILL THE LIVES
OF A HUNDRED MEN!

12-year-old Robert Scott designed and built a home-made glider—and walked away from his first crash. A year later he bought an old Jenny for $75 and taught himself how to fly.

One of the greatest careers in American aviation had begun.

GOD IS MY CO-PILOT is his electrifying account of his wartime adventures; piloting a Flying Fortress over the Atlantic through equatorial storms; fighting the Japanese virtually single-handed over Burma; battling the enemy in the skies of China.

"A record of persistence, determination and courage . . . an inspiration to Americans of all ages."

—C. L. Chennault

GOD
IS
MY
CO-PILOT

This story is dedicated to the man who, more than any other person, is responsible for the Air Force coming of age—GENERAL HENRY H. ARNOLD, Chief of the United States Air Forces.

BY

ROBERT L. SCOTT, JR.
Colonel, Air Corps, United States Army

With A Foreword By
MAJOR GENERAL C. L. CHENNAULT

BALLANTINE BOOKS • NEW YORK

ISBN 0-345-25279-9

Manufactured in the United States of America

Paperbound Edition
First Printing: May 1956
Twenty-second Printing: November, 1976

First Special Printing: January 1976
Second Special Printing: March 1976

contents

Foreword by Major General C. L. Chennault

foreword

The author, Colonel Robert L. Scott, Jr., served under my command from July 1, 1942 to January 9, 1943 as Commander of my fighter force. The only criticism of his actions as Group Commander was that he consistently scheduled himself as a pilot on all possible missions. He led all types of combat missions but specialized in the most dangerous, such as long-range flights to strafe from minimum altitudes Jap airdromes, motor vehicles, and shipping deep in enemy territory. It was often necessary for me to forbid his participation in combat missions in order to enable him to discharge the many other duties of a Group Commander.

His story is a record of persistence, determination, and courage from early boyhood. Having determined early in life that he had to fly, he overcame all obstacles in the way to the attainment of his ambition. This story alone should be an inspiration to every American boy. Having become a military pilot, his determined struggle to meet the enemy and his glorious record, first as a "One Man Air Force," and later, as Commander of the American Fighters in China, should be an inspiration to all Americans of all ages.

Colonel Scott's group of fighters always operated against greatly superior numbers of the enemy. Often the odds were five to one against them. Their planes and equipment were usually battered by hard usage, and supplies were extremely limited. Both Scott and his handful of pilots had one resource in unlimited quantities—courage. They also possessed initiative and a never-failing desire to destroy the enemy. They wore themselves out doing the work of ten times their number. They demonstrated time and again that American pilots and planes are superior to the Japs. The results which they achieved prove indisputably that the enemy can be destroyed or driven from China if adequate equipment and supplies are made available. The offensive spirit displayed by Scott and his early pilots lives on in the men who replaced them. They impatiently await the weapons needed to drive on into the heart of Japan and to final victory.

C. L. CHENNAULT,
Major General A.U.S.,
Commanding, 14th Air Force

author's note

My decision for the title of this book was probably made back there in Kunming one afternoon as the doctor dug those five rivet heads from my back. They had been driven in when a Jap explosive bullet hit the armor plate behind my seat. To keep my mind off the pain the big Cantonese intern of Doctor Manget's kept talking to me. He seemed to find it hard to believe that I flew the little fighter alone—that I dropped the bombs—fired the six machine guns—changed the fuel tanks—navigated and landed the fighter. Finally, with disbelief in his eyes, he looked at me and said, "Colonel, you are up there all alone—you even talk over the radio when you shoot the guns?" As I waited for him to go on with another question, I heard the old doctor say, "No, son—you're not up there alone—not with all the things you come through. You have the greatest co-pilot in the world even if there is just room for one in that fighter ship—no, you're not alone."

I believe when this war is over that we will be closer to God than at any time in the past. I believe this because I have seen instances of real faith on several fronts in this war and have heard of them on all fronts. Take for instance: Just the other day a song came out, "Coming in on a Wing and a Prayer." That could have been conceived as a title or as the theme of the song only by some real event. A ship landed with an engine shot away—the fuselage gutted by fire and the plane riddled with bullets. One of the war correspondents hurried out to the wounded pilot and asked, "How in the world did you bring this ship in . . .?" The pilot shook his head, smiled and replied, "I don't know—ask the Man upstairs."

We who fly are going to get to know that Great Flying Boss in the sky better and better. My personal ambition is that He permit me to go again into combat against the Jap or the Hun; that He help me just a little to shoot down a hundred Jap ships—even a thousand. Then I hope He lets me come back to tell another story. I'm going to name that one—the sequel to this one—GOD IS STILL MY CO-PILOT.

R. L. S.

GOD IS MY CO-PILOT

1
I Knew What I Wanted

EVEN THE angels in heaven must have shrugged their wings after the few seconds of my first flight. For back home in Macon, Georgia, in 1920, I must have been, even at age twelve, the "vandal" type. There I climbed the steeple of the Baptist Church, and from the belfry took twelve whitish pigeons, carried them to a tent-meeting of Holy Rollers, and at the tense moment of fanatic prayer released them. I can remember nearly splitting my sides laughing at what happened—the congregation was rolling on the sawdust floor. They were rolling their eyes and yelling, "Gideon, Gideon—halleluiah—glory, glory!" I suppose the pigeons really did look like doves of peace.

But I had reckoned without the old preacher, who had me arrested for disturbing the noisy peace. When I got out of jail, more embarrassed than anything else, I swore vengeance on the Holy Rollers and the old preacher. Early one morning while delivering papers I took a razor blade and cut off fifty feet of canvas from the side wall of the converted circus tent—took it away and hid it in the woods.

I had no use for the purloined canvas, and to excuse myself from a nagging conscience I tried to forget it. But every morning I saw the jagged hole that I had made for vengeance. Later on I decided to build a glider, and for wing-covering the canvas was ideal. Then, with the cloth stretched over the ribs of the airfoils and varnished for tightening, even with American insignia painted on the fuselage, I found myself ready to fly. Two of my friends helped me pull it to the roof of a high colonial home in Macon, and with them steadying the wings I ran down the sloping roof and flew out into space. Now in those days I knew nothing of "main-spars," "center sections," or "wing-loading." With a crack like the closing of the jail door, the wing buckled in the center and I crashed sixty-seven feet to the ground. The Cherokee rose bush—that sacred State flower of Georgia into which I fell—probably saved my life, but the thorns stayed with me for a long time.

After my father had pulled me from the wreckage—more scared than hurt—I was ordered to tear the glider apart. I did, but saved the ill-fated canvas for other plans. Later on it was used to cover the barrel-stave ribs of a home-made canoe

1

which was intended to transport me down the Ocmulgee River to the sea, some twelve hundred miles away as the winding river ran. I had made about six hundred miles of the trip when the sailing canoe caught on a snag and the current rolled us to the muddy bottom, tangled in the rope rigging of the sail. In the seconds that followed I nearly drowned—I saw my whole misspent life parade before my eyes. Finally the rope broke and I swam ashore; but I had already decided to leave the sacred canvas, seasoning forever, at the bottom of the Ocmulgee River.

Once again my mind turned to flying. I confined my aircraft construction to scale models, and finally made a flying one which won the first Boy Scout Aviation merit badge in that part of the country. I remember when General Mitchell (Billy Mitchell) led a flight of fast-looking MB-3's through the home town. I crawled into one of the baggage compartments in hopes that I would be flown on to Florida in this dawn-to-dusk flight. But the mechanics found me, and I missed making the pursuit ship any tailheavier than it normally was.

It was far back, when I was four or five, that I had seen my first airplane. A pilot by the name of Ely spun in and was killed, and my horrified mother dragged me from the scene. It most certainly should have been an ill omen for my flying future. However, I know that it whetted my appetite to fly. I liked anything that flew and freed one from the earth, but most of all I prayed that destiny would make me a pilot of the fast, little single-seaters—a fighter pilot.

In 1921 I read of an auction sale of war-time Jennys in Americus, Georgia. Gathering the largest fortune that I could collect, I drove my cut-down, Model-T racing Ford to buy myself a real plane. As the auctioneer's hammer hit the block for the first time that morning I opened with my maximum bid—Seventy-five dollars! The auctioneer did look my way, but the look was merely a frown. Far in the back of the hangar a heavy voice called, "Six hundred dollars." And to this fat man the Jennys went, one by one. I must have bid over a hundred times before the morning had gone—the sale had stopped for lunch and had been resumed.

That afternoon I kept bidding, and as I said "Seventy-five dollars" for about my hundredth time, I heard heavy breathing over my right shoulder. I turned to look at the man who had been overbidding me, and the deep voice said, "Now listen, son, I'm going to let you have this one for your seventy-five dollars. Get it and get the hell out of here, because I'm buying all the rest for an airline." Anyway I had a real plane, all crated up. I hauled it home on a truck, hid it in another boy's garage so my parents couldn't find out about it, and began trying to assemble the parts.

For days and weeks I worked, but couldn't get the knack of it. Finally I received a letter from a street-car conductor who said he had been a pilot in the war. He offered to help me put the Jenny together, and teach me to fly and navigate, if I would give him use of the plane for "barnstorming" over the State on weekends.

The partnership began. He taught me some fundamentals, like taxying faster and faster until the ship was almost ready to take off. I went to Candler Field in Atlanta and took several lessons with the instructors there in Eagles and Jennys, until one day I trusted myself to take off from the racetrack of my home-town fairgrounds. I still don't see how I got by with the flight, because I knew nothing about co-ordination of controls or the technique of flying—though no one seemed to know much about them in those days. But the ship was a pretty safe old crate, the wing skids saved me from digging a wingtip in on the forthcoming groundloops, and I got away with murder.

All of this ended very suddenly. The street-car conductor instructor of mine came back to land one night and hooked the Jenny's right wing on the guy-wire of a smokestack. That was the last of him and the last of my Jenny, because they both burned.

As the years went on I moved up in the Boy Scouts until at seventeen, in 1925, I was one of the highest in the country, and had more merit badges than any other Scout in the South. With all of them, however, my schooling had suffered, for to me flying and athletics came before books and such. I sometimes think the only way I ever completed high school was for my patient mother and father to promise to let me work my way to Europe on freighters in the summer only when I could pass studies like Spanish and English. I don't think, though, that my parents knew I had resolved to go to West Point. For after talking to men in the Air Corps I had discovered that if a boy went to the Training Center at Brooks Field, near San Antonio, as a Flying Cadet, his future was rather indefinite. The Government would train you to fly, give you the best course in the world. Then they would order you to active duty as a Reserve Officer for about a year. After that, due to economy programs, it might all be over.

Wanting to fly for the rest of my life, I had charted my course. I resolved to go to the Military Academy and become a regular army officer first; then to be ordered to the Air Corps Training Center as a student officer. After completing the flying course, I would have a lifetime in front of me as a pilot in the Regular Army.

The greatest fight I had was to get into the Military Academy, for appointments were scarce in the South. I wrote all the Senators and Congressmen in Georgia, but found they had promised their quotas long before. All such refusals merely made me more determined to win the opportunity. I wrote not only my own State political leaders but those of other States. Finally, the Congressman of my Georgia district—at the earnest plea of home-town friends who knew of my Boy Scout record—gave me second alternate. This proved of little value; the principal won out by merely presenting his high-school credits and passing the physical examination. The next year I was given a first alternate from a Senator but again the principal won.

Hope of entering the Academy seemed to wane, for I was approaching maximum age limit for applicants. The same year I tried a competitive examination with the National Guard, but failed the algebra subject. This failure at least proved to me that though my studies in high school may have been passed, I had learned very little. My stock in myself was at a low ebb, there in 1926, when the high-school principal did me the greatest favor in the world by his remark: "Well, you really didn't expect to get to West Point did you?" And the smile that accompanied the slur made me swear that by all that was high and holy I would get there.

The things that followed were chronologically peculiar for any boy. I'll bet I'm one of the few in this world who was graduated from high school, attended two colleges, and then returned to high school to really get the foundation I had missed. I know I had at last learned that what one of the old professors said was right: "Not for school, but for life, we learn."

Returning to my old high school, I chose my own courses and subjected myself to several periods of mathematics, history, and English every day. The professors, who remembered me as seldom opening a book, glanced at one another as though they thought they had a psychopathic case on their hands. But I acquired some of the knowledge I had missed, and the next

4

summer—June, 1927—I went to Fort McPherson and enlisted in the Regular Army as a private. There I became Private Scott, Serial Number 6355544, in Company "F" of the 22nd Infantry. Three months later, after a preliminary examination, I began training in the Fourth Corps Area—West Point Prep School. I really put in six months of study there, for there were some eight hundred of us soldiers trying in competition for about fourteen vacancies. As luck would have it that year, these fourteen were cut to eight. Once again West Point seemed a long way off. I got down to business then; I would shut myself in my room and almost memorize the lessons, especially every old West Point examination as far back as 1920. The study bore fruit. I kept at the top of the class and in March took the dreaded examination.

One day, some weeks after the annual competition for entrance from the Regular Army, I was walking guard duty. I was called from Post Number One, around the guardhouse; I had just heard the familiar call, "Number One—two prisoners," and had replied "Turn 'em in." The General had sent for me. As I stood before him my heart felt as though it would beat out through my blouse. He smiled and spoke.

"Son, you have won in the West Point competitive examination and I want to tell you you're starting out on the same road I started out on a long time ago. It's the greatest school in the world—but learn some common sense too. I'm sending you on furlough until you report for duty at the Military Academy. Congratulations."

The world was never so sweet. I gained two inches in the chest that day.

Thus, in July of 1928, I walked through the sally port with my suitcase and began the routine that is familiar to nearly everyone. I had heard of the strict discipline of West Point and the difficulty of studies for one handicapped by a Southern accent. My year of hard work had made me hate books again, but I resolved that after the work I had gone to I most certainly would not be kicked out or "found," as we say in Kaydet slang. I remember my father's ambition for me. He was of course proud of my appointment, and used to wonder why I didn't rank about number one in my class. During my Plebe year, which was easy because I had just about learned the first year's work at the prep school, he used to write and tell me that while it wasn't too disgraceful to be number fifty in a class of over three hundred, he couldn't see why I didn't study a little more and get up into the first twenty. Well, as the first year went by and I got into the more difficult studies, I went lower and lower in a class that dwindled finally to some two hundred and sixty. During the last year, when I was very far down, Daddy would write:

"You just stay there, Son, just stay there."

I still heard the planes flying over and try as I would, I could concentrate on nothing but the Air Corps.

In 1930 I wrote an essay on flying, and it almost got me kicked out. You see, in Military History you have to write a monograph on the strategy employed in one of the major battles of the world. I had always liked military history and had been in the first section of that subject. (At the Academy each student is in a section commensurate with his scholastic standing.) My presence in that group permitted me to choose my battle. I had had a grandfather killed at Bull Run, and I therefore selected the first Battle of Manassas.

There was, as usual, many a slip. Before I was able to write the story we were permitted to travel to the West Coast to play Stanford in football. Coming back under the chagrin of defeat, I did not bother to open my books, believing that even West Point would not expect a student to recite within one hour of his return from California. But I reckoned without the rigidity of the Academy. Our train arrived across the Hudson at Garrison at 6:55, and we marched into History at 7:55. I was immediately assigned to recite on the battle of Valmy. I did not know what war it was in, and therefore knew nothing concerning it. To say that and get a zero, however, would be fatal and in fact could mean disciplinary action. I therefore resorted to the time-worn West Point tactics of evasion—known as "bugling."

Going to the blackboard with an air of confidence, I stood at attention with pointer in hand and began, "Sir, my duty for today is to explain the battle of Valmy. Napoleon declared after this engagement that the forces of an army must be concentrated for battle . . ." At that instant the professor stood up and said he would wait five seconds for me to begin the recitation correctly. I tried again and was ordered to sit down.

The zero I received dropped me from the first section to the last. Furthermore, I found immediately that in this last section the subjects for monographs were not selected by the cadet, but were assigned. The new instructor gave me the battle of Sandepu—some insignificant engagement in an insignificant war. I looked for days in the library for data on the battle, and finally found about one paragraph devoted to it in the *Encyclopaedia Britannica*. It was Sandepu, Haikoutai, or Yen

6

Kai-Wan, fought during the Russo-Japanese War of 1904-05.

A person with my imagination and initiative, I reasoned, would simply waste his talents on such a small battle. I therefore decided to create a fictitious battle. This extra work mattered not, for I had nothing but time, having been placed in confinement for getting the zero in history. I worked out an elaborate plan for the battle and introduced the subject in a manner that I knew would attract attention to even a last-section monograph. I dedicated the work of art to the officer in charge of Field Artillery, Lieut. Pete Nuby—a contraband nickname of a very tough officer. I illustrated the monograph with pictures of New York street cleaners and wrote under them that they were Japanese soldiers waiting to go over the top at the River Ho in 1905. Lastly I tied the book in red ribbon at least six inches wide, completed with a bow larger than the monograph. I doomed myself in the last paragraph by saying that I had dreamed I had observed the battle, but had been awakened by reveille, which, as Napoleon declared at the battle of Maloyaroslavetz, is a hideous noise in the middle of the night. All of which went to prove, I contended, that history could be made in sleep, and it therefore did not require an "engineer" to be a historian.

For the story of Sandepu, I imagined that I went down to a Southern city to inspect the Army's first aircraft. This was a free balloon—the latest invention of 1905. Becoming weary, I went to sleep in the basket of the balloon. But a storm must have torn the craft from its moorings, for when I looked down I was being blown to the East across the Atlantic. For days we drifted over ocean and continents, until, coming close to the hilly ground, I used the first air-brakes ever known. They were composed of one mile of government red-tape and the anchor worn by the captain of the "goat" team of 1904. (This was readily interpreted by the professors, for the traditional football game of the year is one played between the first thirty men in the Second Class, called the "engineers," and the last thirty men, known as the "goats." I was of course in the last thirty; I had been Goat Captain, and had worn the anchor sewn on my football jersey.) These improvised airbrakes worked, and the anchor caught on a hill which I identified from maps as the hill of Chan-tan Honan—the theatre of the Russo-Japanese War. From this vantage point, swinging in the balloon, I watched the two armies in battle. Merely rank facetiousness, I admit, but even then I was completely air-minded.

I was reported for submitting a facetious monograph in

military art and for casting reflections on the Engineering Department. For this offense, I was brought before a board of four officers, known as the Battalion Board—or, as we called it, the "Batt Board." My explanation was that I knew, after being dropped from the first section to the last in one recitation, that I must have inferior intelligence. I therefore had no chance of writing an interesting and worthy monograph on the material of the actual battle, and accordingly I had decided to make my battle fiction, and so interesting that it would be read completely instead of merely being graded according to the tradition of the last section—that is, either barely passing or below. I argued that I had evidently accomplished that purpose for my grade was perfect.

This explanation had just about won the Batt Board around to my side when one of the Board members—a stumpy little officer noted for his preciseness, called behind his back "Fanny" Macon—asked me: "Mr. Scott, I see your point about making the monograph interesting. But what is the red ribbon for, what does it represent?" I looked at him almost with pity. "Sir, how long have you been in the Army?" "For seventeen years," he said, intimating that it was none of my business. Even then I think I could have saved the battle, but the opportunity was too imposing. "Well, Sir," I said, "in that time you certainly should know about military red tape."

The Batt Board agreed unanimously that I should walk the Area one year. For all that, I finally graduated—even if it was just about as the anchor man.

2

Bumpy Landings

IN THE SUMMER of 1932, after being graduated and commissioned a second Lieutenant of Infantry, I went to Europe. In Cherbourg, France, I bought a motorcycle and set out to ride to Constantinople. The one-cylinder Soyer took me down through Paris, then Southeast into Switzerland, and over the Simplon Pass to Italy. I spent some time in Venice; then I went up through the dust into Yugoslavia.

One day I had ridden some four hundred miles into the town of Novo Mesto. Tired and dirty from the heavy dust of the roads, I went to the best-looking of the hotels, and after some delay in making myself understood among Serbians and Croatians, I ordered beefsteak. During the explanation I gathered that somone who lived there in the town spoke English. This of course was pleasant news, for I was, after all, a lonely tourist in a very foreign land. They now sent a small boy to bring back this connecting link between us. I waited and waited, while they all pointed and jabbered about me. Finally the steak came, and got cold while my mouth watered, but I felt I had to wait and ask the American if he would eat with me. At last there was a commotion at the entrance, and I turned anxiously to see my American friend.

Through the door waddled a dark, dirty little man—evidently a former fruit-vendor in New York. He saw me, stopped his Croatian talk, threw out his arms. To my discomfiture the only English he seemed to know was a few words of profanity. But I halved my steak with him and patted him on the back as he tried to talk, and in the end I guess his compatriots really thought their friend spoke American anyway. I could hear them calling me Americanski.

I continued on, keeping clear of the tourist routes, and finally, after a forty-five day trip from Cherbourg, I rode into Constantinople. Here I came close to getting in a real jam. Back through my life I had concentrated on scouting, archery, and flying—anything but girls. I could remember crossing the street to keep from having to talk to them. But that real bashfulness was far behind me. Now I had about gone to the other extreme; I had found dates in Paris, Venice, and other cities, and had had a fine time.

Before reaching Turkey, I had been warned by the head of the American Express in Sofia that I should be very careful in Istanbul and should confine myself to the Americanized Turks in and around the Pera part of the city. They told me above all to stay clear of Galata—the old Greek and Turkish section. As luck ruled, however, my first acquaintance was from Galata, and that night I headed for the city of the veiled women.

Well, even with right ideas the men in that quarter had the wrong idea. I saw the danger just in time, and even then I had to jump through a window—glass and all—into an alley. I can hear the yells even these years afterwards as I ran through Galata back to Pera for my motorcycle. Stopping at the hotel just long enough to check out, I was off in more dust for Scutaria and East in Asia to Ankara.

So raising the veil of a Moslem female shortened my stay in Constantinople. Even in my return to the West from Ankara, I found a way to dodge the city on the Hellespont by getting a Black Sea steamer and crossing North of Instanbul to land at Varna in Bulgaria. From here I crossed the Danube at Rustchuk and went to Bucharest.

My spirits had risen a little after missing the Turkish knives in Galata, but here I found a cablegram awaiting me. The Comptroller General had ruled that the Economy Act of June, 1932, affected all officers on leave. He had decided that I, like many others, was on leave without pay. My orders were to report to the nearest American Embassy for duty; I remember that they were signed by McColl. I sent my champagne back and ordered beer, for the money for this trip had been borrowed against my three months' leave pay. Here I was, thousands of miles from home and Randolph Field, where my flying training would start. If I reported to some ground officer in Europe, I would probably never get to fly.

Anyway, just to make sure, I hopped on my motorcycle that night and headed for Texas by way of Budapest—Linz—Bingen-on-the-Rhine—and Paris. I sold the motorcycle in Cherbourg and boarded the *Bremen* for a quick trip home. I had used pay that I was expecting to get during leave, and I'd be paying the bank for a long time. But I resolved right then and there that I would pay that money back from the Air Corps at Randolph Field and not from some desk in an Embassy.

And so I came at last to the Air Corps Training Center at Randolph Field, Texas.

It's hard to describe my feelings as I walked into the North gate of that field and down the nearly mile-long road to the Bachelor Officers Building, where I was to report. It seemed that all my life I had waited for this moment. Now at last the great day was at hand when I would begin my government flying training. There above me against the blue Texas sky I could see the roaring airplanes in their Army colors. As my feet carried me into the field I could hear the rhythm of the steps seeming to say in cadence, "This is it! This is what I've waited for all the days of my life!"

In October, 1932, I was assigned to Lieut. Ted Landon for primary flying training. I imagine this assignment was about as momentous for him as it was for me—for after all I must have been quite a problem, with all I thought I knew about flying and the eagerness with which I approached military aviation. Though I had flown before in the prehistoric crates of the past, this fact had nothing to do with whether or not I would get through the course. On the side against me was the fact that during my unsupervised flying I had doubtless developed many faults that were not for the Army pilot to be proud of. In a case like mine, some pilots think they know it all; therefore there is nothing to learn. Others make such an effort to please their instructors that this very eagerness works against them as their own worst enemy—the result of tenseness.

My case was more of this last order. I knew I could fly the ship but I tried to carry out my instructor's orders even before he gave them. I listened almost spellbound through our oral communications system in that primary trainer—that speaking-tube which we called a "gosport" and which at best was hard to understand over the rattle of that Wright Whirlwind engine. I used to try to read his mind, execute his every little whim. I even tried to outguess Lieutenant Landon and have the stick and rudder moving in the right direction before he could get the orders out of his mouth.

Now thereby hangs a tale. I was not only trying to look in his rear-view mirror and actually read his lips when I couldn't hear through the gosport, but was diligently looking about the sky for other harebrained student pilots. He must have realized my eagerness, for he gave me every break—and for the many boners I pulled I needed lots of breaks.

One day, at a bare four-hundred feet altitude, I thought I heard the instructor say, "Okay, Scott, put it in a dive." I peered around first and then at the nearby ground, for it looked very low to be going into a dive. Then like a flash I thought I understood: Why, he's trying to see if I'm ground-shy—I'll show him I'm not.

With my teeth clenched and probably with my eyes closed, I pushed that PT-3 into a vertical dive at point-blank altitude. Just as the cotton fields down below seemed about to come right into my lap I felt Ted Landon grab the controls and saw him hastily point to his head with the sign that he was "taking over." We came out just over the mesquite trees, and he roughly slipped the ship into a bumpy landing in a cotton field. Then, while I was trying to add things up and realizing already that I had tied it up again, I saw Ted very methodically raise his goggles and with great deliberation climb out of the front cockpit. He glared at me but said sweetly enough:

"Scott, what in blazes are you trying to do—what was that maneuver? I said glide—G-L-I-D-E. Don't you at least know what a normal glide is in all this time?"

Weakly I said, "Sir, I thought you said a dive." I could see Ted fight for control; then he told me the next time I had him at an altitude so low, not to attempt to think but just try to keep the ship straight and level.

On another day, after about two weeks of instruction, we had been making only take-offs and landings, and I knew the time was approaching when I would solo. As usual, that realization made me more and more tense as the end of the period neared. On the take-offs I'd tense up and forget all about holding the nose straight, and on the landings I'd jerk back on the stick instead of easing it slowly back into the approach to landing stall. All I could do was day-dream about: Here we are, Scott, just about to take over and prove to the world that we can do all of this by ourselves.

Around the field in traffic I couldn't hold the correct altitude, and my instructor was cussing a blue streak. He'd yell about my having graduated from West Point and say that he knew I was supposed to have some brains but he hadn't been able to find them. After each bumpy landing he'd look around at me and hold his nose—that was symbolic enough for me. I finally bounced into another landing that nearly jarred his teeth out. Then, as usual, he showed what a prince of a fellow he was, and showed me that an instructor had to become accustomed to students' making mistakes—knowledge which stood me in good stead years later when I became an instructor.

Lieutenant Landon got out of the front seat, taking his parachute with him, and I knew the moment of moments had come. As he leaned over my cockpit and reached inside the ship for the Form One, the time-book always carried in Army ships, I saw only his hand and thought he was offering to shake hands with me. So I grabbed the hand and shook it. He just grinned and growled:

"With landings like those I can do you very little good, and I'm not going to let you kill me practising. Do you think you can take this thing around the field all by yourself and get it back down?"

"Yes, Sir," I yelled.

"Then take it around and make a landing as close to me as you can."

I had never felt so good. Taxying out I could see the world only in a rosy light. My head was really whirling. Pointing the ship into the wind, I over-controlled into a normal student take-off and was in the air. Honestly, the living of this life was wonderful—here I was an actual Army Pilot with my own ship, and up here free from the shackles of the earth. I envied no one. Circling in traffic I'd "get my head in the clouds" and gain or lose altitude but that didn't matter. I was soloing.

Then, at the fourth leg of my traffic pattern, I began my glide in towards Lieutenant Landon. By the gods he had said, "Land as close to me as you can," and I was surely going to make that ship stop right by him—I wouldn't have my instructor being ashamed of his student. Even before I got to the moment to level off, I could see that I would land right on top of him. But the Lieutenant was running, throwing his parachute away just to get clear of a student who had really taken him literally.

Anyway, I missed him and plunked the ship into the ground after levelling off too high. Well, I held it straight and there was no ground-loop. As it stopped I breathed again, and I could feel the smile that cracked my face. A pilot! I had landed the ship and it was actually in one piece!

Looking back over my shoulder I saw Lieutenant Landon. He was just standing there about a half mile away. Then I made another mistake. He raised his hands and I thought he waved me in—I didn't know until the next day that he had been shaking his fist at me for trying to land right on him.

So I taxied in, never giving a thought to how my instructor was going to get in with his chute—you see, Randolph is a big field and I had left him more than a mile from our hangar. I had parked the plane and was in and beginning to dress when I began to realize what I had done. Looking out the window I could see him trudging across the hot soil of Texas, in the sun, with ships landing all around him. My Lord, I had tied it up again! I tried to get my feet back into my flying-suit, tripped and fell, got up and ran out of the hangar door. I guess I was going to take the ship and taxy out and pick him up. But I had lost again—the ship was being taken from the line by the next student. I just stood there with sinking heart as he came up. But he didn't even look my way, except to say, "It's kinda hot out there." Then he just glared and threw his chute in his locker.

Well, I nearly worried myself to death that night. I knew he'd more than likely tell me after the next day's ride that I was the damnedest student he'd ever seen, and that I didn't have a prayer of making a pilot. But next day he didn't say a word. All day I started to go over and tell him how sorry I was, but I guess I didn't have the nerve.

My time came to ride with him. We went out over the rolling hills of Texas, went through our chandelles and Lazy 8's—spins and stalls—shot a few landings. Then, as we put the ship down on Randolph Field, he taxied to the exact spot I had left him the day before. Looking back at me he said sweetly:

"Scott, you were kinda inaccurate in your landings yesterday. You get out and watch me. I'll show you what I wanted."

Getting out with a puzzled expression, I stood aside. First he pointed the tail at me and ran the ship up full gun, blowing Texas dust all over me. Then he took off and came around to land. Three times he did this, each time making me run like hell to get out of the way. Just as I was completely out of breath he landed, looked back at me, and began to taxy in to the hangars—leaving me to the long, hot walk across Randolph Field with the parachute.

I shall never forget the smile he wore as I trudged in past him where he sat smoking a cigar. His look spoke volumes, though he said nothing. I felt good, too, and happy. He could have used no better method to make me relax, to make me feel as though I had actually joined the brotherhood of Air Corps pilots. Next day I soloed again, but definitely remembered to taxy over and take him back to the line with me.

3

84,000 Miles of Girl-Trouble

DURING MY FLYING training, I had girl trouble, too. You would no doubt call it "trouble," but I knew it was the real thing. I had a Chevrolet then, and every week-end I just had to see my girl, even if she did live over thirteen hundred miles away in Georgia. To get to see her, I would drive that thirteen-hundred-odd miles to her college or her home in Fort Valley, spend anywhere from ten minutes to two hours with her, then jump back in the car and drive madly for Texas and the Monday morning flying period. I always had to delay my start until after Saturday morning inspection. That meant that I had to average just about fifty-four miles an hour, even counting the time I saw the girl, in the forty-seven hours that I had from after inspection on Saturday to flying time at eight o'clock Monday mornings!

Week-end after week-end I drove madly across the South from the middle of Texas to the middle of Georgia. On one of these cross-country dashes, I weakened and was fool enough to ask the Commandant of Student Officers if I could go to Atlanta. I can still see and hear Capt. Aubrey Strickland saying, "Atlanta what?" And me meekly replying, "Atlanta, Georgia, Sir." He just said, "Hell, no," and I turned and walked from his office with the good intention of obeying the order.

But within the hour I had weakened. I filled my rumble-seat tank, which held fifty-five gallons of fuel, and was off to see her for the short time available. (Yes, she was, and still is some girl.) On the return trip I burned out two bearings near Patterson, Louisiana. Jimmy Wedell, one of the well-known speed flyers, helped me to get it fixed after I explained the predicament I was in. But even with five of us working on the number one and number six bearings of the Chevy, I was twelve hours late getting back to Randolph Field.

As I walked into the bachelor officers' quarters that I shared with Bob Terrill, I expected any minute to hear the sad news. But I was too afraid to ask for details, so I just waited for Bob to say, "You are to report to the General tomorrow for court martial for A.W.O.L. in violation of specific instructions." Finally he put down his letter writing, looked at me almost in disgust, and broke out:

"Scott, you're the luckiest man that ever lived! You didn't get reported today. No! This is the first time in the history of Randolph Field that it's been too cold to fly. And it wasn't only too cold to fly, it was too cold to have ground school, because the heating system had failed. We haven't flown today, we haven't been to ground school. So they don't even know that you've been over there to see that girl."

In all of these trips to see my girl over in Georgia, I drove 84,000 miles. I wore out two cars—and you'll probably agree that her father had full right to say to her: "Why don't you go on and marry him? It'll be far cheaper than his driving over here every week-end." But I found that I still had some talking to do.

When I had finished Primary and Basic training at Randolph, I almost let down my hair and wept, though, on the day that Commandant of Student Officers called over and said that now I could have permission to go to Georgia, to see my girl. I thanked him and went, but I of course didn't have the heart to tell him that I had been heel enough to go many times before, in secret.

At Kelly Field we moved into the old quarters of that World War field and began the last phase of our student flying. Once, after one of the cross-country flights to Brady, Texas, and back, I arrived over Kelly Number Two—an auxiliary field about ten miles west of Old Kelly—and decided to have some fun with my P-12 by making landings in all directions on the empty field. I dove down across the field to see that no other ships were there. Beginning from the proper direction, I made a landing to the North, then one to the South, one to the East, and one to the West.

But about that time a P-12 No. 1 screamed down over me and I saw a man waving his hand. I saw the hand and saw the pilot there, too, but I merely thought it was one of my classmates coming back from Brady. So I pulled up close to the ship and slashed across its tail in a mock attack, then went down and made another landing, bouncing across the rough field downwind. No. 1 dove down again—and then I realized that it was Lieutenant Gaffney, the head of all pursuit pilots, and that he was motioning me to come home. So I sheepishly followed him back to Kelly Field and landed.

When I taxied up even the mechanics looked funny. One of them came over and said, "Lieutenant Gaffney wants to see you." So I went on in to him and he was raving mad! I have never seen a man in such a rage in my life.

"I don't mind my students taxying around like you were and landing from all points of the compass," he said, "but when I come down and try to tell them to come home and they wave at me—well, I quit. Now you go over to the hospital. I want you to get a physical examination and see what's wrong with you."

Well, I didn't know what was wrong myself, but instead of going to ground school that afternoon, I had to go to Duncan Field to the hospital, and had to wait about two hours before the Major called me into his office. He said, "Scott, are you married?" and I said, "No, Sir." He looked at me a minute and said again, "Scott, are you married?" And again I said, "No, Sir." He walked around the room a while; then he looked at me again and said, "Are you married?" and I said, "No, Sir."

Then I realized what this was: he was giving me a psychoanalysis. And I said, "Well now, look, Major, I know what you are trying to do—I don't think there is anything like that wrong with me anyway."

"What have you been doing this morning?" the Major wanted to know. So I told him the whole story, about making the landings in different directions.

"Has anybody over there got anything against you?" And I said, "No, Sir, they haven't got anything against me—I probably don't catch enough hell, for I do some queer things, but

16

in this case I was just out trying to train myself to land down-wind and cross-wind." So after we talked it over, the Major gave me a piece of paper which went like this: "Lieutenant Scott is physically and mentally qualified to perform in the Arm of Service that he has chosen." I carried the affidavit with me for years because I always say I can prove that I'm not insane. I don't know whether it works or not, but my wife still keeps it.

Well, when graduation came at Kelly and I had those wings pinned on my chest, I had the wonderful feeling that I had gone a little way towards the goal I wanted. I was at last an Army pilot. Never did the world seem so good. And then out of a clear sky came orders for me to go to duty in Hawaii. That was pretty bad because I wanted to get married before I went out of the country, and as yet the girl hadn't gotten her degree from college. Probably if I had gone to Hawaii, I would have figured out some way to have flown a P-12 back over every week—but I didn't have to do it after all.

The Chief of the Air Corps came down a few days later and I waited until he had had lunch in the Officers' Mess. Then I walked over and said, "General, can I ask you a question?" "Sure, sit down," he said, and I told him the whole story—and I made it like this: "General, I know that I'm supposed to go where I'm sent because I'm in the Army, but I've got a girl over in Georgia, and I think I can do a lot better job wherever you send me if you can give me time to talk her into marrying me." He didn't appear to be very impressed at first, but he took my name and serial number, and two or three days later, when he got back to Washington, I was ordered to Mitchel Field, New York.

As I drove my car towards my first tactical assignment I kept reaching up to feel my silver wings on my chest—I wanted to prove that it wasn't a dream. This was what I had been working for since 1920. Now I was actually riding towards the glory of tactical Army aviation.

I recall that I had just about completed the trip to Long Island, when something happened that will keep me remembering the fall of 1933.

Just before I reached the Holland Tunnel, I was suddenly forced to the curb by three cars all bristling with sawed-off shotguns and Tommy-guns. I jumped out pretty mad, but saw that many guns were covering me and that it was the police. They looked at my papers, but said anyone could have mimeographed orders. They searched the car and me, took down the

17

Texas license number, and even copied the engine number. All the time I tried to talk with the flashlights in my eyes.

It took them thirty minutes to find out that the mere fact that I was travelling in a car with a Western license plate didn't make me Pretty Boy Floyd, who they said was on the prowl in that area. I finally had to telephone the Commanding Officer of Mitchel Field, and as he didn't know me, all he could say was that an officer by the name of Lieutenant Scott was supposed to be on the way to Mitchel from Kelly. Anyway, I still didn't think I looked—even then—like Pretty Boy Floyd.

My arrival at my new station was the start of a hectic time for the Air Corps. First I began to try to work in some flying time by volunteering for every flight I could get. I had an especially good break when I got on the Department of Commerce weather flights. I used to have to get up at two o'clock in the morning and take off—no matter what the weather was —at 2:45 A.M.

On one of these I found myself in quite a bit of trouble. As soon as I took off I went on to instrument flying and climbed up through the heavy clouds in the Curtiss Falcon—known then as an O-39. Out to the side, fastened to the "N" struts, I could dimly see the barometrograph which was to record the changing weather as we climbed to as high as the ship would go. It was necessary to climb at a constant three hundred feet a minute, which in several thousand feet became fairly monotonous. I finally adjusted the stabilizer so that the ship would climb this altitude, and then all I had to do was to keep the wings straight and level with the turn and bank indicator and the course constant with the gyro.

But I had reckoned without real knowledge of flying. My first indication of trouble came at some seventy-five hundred feet, when I was surprised to see the reflection of the moon down directly beneath my ship. I then forgot all caution and tried to fly partly on instruments and partly by visual reference. This I learned pretty soon was about impossible, for I went into the nicest spin I have ever seen. Recovering about four thousand feet below, I tried it again but the same thing happened. I then realized that after I had set my stabilizer for the steady climb of three hundred feet per minute, as the fuel was used the weight of the ship decreased and the nose went up, for the fuel was of course forward. This gradually precipitated a stall which turned into a spin as the big Conqueror twisted the fuselage from propeller torque. I had to resolve to do all my instrument flying by hand until the automatic pilots were perfected later.

That afternoon I looked at the graph paper of the barometer recording, and there were two little jagged lines, plainly showing where the ship had lost nearly four thousand feet in two spins.

The weather flights got pretty monotonous, and I would take off from Mitchel and fly up over Boston, then let back down to my home base. Finally the meteorologist caught on and told me to please stay right over the area, as he had other weather ships taking the same readings over Boston.

These flights taught me enough to save my life when the Army took over the airmail contracts a little later in the year.

4
When Death Flew the Mails

IF YOU REMEMBER 1934—there was trouble between the Government and the air lines concerning airmail contracts. To me even this was a life-saver in securing flying time, for all of us had recently been ordered to fly no more than four hours a month. This was the bare minimum to receive flying pay, and, as it turned out for many, the best way to get killed in airplanes. It's still a game that takes constant practice.

The first incident to permit us to keep flying temporarily happened when the youngest pilots at the station were sent to Chapman Field near Miami for gunnery camp. We left the snows of the East and went to the sunshine of Florida, about February first. From this camp we were saved again from going back to Mitchel Field and to the rule of no more than four hours a month. On February thirteenth came orders to take off for Cleveland, for the job of flying mail over the Alleghenies from Chicago to New York. I completed loading my Curtiss Falcon, got my Crew Chief, Sergeant Tetu, aboard, went to the downwind end of the single runway, and gave the ship the gun.

We took off and as we pulled up over the big Bellanca transport at the other end of the field I felt something peculiar about my ship. I began to climb slowly to the left—and then I noticed a blast of wind across my face. I was skidding. I tried to correct it with the rudder and it became worse instead of better. Exerting more pressure on the pedals, I looked down, and I could see the springs of the rudder-control moving. But the rudder itself was not moving. It was stuck. I looked back over my shoulder with a peculiar feeling at my heart and saw the rudder locked in the full left position.

I didn't know what to do. I pushed the nose down, and as the speed increased the skid got worse. I turned to Sergeant Tetu and started to yell to him to bail out, and then I thought: We're too low for that. So I just began to fight the ship. I would give it full gun and then slide the throttle gradually back to see if by crossing the controls (by keeping the stick forward and to the right) while the rudder was locked to the left, I could keep the ship in a mild slip but still have control. I don't know whether I figured this out or just luckily did it—for things happened too fast.

We circled the field and came around, while I tried to land on the runway into the wind, but as I went to cut the gun the ship nearly spun in and I almost hit the transport as I dove out to recover. I gave it full gun again and climbed, with my right leg braced against the rudder trying to bring it free. I then thought: This is a time for a cross-wind landing if there ever was such a time—because the wind is pretty strong and if I come around with full left rudder on and can push the stick far over to the right, it will be the same as slipping towards the ground, and if I'm slipping towards a twenty or thirty mile wind it may hold us straight till we get the wheels on the ground.

At any rate, I did this and we scraped the trees coming over the mangrove swamp near the field boundary. I slipped and skidded towards the hangar and the ship hit the ground. I cut the switch and climbed out, and I assure you that the first thing I did was to reach down and pat the ground lovingly.

Then I looked at Sergeant Tetu, who was a kind of greenish color. "Lieutenant," he said, "I thought you were just showing off at first. When you dove down on that transport I thought you were giving them a scare, but when you did it the second time I knew there was something wrong." We unzippered the fabric inspection plates from around the tail, and in the empennage section we found about a bushel of empty machine-gun cartridges, one of which had jammed in the rudder pulley and had locked the rudder in the full left position.

We proceeded on up into the cold of the North, landing in Cleveland, Ohio, that afternoon. And then began the greatest training that I have had. I wasn't going to training school this time: I was in something more important. Here was what we had been prepared to do—or unprepared to do. Here we were, about to start out flying the mail in tactical planes with open cockpits, in the blizzards of the Great Lakes region, the Rockies, the Northwest, in the cold of the prairies. Would they work or not? We certainly didn't know.

The weather we flew in to carry the mail during the winter of 1934 was about the worst in history. I sometimes think the powers on high collaborated to give us a supreme test. There were fourteen pilots killed along that airmail run, and most of them were killed because we had no instruments for the ships, or at least not the proper type for flying blind. We flew pursuit ships, which carried fifty-five pounds of mail; we flew old B-6 bombers that would carry a ton of mail at a speed of eighty miles an hour, providing the wind in front of you wasn't too strong—sometimes they almost went backwards. We flew everything from a Curtiss Condor which Mrs. Roosevelt had been using, to the old tri-motored Fords. And we flew through the worst weather in the country.

The route I flew from Chicago, to Cleveland, to Newark, was what was known to all airmail pilots as the "Hell Stretch" —and it was just that, as I found out pretty quickly.

We stepped out of routine flying into something we knew nothing about. I took ships that I had never seen before and flew them on orientation flights towards Chicago. I had never been to Chicago. One of these ships—a P-12-K with a fuel injector system—I flew West out of Cleveland one morning, but I didn't know anything about changing the fuel tanks. You see, usually you just let the gasoline run out of one tank and then you turn another on before the engine quits running from lack of fuel. But in this type of injector system, if you should let the fuel run all the way out of the tank, the engine wouldn't pick up when you turned on the selector valve!

Over Michigan City, Indiana, running out, I reached down to turn on the other tank. The prop just windmilled and I had to land down on a broad, open, snowy plain. When I landed I found it was the airport of Michigan City, which had been hidden by three feet of snow. I opened the technical pamphlet carried in the ship, read in the book how to work the fuel system, turned the tank on there, and using a wobble pump got the fuel back up to the engine. But then I found out that there was no crank for this type of ship—you had to use a shotgun shell to start the engine. I was learning things every day.

Well, I crawled around and finally after reading everything again, I got the engine started by pulling a trigger and exploding the shotgun shell. And after losing about three hours, I bounced across the snowdrifts and went on to Chicago. I figured that everyone would be standing out on the field, worrying about what had happened to me and the P-12-K. Landing, I ran hurriedly into the Flight Officer and said, "I'm the pilot who came here from Cleveland, I had to land in Michigan City . . ." and so forth. One of them said, "Well, we didn't even know you were on the way—our radios aren't working and the PX systems haven't been installed by Western Union." That began to show me that things weren't so well organized.

And so we began our airmail flying—slightly SNAFU, as we have learned to say from the gremlins in World War II. There were tragedies and there were funny things. Among the tragedies, I remember one man had three roommates killed—so many killed that he refused to have anyone else live with him. Finally when my second one was killed, we lived together—figuring rightly that better things were coming.

On February 19, 1934, we made our first real airmail runs from Cleveland, some of them going to Newark, some down towards Cincinnati, some to Chicago. One of the funniest things I remember happened that night. We had got the first ship out, Lieut. Bob Springer in a P-12-B for Cincinnati. We had worked over his ship to get him off on time, which was somewhere near two o'clock in the morning, out in the freezing snow of Cleveland airport. It must have been thirteen below zero. Anyway, we got the ship started, saw Springer's light disappear in the dark, breathed a sigh of relief, and went into the hangar again to get another ship ready to go out. Just as we started to get settled down over the manifest for the next load West, we heard the roar of a P-12 come over and land. Outside we could barely make out the wing lights as it taxied back in the blizzard.

It was Bob Springer. He leaned out of his ship and yelled, "I can't see my compass—the light up there is out—get me a flashlight so I can find my way out of this town." We got him a flashlight. Even then, when he finally got away carrying something to read his compass with, one of his gloves blew off and he had to sit on the ungloved hand to keep it from freezing.

Sometimes people on new jobs got mixed up and sent the Cleveland mail in the wrong direction from Chicago, towards Omaha, or sent the Chicago mail from Cleveland to New York, the reverse direction—just normal events amid the "growing pains" of an Army flying the mail.

22

Once the control officer finally got a man in the air after sweating the weather out to the West for days. I saw his ship take off and disappear in the snowstorm. Then I saw Sam Harris jump up, for the U. S. mail truck had just driven up. It was late, and in the excitement of getting the ship's clearance the eager pilot had forgotten to wait to have the mail loaded. The control officer had to call him back and start all over.

Buster Coln, a former college boxer from Clemson, used to give the newspapers some wild stories of the trials of bad weather flying. I'd say to him, "Buster, you told the papers you landed last night with about a pint of gas—just enough to get you over the fence. Well, I looked at the record and you had half a tank." Buster would look up and say, "Well, you got to give these paper boys something good—they wait for us out here all night and I'm not going to land and tell them everything was routine."

His most exciting yarn grew out of a flight when he was really about to give out of fuel over North Platte, Nebraska, in a snowstorm. Buster told it like this:

"I decided to jump. So I climbed the A-12 to six thousand, got it straight and level. Then, after getting out on the wing—still holding the stick—I said to myself: 'Buster, you don't want to do this and leave this fine attack ship to crash from up here.' So I got back in, buckled my safety belt, and tried again to fly down low enough in the blizzard to see where I was. Finally I saw a light and dropped a flare—I cut the engine and glided down to try to land. I hit the ground pretty easy without even seeing it, dodged trees and snowdrifts, and finally came to a stop.

"A farmer came out and took me and the mail to the train, and I was taken to the home of the Mayor of North Platte, where there developed quite a party which lasted until the storm was gone. We then went out and dug the ship out from under the snowdrifts. I had landed on the levee of the Platte River and had come within inches of hitting trees—so I guess the Lord was with me. The Mayor had the W.P.A. boys in the city pull the plane to the best place for take-off, and then after getting it serviced and the top of the levee scraped smooth with a snowplow, I climbed in to go on to Omaha.

"When I finally got the engine started after wearing out most of the W.P.A. boys on the crank, I looked down the improvised runway and contemplated the take-off. The Mayor ran over about that time, and holding his hat on his head in the slipstream, he yelled, 'Can you get over that tree down there, Lieutenant?' I said I didn't know; so the Mayor waved his hand at the W.P.A. men and yelled: 'Cut it down.' I climbed out and waited. When this obstacle had been removed I got back in, but the Mayor pointed towards an old barn far down the runway and asked if I could get over that. At my second reply of 'I don't know,' he called to the men and said, 'Burn it down.' So, I had to stay with him that night for another party. Next day I got the ship started again and finally got away."

The Mayor of North Platte was quite a boy, and so was Buster Coln. His best stories used to rival those of airmail pilots on the West Coast, and the best of them all was good enough for the Liars' Club—which is the classic of the Air Corps.

A pilot out there was having trouble over some very thick weather. He tried several times to land in a tule fog in the San Joaquin Valley, on the Fresno Airport. Each time he'd come closer and closer to the ground, and then, seeing nothing, he'd have to go around again. Finally the plane touched the ground, light as a feather, and without rolling more than ten feet it stopped. The tired pilot looked all around but could see nothing. He climbed out and with his hands outstretched to keep him from walking into something, he took three slow steps and felt his hands touch a hard brick wall. He walked forward, holding one hand on his plane's wing, stretched out his other arm, and found another wall. Continuing all around the ship he found to his surprise that there was a wall all about him. Next morning the tired pilot, having slept in desperation under the wing of his plane, found that he had landed in a silo.

My most amusing experience came when I took a single engine plane to Chicago from Cleveland, about the last of March. I came in with the new P-16 pursuit ship, expecting to take the same plane on back to Cleveland, that night. But as usual, plans were changed. The control officer told me to go to a hotel and they would telephone me when my load of mail was ready.

I had hardly climbed into bed—so I know they planned the time angle perfectly—when they called for me to come to the airport. I got there and found a brand new B-10—a twin-engine bomber, at that time the most advanced ship in the world. It was warming up, so I knew it was my trip. I went over to the control officer and told him that I'd tried to get them to let me fly that ship in Cleveland, all week, but they had said I was too young.

"Well," he said, "it's your ship now and you had better learn how to fly it before you take off, because you leave here at 2:35 this morning." I called up one of the officers at the hotel who was supposed to check pilots out, and he said, "It's got a stick and a rudder like every other plane. You know about as much about it as any of us, so just get out there and learn the cockpit." I did that, and when they put the mail aboard I climbed in and worked my way out into the runway of Chicago Airport.

Now you've got to remember that back in those days a B-10 was one of the few planes with retractable landing-gear. It was pretty much of a modern ship for someone to be jumping into who had been flying the old P-12's, P-6's, and A-3's. But I got down there, pointed it into the wind, gave it the gun with the two throttles, and we took off down the runway. As we went up over the other end of the field, I tried to work the landing-gear, but I didn't know how. I tried to read on the side of the fuselage how to do it, but I had too much else to do—it was snowing and it was dark and I was trying to fly a bi-motored ship that I hadn't the faintest idea about. And I said, "This trip will be a cinch—there are lights all the way to Cleveland."

So I went down to the tip of Lake Michigan where the lights begin their turn to the East, and I have never in my life seen so many lights winking at me from the ground. They seemed to point in all directions. And then it dawned on me that there were more lighted airways out of Chicago, and not just one from Chicago to Cleveland. Anyway, I took a line of lights that looked as if they were going in the right direction, and I went on and on, fumbling around trying to get the wheels up and trying to get the props synchronized and running smoothly. Finally I got a little settled down, and after pulling and pushing everything I got the wheels up about eighty miles from Chicago.

Then I looked at my compass and it read sixty degrees. Now anybody knows that from Chicago to Cleveland is pretty close to ninety degrees. So I looked at my map and I saw rows of lights going down to St. Louis, going to Cleveland, and going to Kalamazoo—and I was on the way to Kalamazoo! And scared as I was, I remember laughing, because if I had had to land in Kalamazoo, Michigan, with the Cleveland mail, there would have been more jokes on me than there had ever been on anyone. Until that time, Kalamazoo and Timbuktu to me had been just fictitious names—and now here I was, headed for Kalamazoo with the Cleveland mail.

Swinging down to the South, I found another lane of lights, but by that time my "time elapsed problem" was ruined. That is, after flying at so many miles per hour and having been out on an unknown leg of a course for so much time, I didn't know exactly where I was. But I headed on down over the lights until I came to a green one, which meant a landing field, and then I circled around, hoping that I was landing in Toledo, but not knowing exactly. I landed in the snow there and taxied up towards a sergeant who was waving his flashlight. When I pushed the cockpit cover back and looked out at him and cut my engines off, I still didn't want to embarrass myself by saying, "Sergeant, is this Toledo?" After all, you see, a pilot who is flying airmail is supposed to know where he is—not be asking after he lands.

And then I remembered I had flown a friend of mine over here, a classmate from the Academy, several days before and he ought to be here. If this is Toledo, then I can identify it, I thought. So I said, "Hello, Sergeant, how is Lieutenant Wold getting on?" The sergeant looked over at me and said, "Just fine, Sir."

Well, you talk about a sigh of relief. I breathed a big, long one—then I said, "Okay, Sergeant, take off the Toledo mail." With that done, I went on to Cleveland. When I walked in to the control officer there and told him my experience, he said, "Okay, you take that ship out tomorrow and fly it all day." I did it—and learned how to get landing-gear up, and the myriad of other new things. It was just a case of having to do something in a hurry, just a first taste of what a war might be. We made a lot of mistakes doing airmail, but we learned things we could have got in no other way.

It was during this airmail business that I really began to realize how lonely is the life in flight of a pilot alone in a ship, up at night with just the stars for company. We would take off on courses towards New York and Newark from Cleveland, and we were afraid—all of us knew that—because the weather was bad and we were in pretty sorry airplanes, and we hadn't flown routes like this. An airline pilot flies the same route most of the time. He learns the country over which he flies; he learns the weather conditions. But we had come from all sorts of posts in the United States. Some of us had flown only around San Antonio, Mitchel, or Miami. On Air Corps posts you do more or less local flying, working on combat maneuvers, but out here we were trying to do a job that we had not been prepared for.

I went to all the airline pilots and they were very nice to

26

me. They told me what to do in case of bad weather in some places, and said that when I had to make a decision and didn't know exactly what to do, not to be afraid to turn around. That sometimes when I hit weather that I couldn't turn around in, to go up instead of going down, in order to seek levels where ice didn't form. And, in general, just not to get excited and never to hesitate and circle.

About that time, when men had begun to die on airmail, I wrote a letter to this girl, the same one I had been going to see by automobile from Texas. It was addressed to her in case the "old ship hit something," and I carried it around in my pocket during all my trips of airmail—I nearly wore it out, just carrying it. But the ship didn't hit anything and she didn't see it. In it I must have just asked her to marry me—that's all I used to ask her anyway.

One night I took off from Chicago and came to Cleveland. They couldn't find the man who was supposed to take the mail on to Newark; I found out later that he was sick. So I talked them into letting me take the ship on East. I climbed in and headed out towards the bad weather. When I got to it, following the experience I had gained in the months before and the advice I had received from the airline pilots, I climbed instead of diving, to hunt for a way through. At 18,000 feet I came out and over the clouds. I was alone, for as far as you could see. There were stars and a moon, and down below were the swirling clouds over the Alleghenies, dropping their snow and ice. If I had turned back towards Cleveland, I would have had to let down in the dark and probably would have crashed. So I decided to head to the East with New York as my goal. I went on and on into the clear sky of the night, at 18,000 feet, and as the dawn came the next morning I started my let-down, for at least I would have light in which to make the landing.

My radio had not worked since I had got into the snow and ice; so I was flying merely by dead-reckoning. I let down somewhere over what I thought was northern Pennsylvania, but after buzzing the town and reading the name, found I was over Binghamton, New York. I flew on South, having remembered a field at Scranton, Pennsylvania, and there I landed.

The landing was quite an experience. As I dove over the field I saw workmen there, frantically waving their arms. They were repairing the field. But I was about out of gasoline, so I came in, motioning with my hand for them to get out of the way. The only damage was caused by my landing on one of the small red flags on a stick that one of the workmen had

27

been waving—he had hurriedly stuck it in the ground when he saw me landing regardless, and I came down right on top of it; but the small tear was of no consequence. I repaired it, had coffee with the man in charge of the airfield, and went on toward Newark.

They had long ago given me up for lost, for in that same night two other army pilots had met their death over the Alleghenies. Once again I felt that something had told me to climb when I got to the bad weather, and if that same thing had told those men to climb they would have flown through instead of going down—they might have disregarded a warning. In a case like that we think it's luck, but maybe it's not. To me something had said, "Get altitude, don't roam around down here, get altitude and go on." And I think that after that things just took care of themselves.

5

Hazards of Being an Instructor

WITH AIRMAIL over, we went back to our usual duties at Mitchel Field. Things sort of settled down, and I began to make more flights and more automobile trips towards Georgia.

Finally I talked the girl into it. We went on up to West Point and were married. Catharine really fits into this story because it was the trips over to Georgia to see her, from every place in the United States, that not only made me drive an automobile but taught me cross-country flying, since I had been flying in these later months from wherever I was—by way of Georgia.

From Mitchel Field I was sent to Panama. And then began my real pursuit training. In P-12's I roamed across the country of Panama up into Central America and down into South America. I was given a job constructing flying fields, which we figured would some day protect the Canal. These fields were put in for the purpose of installing radio stations and also air warning devices to tell us when enemy planes approached the Panama Canal. I would have to go down on the Colombian border and contact the natives, some of whom were head-hunters, to work on these fields that we were building. We would have to get the grass cut off, and I would make motions with a machete—the long knife of the Darien Indians

—and show them what we had to do to keep that field so that airplanes could land on it.

The natives didn't work very well with us at first. But we doctored a few of them for chiggers and for other infections under their fingernails which had become very inflamed, or we flew men in to hospitals who needed operations, and soon they began to appear more friendly. By the time we left there they were calling me "El Doctor." The only thing I want to bring out by this is that by doing simple kindnesses to these Indians, we were able to get them on our side, and they added materially to the value of fields that we constructed in Darien, and on the Chucunacque.

On some of my trips down there I would see orchids growing in the tops of the trees. I would measure the course out to the nearest river, take a boat and go as close as I could, then walk in through the jungle, climb the tree, and cut the orchid away by cropping off the entire limb upon which the epiphyte was growing. These I'd take back to my house at Albrook Field. It was the start of a hobby. I finally collected several hundred varieties of these beautiful plants and grew them for the last year I was in Panama. When they learned what I wanted, I had the natives around the villages bringing the various kinds in for me to fly back to my station.

Returning with my field crew in a Bellanca transport on one of these orchid-collecting trips, besides the fourteen men I loaded in six bunches of bananas of at least one hundred pounds each, one thousand oranges, one thousand avocados and limes, and an eight-and-a-half-foot jaguar tied to a pole with another stick in his mouth, and his jaws of course clamped down on that. There was a sack containing a bushmaster, the most feared snake in all of Central America— called by the natives Barba Amarilla, or Old Yellowbeard, because of his yellow throat. There were also ten green parrots; we just tossed them in with their wings clipped and left them back in the tail of the ship.

As that old Bellanca took off from Jaque' in the Republic of Panama, leaving behind the village governed by the Chinese mayor, Simon Mong, and heading on across the Bay of Panama, over water all the way to Albrook Field, I could hear the parrots scratching around inside. I looked back and saw the green birds reaching forward and taking hold with their bills, then putting one claw up where their bills were and pulling themselves up. They kept working themselves up toward the window of the airplane, and when one of them finally was perched on my shoulder he would try to jump out the window.

But the 140-mile-an-hour slipstream was too much for him—it would just blow him back. All through that two-hour flight back to Albrook Field, however, the parrots never did give up, one by one working their way up and then being blown back towards the tail.

When I landed at our home base it was quite a field day, a gala event more or less, because Dr. Marsh of the Panama Zoo had come out to receive this cargo that I was going to give him. He was very interested in the bushmaster, for his every hour there in the tropics was being devoted to an attempt to develop an anti-venom against the poison of that snake. The thing that pleased him most was the conglomeration of pets and reptiles. But the men in the ship said you could take it from them that it was illegal to transport snakes and tigers by air—they'd prefer riding in ships filled with men and dynamite to a repetition of a ride in a menagerie.

And so, collecting orchids and flying every minute I could beg or chisel, and shooting all the ammunition I possibly could at targets on the gunnery range at Rio Hato, as well as at hundreds of sharks in Panama Bay, I learned to navigate anywhere and to shoot as an expert from a single-seater pursuit ship. Finally, after nearly three years there, I was ordered out of Panama to report to Randolph Field as an instructor of flying students.

When my training of other pilots began, I realized the terror I must have caused my own instructor. For in training I perceived my own faults better, learning even to anticipate the mistakes the student would make. And I learned much about the peculiarities of man, for on one occasion I had a student who attempted to kill me. I don't know why—he would have killed himself, too.

One day I was told to take out a cadet listed as an incorrigible and try to find out what was wrong with him. I gave him forced landings and such, and when he tried to glide down and land on a highway, I would take the ship and caution him about gliding low towards trucks and automobiles. On one of these tries, as I gave him a forced landing—you do this merely by cutting the throttle to idling speed to see what the student will do—he rolled the ship on its back and pulled it down in a dive towards the ground. I waited as long as I could and then I took it away myself. I found that the man was glaring straight toward the trees we had almost hit. I landed the ship and asked him what was the matter. He appeared very sullen, and so I took him aloft again.

Once more I put the ship on its back and told him to bring it out. Immediately he pulled it toward the ground, and I knew it was intentional. With alarm I realized that with him almost frozen to the controls I would have extreme difficulty taking the ship from him by force. I hurriedly kicked the right rudder, which carried the half roll into a complete snap roll. Then I went through every acrobatic maneuver I knew until I made him sick; after that I flew him back to Randolph Field with my own heart beating a little wildly.

As I landed the ship two men stepped from behind a plane, asking to see the student. "You just wait a minute," I said. "After all, he's my student and I have some things to say to him." Then they pulled gold badges out of their pockets to show me they were F.B.I. men. They had been looking for this student for a long time. He had been a pilot before and had smuggled dope across the Mexican border, and I believe to this day that to evade the arrest that was waiting for him, he was trying to end it all. But the worry I had here was that in ending it for himself, he would have been ending it for me.

One of the most amusing things that ever happened to me while teaching men to fly concerned a man named Belonby, who I'm sure always will remember the incident. I was teaching him how to glide—how to know a normal glide in a primary ship. I had told him time and again that there are three ways of knowing the normal glide. First of all, I would say, look up there and see the distance your nose is below the horizon, then listen to the sound of the wind in the wires, and feel the pressure on the controls. Those three things will tell you whenever you are making a normal glide. Now look at this: If I pull the nose up it approaches the horizon, that tells me right there the glide is too flat. This is the visual test. Now listen to the sound of the wind in the wires as it comes down from the steady scream to a lower hum. Now feel the controls become slack.

I let Belonby try this two or three times, but every time his nose would drop down, and I would keep cautioning him, showing him how to pull the nose up, and telling him once again to note how the sound of the wind in the wires was changing, how the pressure was changing and the controls becoming sloppy—and to bear in mind that after all he merely had to look up there and see that the nose was approaching the horizon. Finally in desperation I yelled, "Hold your nose up, Belonby, hold your nose up!" But the nose of the ship continued to go down. I looked in the rear-view mirror and what I saw nearly made me fall out of the ship. Mr. Belonby was sit-

31

ting back there with his right hand on his own big nose, pulling it up with all his might. His eyes caught mine in the mirror and he realized what he had done. Never have I seen on a man's face such a sheepish expression as that which came across the blushing visage of Mr. Belonby.

When I first came to Randolph we worked only half a day and had the rest of the day to play around at golf, to hunt, or do anything we wanted. But as the belief that war was coming got into a few American people, we started the limited Air Corps expansion program. We then began working all day, and I was moved up to a Flight Commander and taught instructors, for the Government was giving contracts to civilian corporations to train Army pilots. The Air Corps was beginning to grow. As the years rolled into 1939, I was moved to California to become Assistant District Supervisor of the West Coast Training Center. This job was to check all flying cadets in the three schools at San Diego, Glendale, and Santa Maria. Later on I received my first command—that of the Air Corps Training Detachment called Cal-Aero Academy, at Ontario, California. I worked this up from forty-two cadets, until after one year we had nearly six hundred.

By this time, war with certain countries appeared imminent. I had always believed that we would fight Japan, and had always believed that Japan would make the first thrust. And I tried to "figure out" every cadet that came through our school —tried by talking to him to find out whether or not he had the urge for combat, for I knew that the urge was positively necessary. Not only did a man have to have that certain incentive to fly and keep on flying, until flying became second nature, but he had to have the definite urge for combat. When he learned to fly automatically he would control the ship without thinking about the controls and have his mind free to concentrate on navigation and the aiming of his guns—besides watching his tail for the enemy.

I talked with the cadets many times, and I was surprised to find that a lot of them didn't seem to know whether they wanted to fly or not. Many of them still thought it was wrong to want to get in the air against an enemy and fight. Sometimes I was disappointed to find that men lacked fighting instinct for the coming war. Youngsters seemed to think that combat was unnecessary. Many of them, it seemed to me, were learning to fly merely for the high-paying airline jobs of the future. But as time went on, I changed my mind. There would always be a few who didn't want to fight, there would be some who were uncertain, but from their attitude as the war tension increased

I knew that when war came, as it inevitably would, these youngsters in the fighting ships of America would do their part.

From Ontario I went to Lemoore, in the San Joaquin Valley of California, and there I went through one of the low periods of my life. It was not that Lemoore was bad, for the people were wonderful—but war was getting closer and closer, and I was getting farther from combat duty. Finally, after war had opened on December 7, I began to write Generals all over the country in an effort to get out of the Training Center. After all, I had been an instructor for nearly four years and it was pretty monotonous. I knew that instructors were necessary, but I wanted to fight, and I thought if I could get out to fight with my experience, I could come back later on and be even more valuable as an instructor of fighter pilots.

6
Too Old for Combat

AT LAST THINGS began to happen. On December 10, I was hurriedly ordered to report to March Field. When these secret orders came, I thought the day for my active entry into the real war was near. Hardly taking time to get my toothbrush—the radiogram said, "immediately"—I jumped into a car and drove madly through the Valley and over the pass of Tejon through the snow at the summit at nearly ninety miles an hour, to March Field. I arrived there in a blackout, and though I was to see plenty of combat later on, I'll take an oath that the nearest I've been to death in this war was when I rode into March Field with my lights out, trying to follow the line in the highway that was not there. Army trucks went by with dim, pinpoint blue lights, and as I looked out of my car the trucks would almost hit me.

When I finally got on the post with my radiogram for admission, I tore up to the headquarters and operations office, expecting any minute to be told to jump in a P-38 or a P-40 and go up to protect Los Angeles. There were many others like myself, for apparently all pilots with pursuit experience had been assembled.

No one knew what we were to do. No one knew we were supposed to be there. We could get no flying time, and some of the old pursuit pilots hadn't been in a single-seater for years. We waited and waited while rumors increased. Some said we were going to the Philippines by carrier; some ventured that our destination was Java or Australia. After that, I saw some of the men in India and China. Their ways to war must have been as circuitous as mine.

Squadrons of pursuit planes would come through daily on the way up the coast and we all grew very envious watching them. The only cheering thing was the radio broadcast which told of Capt. Colin P. Kelly and his crew sinking the Jap battleship *Haruna*. In this engagement Kelly became the first hero of the war, and I was very proud. For Captain Kelly had been under my instruction at Randolph Field. I could well remember that fine student's excellent attitude for a combat pilot. He had broken his collar-bone in a football scrimmage at Randolph and had told no one on the flying line. Looking in the rear-view mirror, I saw him flying with his left hand on the stick; when I corrected him, I learned of the accident. Fighter Kelly had been so anxious to get on with the course of instruction that he was completely ignoring broken bones. Of such material are heroes made.

As the days went on we noticed that pilots whom we had trained were doing the things in this war, in every theatre, with the few airplanes we had. It was some consolation to know that we had trained the youngsters who were sinking the Jap ships and shooting down the enemy planes. But it was not enough.

I still wanted to fight myself. I could well remember the years and years I had trained in Panama with the 78th Pursuit Squadron; I had always been too young to lead an element, a flight, a squadron, or anything. Then suddenly I was told here that I was not only too old—imagine that, at age 34!—to lead a squadron, but also too old to lead even a group. In fact I was too old to fly a fighter plane into combat. I used to tell the Generals that from being too young, I had suddenly jumped to being too old. There had never been a correct age.

But all the argument was to no avail, and after waiting around March Field for ten days we were ordered back to our home stations. I returned to Lemoore in the San Joaquin. I know there was no man on Bataan any sadder that night than I. Then came orders to report to Victorville—at least here was a change, and I welcomed it. I found myself director of training in a twin-engine school—I was still getting farther and farther from the war.

It seemed to me now that all was lost. I had tried desperately for the last six months to get out of the Training Center, and now that war had come it seemed that the powers at the top had decided that all of us, whether we had been trained as fighter pilots or as combat pilots, bomber pilots, or transport pilots, were nevertheless to stay there in the Training Center. December, January, and February went by, and in these months I wrote from Victorville to General after General. I remember saying to one of them:

"Dear General, if you will excuse me for writing a personal letter to you on a more or less official subject in time of war, I will certainly submit to you for court martial after the war. But if you can just listen to me I don't care whether that court martial comes or not. I have been trained as a fighter pilot for nine years. I have flown thousands of hours in all types of planes. I've been brought here as an instructor and I think I've done my job. Please let me get out to fight. I want to go to Java, I want to go to Australia, I want to go to China, India, and anywhere there's fighting going on—just so you get me out of the monotony of the Training Center."

An answer came back from this General: He would do all he could, he would even forget the court martial, but men were necessary in the training centers. Even with these kind words, it appeared that my cause was lost. Then, when the future looked worse than at any time in my life, a telephone call came from Washington, from a Colonel.

"Have you ever flown a four-engine ship?"

I answered immediately: "Yes, Sir." I had flown one for a very few minutes, at least I'd flown it in spirit while standing behind the pilot and co-pilot—but that was the only time I'd ever been in the nose or in the cockpit of a Flying Fortress. His next question was, "How many hours have you flown it?" I told him eleven hundred; there was no need to tell a story unless it was a good one, and after all, I considered this a white kind of lie—a white lie that was absolutely necessary if I was to get to war.

After giving this information I went back to waiting with my hopes way up. One night in early March, 1942, they came true —and to me they read like a fairy tale, too good to be true. I was to comply with them immediately, reporting to a field in the Central States. There I would receive combat instructions from the leader of our mission.

As I drove over from Victorville to my home in Ontario that evening, it seemed as though I was already in the air—adventure had come at last. Even then the fear tugged at my heart that the orders would be changed before I could start. I told my wife that I was going to combat, but the nature of the orders forbade my telling here where, or what type of mission. Not even at the look of pain that crossed her face did I lose my feeling of victory. She was trying to act happy, but I knew it was only because she remembered that I wanted duty in combat.

That night I began to pack hastily, resolving at the same time to take my wife and little one-year-old daughter back towards Georgia, where they could be among relatives. As I packed and arranged for the furniture to be shipped I still had my exalted feeling of victory. When I got into bed, very late, I thought I would drop right off to sleep. But as my mind relaxed for the first time after the orders had been received, I felt myself come to complete wakefulness. I even sat up in bed, for I had realized for the first time what I had done.

Here was my home, with the two people whom I loved more than any others in all the world—my wife and my little girl. Here, in this wonderful place, I could possibly have lived out the war, behind a good safe desk at Victorville or some other training field. By my love of adventure, by my stubborn nature, I had talked myself out of this soft and wonderful job of staying home with my family. I was about to leave that girl I had driven all those thousands of miles to see—for even ten minutes. . . . Tears came to my eyes—I knew I had been a fool.

For hours I lay awake. And then, in the darkness, I think I saw the other side. Suppose I called that officer who had telephoned me from Washington. Suppose I called and told him that I had lied—that I had never flown a Flying Fortress. I could easily get out of this mission—but the thought was one that I couldn't entertain even for a second. For now the seriousness of war had gradually come to me. Unless men like myself—thousands and millions of them—left these wonderful luxuries in this great land of America we could lose it all forever. I loved these two with all my heart, but the only way in all the world to keep them living in the clean world they were accustomed to was to steel myself to the pain of parting with them for months or years—or even forever. The actuality of war, grim war, had come. I knew then that the theoretical word "Democracy" was not what we were to fight for. I knew it was for no party, no race, creed, or color. We were going to fight, and many of us were to die, for just what I had here—my wife and family. To me, they were all that was real, they were all that I could understand. To me, they were America.

7

Dream Mission

NEXT DAY we got the household goods packed. We piled on an eastbound train and left California. The ride for me was the saddest thing that has ever happened. I would look at those two and see that my wife was thinking my own thought; even the little girl seemed to sense that all was not well. At Memphis, I almost casually bade them goodbye, and we parted. But as I watched their train disappear down the track I knew that part of my life was gone. My world was grim.

Reaching my assembly point for instructions, I found that I was reporting to Col. Caleb V. Haynes, one of the greatest of big-ship pilots—the pilot in our Air Force who had devoted much of his life to making the four-engine bomber the weapon that it is today. The entire group of officers and men made quite a gathering. I learned that they were all picked men, and that they had volunteered and almost fought for places on the crews of the Fortresses. And as I heard the explanation of the flight from Colonel Haynes I saw the reason for their excitement.

This was a "dream mission"—one that was a million kinds of adventure rolled into one.

We were to fly thirteen four-engine bombers—one B-24 and twelve B-17E's—to Asia. There we were to "bomb up" the ships after we had gone as far East as we possibly could, and then were to bomb objectives in Japan. Our orders read that we were to co-ordinate our attack from the West with another attack that was coming from the East.

The sadness that had been with me since leaving my family vanished. Once again I saw the war in a spirit of adventure. Here was what any soldier might have prayed for—here was what the American public had been clamoring for during the months since Pearl Harbor. I was fortunate to be one of the pilots; it almost made up for my failure to finally get into single-seater fighter ships again—almost, but not quite.

That night we talked things over and met each other, and next morning we left for Washington, with our newly drawn equipment. Our planes were in Florida, being made ready for combat, but we were obliged to go by way of Washington for the purpose, astounding in war, of securing diplomatic passports. I remember that even in the joy of the mission, I couldn't help wondering what kind of a war this one could be. We were having to secure passports in order to be able to fight. Visas were obtained for all countries we were to fly over and through—Brazil, Liberia, Nigeria, Egypt, Arabia, India— and China, especially! Visas—to go to war!

Properly inoculated against fourteen diseases, with visas for everywhere, with trinkets for trade with natives in Africa, Arabia, and Burma, we went on down to Florida. The instant I landed I hunted out my ship—B-17E—Air Corps number 41 9031. I soon painted on its nose the red map of Japan, centered by the cross-hairs of a modern bombsight, with the cross right over Tokyo. In my poor Latin was inscribed *Hades ab Altar*—or roughly, *Hell from on High*.

I climbed into the control room of my ship and met my crew. Each man was a character, each man wanted badly to get started.

The co-pilot was Doug Sharp, another dark-haired Southerner, a first Lieutenant who was destined to get shot down in another Flying Fortress over Rangoon. He coolly got most of his crew out of the burning ship; then, with those who were unable to parachute to safety, he landed the flaming ship in the rice paddies of central Burma. From this point he led his men —those whom he did not have to bury beside the ship—out through the Japanese lines to safety in India. He was made a Major after this gallant act.

Doug was an ideal flying officer, and it was to him that I first turned for advice on how I should make myself acquainted with this big airplane. Doug had learned to fly at the period when I had been instructing. I had taught his class to fly; now the tables were turned and he would have to be the instructor for a while. Don't forget that as yet I hadn't flown a B-17E.

Introducing myself to my co-pilot, I said, "How about showing me how to fly this ship—I want to see how to work these turbos and such." He merely grinned at me in disbelief. "Aw, Colonel," he said, "you can fly the thing—why, you taught me to fly." I finally got him to give me some cockpit instruction by explaining that though I had many thousand hours in PT's, BT's, and other trainers, and knew lots about single-seaters and fast twin-engine medium bombers, I knew nothing about such planes as this big devil.

He showed me the approved method of starting the four engines, when to use the booster switches, how to set the turbos, how to lock the tail wheel—and generally how to pick up that fifty-seven thousand pounds of flying dynamite and take it around the field. I flew it for two landings that afternoon, and that night I climbed all over the Fortress, read the entire maintenance manual, and learned from scratch what made the big ship go. Next day I soloed it for over four hours, and after the twentieth landing I felt as if I was ready to start for war.

Then we tested everything—fired all guns at targets in the everglades, and the cordite from all those roaring fifty calibres gave even the swampy "glades" a sweet aroma. My gunners were eager to be on the way, and I soon found that they knew exactly what they were doing.

Private Motley was my tail gunner. During the entire trip I think he stayed in the tail ninety per cent of the time, just to get used to the way to handle the tail turret. I used to say of Motley that he just didn't care where he was going—he wanted to see where he had been.

Sergeant Aaltonen, the engineer, was charged with keeping the engines functioning properly, and in general the entire enlisted personnel was under him. He was a diligent Finn and one of the bravest men I have ever seen. I can see Aaltonen now, standing there behind my seat and the co-pilot's seat, unperturbed in the roughest of storms, from the violent currents of the equatorial front of the Hamadans to the Shimals of Africa and Arabia. Eternally watching the many instruments, waiting to correct the slightest trouble even before it happened. When we were lost over trackless seas he was never ruffled, but ready at all times with information as to fuel consumption and the best RPM's for cruising. Once when he was told that we would probably have to land in the Atlantic there was no change in the expression on his face; he simply began to move the provisions to a point where they could be quickly placed in the rubber boats. His job in case of attack was to man the top turret with its twin Fifties.

Sergeant Baldbridge was the head radioman. His secondary duty was to handle one of the waist guns back aft of midships. Corporal Cobb was second radioman; he would leave that to enter the lower turret. The other waist gun on this flight was to be handled by a radio officer, Lieutenant Hershey.

The navigator was a Lieutenant whom I'll call Jack. He was a nervy kid who liked his job. I know that after our mission he made many raids as navigator to bomb the Japs in Rangoon.

We tested the bombardier and the bombsight, too, before we started the flight. Lean, lanky, six-foot-three Bombardier George—I never did see how he managed to wiggle into the

39

nose of the Fortress. I can see him there now, tense over his sight, waiting for the bombs to go—ever with the cross-hairs on the target. George had a couple of fifty calibre guns up there in the nose with him, too. He was just the opposite of the tail gunner—he never did know where he had been but always got there first.

And so the eight of them made up my crew—eight good soldiers who had volunteered and who wanted to hurt the enemy. None of them worried about whether or not he'd get home—for he knew of bigger things that had to be done.

We had to test everything, for it was over sixteen thousand miles to Japan the way we were having to go; there couldn't be a slip-up on this mission, and so we didn't take a chance. When finally all was set I was about nervous enough to bite my nails off, for my ship was to be last to leave the States. I had worried every minute of the time we had been waiting for fear that some brass hat would get my orders changed before I could get on my way. The other twelve ships had gone, with Colonel Haynes leading in his B-24. They all made their way to the East separately, with instructions to meet in Karachi, India, for final orders. And Karachi was 12,000 miles away.

As soon as we could leave the West coast of Florida, we loaded up and crossed the State. Going on East over West Palm Beach, I rang the alarm bell, putting all men on the alert, and we dropped down, with the crew firing at the whitecaps out over the Gulf Stream. The guns were working fine but we couldn't take a chance. I had to learn right now whether the crew could work as a team, for once we started it would be too late.

As we came back towards the last field we were to land on in the U. S. A., something strange met my sight, something that made the blood pound a little harder in my temples. There, along the entire beach of Florida, was a jagged black line— the clean sand of Florida's beaches had been made black and terrible-looking by the oil from many tankers sunk by the Axis submarine war. It gave me a queer feeling, for along the beaches there was also the beached wreckage of several ships. This war was meaning more and more to us as we prepared to shove off for the first stop out of America.

Now we were poised for our flight to Puerto Rico. In our two-day wait for technical changes on the engines I worried more than ever, for the other twelve ships were gone and I was getting frantic lest something might change the orders.

Finally, after having to wait during days of perfect weather, we took off in heavy rain for Borinquen Field, P. R.

The take-off and first two hours of the flight were "instrument," as we were flying through a moderate tropical front. We finally broke into clearing weather over Long Island Key, British West Indies. This was on March 31, 1942.

Just after noon we sighted Hispaniola at the point of Cape Frances Viejo. Sergeant Aaltonen passed out some hot coffee from the thermos jugs. Our spirits were high, for now that we had passed the bad weather this was like a picnic. The big ship was handling like a single-seater. We turned from the dark, mysterious Hispaniola, crossed Mona Passage, and landed at Borinquen Field at 15:07, just three minutes off our E.T.A. (Estimated Time of Arrival).

Two of our flight's Fortresses were waiting in Puerto Rico for minor repairs, so we felt a little less lonesome. Just in case the authorities in Washington decided to stop the last ship or the last two ships in our mission, I got my crew up long before daylight next morning, and we soon were heading South for Trinidad, ahead of the other two. The weather was perfect, with scattered clouds and a light tail wind, and we flew low, looking for enemy submarines. Thirty miles West of Martinique we thought we saw one, but could not verify. We passed over the Grenadines near St. George, Grenada, and soon saw the hills of Trinidad rising out of the Caribbean.

With our ship serviced and ready for a very early morning take-off, we now took the most dangerous ride we experienced on the trip. This was a trip into Port of Spain in a combat car. It seemed to me that the natives just waited in side roads to try and run into us in blind areas where we could not see them. Besides, it has always seemed to me that drivers who take pilots from their ships into towns religiously try to show them how to turn corners on one wheel, and to show that they can easily drive into said town at the same average speed that the pilot could fly.

In the city we picked up a case of Scotch for medicinal purposes—the purifying of water and snake-bites. We joked about the recipes on the way back. I recommended one cup of Scotch to a jigger of water—it works.

A real night take-off from Trinidad—we were airborne in the darkness at 5:20 A.M. As the wheels left the ground I realized very quickly how great a load we were lifting. This was the first time we had taken off with full load of fuel, and it seemed to me that I almost had to break my arms to keep the tail from going all the way back to the jungle—for all practical purposes the Fortress tried a loop.* Finally we got the ship rigged properly and climbed on top of the clouds at eight thousand feet. Later we had to go higher to keep from going through the heavy tropical thunderheads; with our overload, neither Doug nor I wanted to risk the turbulence that we knew was there.

As the sun came up we could look down through holes at intervals and see the dark Atlantic near the Guianas. There was a thick tropical haze from the base of the clouds down to the water, giving it all an eery appearance. Later on, through the breaks I saw the mouth of a big river emptying Northeast into the sea. It was the Rio Maroni, which divides French and Dutch Guiana, and it reminded me that in 1937 I had made a flight up this same jungle stream, looking in vain for the lost pilot, Paul Redfern.

Over Devil's Island at 9:20, I saw by our chart that we were only five degrees North of the equator. Coming down lower to look at the French penal colony, we found that although the temperature was comfortable on top of the haze at six thousand feet, down in the soup near the water we had difficulty breathing. Passing on over another river identified as the Rio Oyapok, we went out of the Guianas into Brazil at 9:55 A.M. Cruising low at eight hundred feet, we got some unforgettable views of the steaming Brazilian jungle.

Looking out to sea, we noticed that the blue color already was changing to the murkiness of the Amazon, though we were about a hundred miles from its mouth. Flying low, I noted that the hump of Brazil near the coast was flat and green and hot as hell—temperature ninety-six and humidity about ninety-nine per cent at 10:55 A.M. We reached the mouth of the greatest river in the world at 11:35 E.W.T. Here the width of the Amazon is about one hundred and fifty miles.

Boys will have their fun too, no matter if you are flying low over the greatest of rivers. As we crossed the equator—old Zero Degrees Lat. at 11:56 A.M., at West Longitude 49 degrees 32 minutes—I saw those of my crew who had been in the South latitudes before take paper cups of water and drop them on the heads of those who were uninitiated, thus making them subjects of the sacred realm of Jupiter Rex as identified from the realm of Neptune Rex on the sea. We crossed the Amazon, from just West of Point Grossa over Bahia Santa Rosa to Mixiana Island, thence to Isla da Marajo. This last island in the mouth of the river is one hundred miles wide and reputedly

---

* It must have been that case of Scotch, added suddenly to the other sixty thousand pounds.

has more cattle on the single ranch than any other ranch in the world. Soon we came to Rio Para, crossed it in a thunderstorm, and were over Belem, where we landed in the blackness of a tropical rain at 12:40 E.W.T.

On April 4, we left Belem for Natal at 6:55 A.M., and climbed to ten thousand feet in order to top as much of the cumulus as possible. We had to skirt one great anvil-head reaching up into the sub-stratosphere near Bahia San Luiz. This storm covered about fifty miles, but we got around it without going into its turbulence. As we went on South of the equator the haze diminished gradually and the country became dry, making us think we were over western Texas. We landed at Natal, our jump-off point for the South Atlantic crossing, at 12:25 E.W.T.

This was to be a real day's flight. For we were not to be able to spend the night at Natal. Our run from Belem to Natal of nine hundred miles, then the crossing of nineteen hundred miles to Liberia, plus the run down the hump of Africa to a Pan-American base on the Gold Coast—this last almost nine hundred miles—had to be made without stops, except short ones for fuel. For all practical purposes, then, we had thirty-seven hundred miles to make in one day.

We got the big ship serviced and ready for the trip, then went to the Ferry Command Hotel. There we found two more crews of our thirteen heavy bombers. One group of these had turned back the night before with one engine out. The other, piloted by Col. Gerry Mason, had nearly come to grief on the way in from Belem. The rubber life-rafts in the Forts are carried in two compartments where the wing of the B-17 joins the big fuselage. This is to facilitate their automatic release upon contact with the water should the ship have to land at sea. They are of course tied to the airplane with strong manila rope, and it is on this hemp that the present tale hangs. In the flight down the coast some malfunction had caused one of these compartments to spring open—and out came the heavy, five-man boat. At the speed of two hundred miles an hour with which it struck the tail section as it went back on its rope in the slipstream of two engines, it nearly took the entire horizontal stabilizer off. Only by very skillful piloting had Gerry Mason managed to get the Fort and his crew of ten to Natal.

Just the same, in my attempted nap that afternoon, I grinned at the thought that we in old "Hades Ab Altar" were passing ahead of two more ships of the flight. Boy, I dreamed, they'll have a tough time getting me back there into the training

43

center now! It's four thousand miles back to Florida and in the morning I'll be across the Atlantic.

But I was to find—before we got to Africa—that many slips can develop. Things had been going very smoothly, but Fate was deciding to test me and my crew on the run across the South Atlantic.

8

Take-Off from Brazil

WE WAITED until darkness for the take-off, to insure our arrival on the West coast of Africa in the light of early morning. At six o'clock, local time, we went to the field. That evening I had tried to eat, but the more I chewed the food the more it stuck in my throat. Nervousness—anticipation—I don't know which. But even this place, far down in South America, was tied on to North America and my home in Georgia by the narrow lands of Central America. In a pinch one could still walk back home from here—but after this hop across the ocean all that would change.

On the drive to the airport I talked casually to the entire crew. They were all anxious to get into the air and get on with our mission, but from their answers I knew they were thinking as I thought. One person whose confidence I was especially trying to get was my navigator. I told him that I had been flying over ten years, and that was a pretty long time, considering. I tried to make him see that even in those ten years things and conditions had changed. I always navigated by dead-reckoning—that is, I drew a course and followed that compass course with corrections from deviation and variation. Then as I flew along, I passed over certain known places we called "check-points," and on to my destination. Of course out over the oceans there would be no check-points—but even without them it would have been possible in many cases to fly a ship, with just a compass course corrected, from South America to Africa.

Nevertheless the best way was by means of celestial navigation, and that, I told Jack the navigator, was where he fitted into the picture. I tried to impress on him the realization that I was going to have explicit confidence in his navigation, for I knew in many cases that older pilots are hard to change from dead-reckoners to the more modern and efficient method.

Jack took the talk well, worked hard over his charts, and told me the initial course was eighty-one degrees—this would

44

change slightly from drift, from the wind, and as we made a great circle. We all knew that this ship had to get safely to the battle zone; we all knew that it would take all of us functioning as a team to get it there. On this navigator rested the responsibility of taking the ship either to some spot lost in the sea, or to an infinitesimal point on the West coast of Africa—our goal.

I got aboard last, going through the fuselage door in the rear of the ship. Each man as I passed appeared light-hearted but I knew that was the American way of facing adventure. As I talked to them, one by one, I would notice that after replying, each man's eyes would turn towards the door through which I had come. It was as though each man knew that when that aluminum door closed, it would close for months, years, or maybe forever, on the world in which he had lived. Each man may have been wondering how many of the men in this ship would ever get back; he was perhaps wondering if this great weapon, before it was worn out, lost, or destroyed, would do enough damage against the enemy to compensate for its loss.

The door closed at my order. I crawled under the top turret after side-stepping through the narrow beams of the bomb bay. I slid into the left-hand seat. Sergeant Aaltonen was at his place behind Doug and me. I nodded to the co-pilot, and he started the four engines. As the roar and vibrations came from our power plants I could feel the thousands of impulses through the throttles. They seemed to flow up my arm to my body—the ship seemed alive.

A light rain was falling. We taxied down for take-off practically by instrument, for even on a clear night it's almost impossible to taxy visually, and the rain on the windshields plus the lights from the cockpit made everything fuzzy. Our world was the cockpit; all else was invisible and unreal. With the turbos set, we gave the Fortress the "needles" and took off towards the sea. As I felt the big wheels draw up into their wells, I heard Jack, the navigator, say, "Off at 10:03 G.M.T."

All about was darkness. I didn't even see the beach as we went over it, and I was momentarily disappointed at missing my last possible glimpse of the Western Hemisphere. Just the same, we'd gotten off with a load of nearly sixty thousand pounds and were rolling towards Africa. I felt my face crack into a grin—I nudged Doug and yelled: "They can't get me back to the Training Center now!" And I pulled my radio-plug free from my headset. This was enough for Doug—he got it. Cut off from the world by merely disconnecting my radio headset! We laughed.

We climbed on up through the rain and broke out into the clear sky and the millions of stars at eleven thousand feet. No one but an airman will ever realize what it means to climb out of a storm and see the friendly stars. I felt as though the mill-stones of anxiety had fallen off, in the confidence that mounted in me, and I called for coffee. The engineer passed it up to me. I drank the second cup as the moon rose out of the white clouds at 11:00 G.M.T. Down below I could see the navigator's dome light going on and off as he took his "shots" of the stars. Jack was beginning his long job, which would end only when we got a definite "fix" on the West coast of Africa. Then he'd put away his navigation instruments, pencils, and charts, and come to stand behind our seats and watch for the landfall that he'd foretold. Then he'd see if the E.T.A. was as he had predicted.

The miles lengthened out behind us, as we kept a course very little changed from the one we'd started with. In four hours the navigator told me we'd made seven hundred miles. That was all right, considering the climb and the fact that we had the headwind ever present in an easterly crossing over the South Atlantic. Down below the clouds were broken, beautiful in the light of the full moon that was climbing fast as we went towards it. Every now and then we'd bump through the tops of higher cumulus clouds. Far up ahead and coming closer were winking flashes that I knew were the lightning of the almost stationary equatorial front.

We'd been told about this equatorial front in our pilot's "briefing" in Florida. The advice was to fly our computed course until the approach to the equator placed us within the rough area of this front, which moved very slowly between four degrees North of zero degrees latitude and about the same number of degrees South. Then, as this front stretched from East to West and our course was very nearly parallel to it, we were advised upon reaching it to turn almost ninety degrees to the left, which would be North. Thus by flying for a very short time perpendicular to the front, we'd be through it. After crossing the front we were to turn back to the normal course.

The flashes of lightning ahead drew closer and closer. I could see the heavy black storm clouds now, and I couldn't help tensing up. For after all, the instructions we had for evading the turbulence were based on theory, and I'd seen theories tumble before. The air grew rougher as we moved in on the front; the lightning looked like a fireworks display at Coney Island viewed from far away.

At first we went into the tops of whitish-gray clouds, and then burst out again into the light of the moon. Finally the clouds seemed to be growing in size and rising. As the light of the moon grew less I could see the cumulo-nimbus thunderheads boiling as if they were steam escaping from a cauldron.

Then we went into them and didn't come out. I held the course steady, for I knew we were now entering the solid wall of the front—the point where two air masses of greatly different temperatures have met. As the flashes of lightning crackled down through the dark clouds, I'd try to turn away from the blue streaks.

Suddenly there came a real thrill: as the lightning played about us the wing tips appeared to glow a dull blue. About the whirling propellers was the same blue fire, and as I reached out towards the instrument-board to take the ship off the automatic pilot, the space between my hand and the board glowed with a soft blue. Then I remembered what this phenomenon was— Saint Elmo's Fire, caused by special conditions of static electricity. The eery sight recurred periodically but I never did become used to it. How can you when you are riding along with practically a railroad tank-car of one-hundred octane aviation gasoline, and the little gremlins and fifinellas are running around with torches of high priority blue flame?

As I settled myself on instruments, hand-flying the ship, the turbulence increased and I remembered the instructions to turn to the North. As I went into the turn it seemed that all hell broke loose—I must have entered the center of the storm just at the instant of turning. The violent up-drafts would clutch the big ship, and we'd go kiting up like an elevator. At first I'd try desperately to hold the altitude constant but it was to no avail. The ship would be flying straight and level, but we'd be climbing twenty-five hundred to thirty-five hundred feet per minute. Then, just as suddenly, we'd hurtle through the up-draft into a down-draft, and it would seem as if the wings were going to be torn from the fuselage. Down we'd go, at the same indicated speed that we'd come up. Looking out the side glass, I could see the aluminum skin of the big Fortress wing shimmering in the lightning as the very metal wrinkled under the heavy stresses the ship was undergoing.

I got the gyro set and headed North, hoping to get out of the turbulence. Doug had to help me—he'd keep the gyro on zero with the rudder and I'd hold the altitude of the ship level with the wheel. It seemed that the clouds were endless and that each new center in the front was rougher than the last. Perhaps this front reached all the way to the North Pole—I'd begun to think so, anyway.

And then, with one final shake of the Fortress, like a giant dog shaking a pup, the elements threw us out from the hills and valleys of the front and we saw the moon and the stars again. Once more came the feeling of exhilaration. We got the ship back on course for Africa. Off to our right in the South the lightning continued to play. If we hadn't turned as the briefing pilots had advised, that flight through the front would have shaken us for another hour or longer. We had gone through in a few minutes, but under the tension time had seemed to drag out for endless hours. As confidence surged back, with better weather indicated, I could relax again, and Sergeant Aaltonen passed me another cup of coffee.

The world was good again, worth living in—and somewhere out there ahead was Africa!

9
Lost Over the Atlantic

THE RADIO MAN called to us to listen on the command set— that the music from Rio was really hot! I switched over to the big set, and as we passed over the very center of the Atlantic I did very gentle turns with the big ship, as if it were S-ing in rhythm with the jazz. Jack gave me another "fix" and said we were halfway across. The engineer checked the fuel consumption, for it was up to him to give me the go-ahead or the turnback signal. He also checked the engines with Doug and me.

We had reached what we called in pilots' lingo, "The Point of No Return." You see, from here on it would be farther back to South America than on to Africa. I remember feeling very glad that we didn't have to worry about going back through that front.

All about us now the night was beautiful. The moon had got back over behind us in the West. I could hear part of old Kipling's "Ballad of East and West" keeping time with the steady roar of the engines. . . . "We've ridden the low moon out of the sky." Outside I looked at the props shimmering in the moonlight, and could not help marvelling at how modern engineering had perfected such engines. I thought of the millions and millions of revolutions those propellers had made and how many more they had to go, how many billions of times the sparkplugs had fired—and still, after years of flying,

I could not quite understand what held such weights as this ship in the air. Down below in the breaks now, we could see the moonlight on the water.

The hours went by and the miles went astern, and I began to let slowly down, for the sky was beginning to turn gray ahead. It's a short night when you travel East towards the sun at over two hundred miles per hour. We had been cautioned to let down early in our approach to the African coast, for there are usually clouds, and always a dense haze. To continue on too far would place us over the hills of the interior and would complicate our arrival at destination.

As the dawn of April 5 came, we continued going downhill, from eleven thousand feet to one thousand. At this low altitude we skated along over the calm sea, looking ahead for land with anxious eyes, for after nearly two thousand statute miles of ocean flying we were tired. We knew we must be two or three hundred miles offshore still, but we were eager to glimpse the Dark Continent. I could see all the crew pressing up from the rear of the ship, trying to get up with us. We were all peering through the windshields, each wanting to be the first to cry "Land Ho!" But the cry didn't come, and we kept flying our course down close to the water.

Then something queer happened. We had been flying approximately 81 degrees all night, but suddenly the navigator called on the interphone and said, "Change course to 135 degrees." At that time I was munching a sandwich—and, boys, I nearly dropped it. I know the piece that I was chewing got bigger and bigger, for I finally had to wash it down with the sweetish coffee that had been fixed for us in Natal.

I looked over at the co-pilot, and he had heard the new course and appeared puzzled too. I looked down at the sea, wondering why in hell we were making such a radical change in direction. Then, just as suddenly, I remembered that I had told this navigator that I was going to go by what he said. So I changed to 135 course.

The ship rolled on, just about one thousand feet off the water. Both Doug and I just forgot all about food. We settled in our seats thinking: Now maybe this is something else. And then I thought: This is a sun-line he's trying to get. Oh! yes, a sun-line! And then I remembered the sun wasn't up. How could anybody be shooting a sun-line when the sun hadn't risen?

But we went on that way for thirty minutes while Doug and I anxiously waited for the navigator to tell us another

49

course to fly. When he did tell us it was some other crazy change, 145 degrees or something. And I said,

"Doug, you take it a minute. I'm going down and see what's the matter here." I went down into the navigator's compartment.

"Look here, Jack," I said, "we've been doing all right, we ought to hit Africa in about an hour, and we suddenly make a radical change of about ninety degrees. What's the matter?" He looked a bit worried. Then I remembered that I had seen his lights go on and off all night, and also that he had seemed a little nervous about what he was doing.

Jack frowned and said, "Well, Colonel, I don't know . . ." I distinctly choked before I was able to ask: "What do you *mean* you don't know?" And the terrible fear that came to me was like this: Here we were in a wonderful ship with nine men supposed to be trained as a team and on the way to war. How could we afford to lose something like that in the Atlantic? I didn't think about losing our lives or having to float about on the Atlantic in a rubber boat for days and days, and I know that none of those men would have thought about that. I thought about the ship we were supposed to take to war, and I looked back at Jack and said, "What did you do? What are you doing? We've been flying a straight course?"

"I made a mistake," said Jack. "When I set my watches last night in flight after we took off."

Now the watches that you set on a ship that you are navigating celestially are your chronometers, and they are of course very sensitive. There were two of them, and Jack went on to tell me that while he'd been listening to Rio during the night the radio had given the time and he had tried to set the two watches. But he had made the mistake of forgetting to pull out the stem on one immediately. At any rate, there was a difference of a few seconds in the time he had and the time it was supposed to be, and even those few seconds, he felt, had thrown us off course.

Well, I didn't know what to do. I went on back to the left-hand seat in that Flying Fortress and I think I staggered a bit; I know I stared out of the window and didn't know what to say. Then I told Doug about it. We kind of cussed, and I remember saying:

"Look, Doug, I've always been a dead-reckoning pilot. Africa's a big place; I think I could have hit it by pilotage alone. Just by pointing the ship at the bulge of the continent and flying straight. I might have missed the field that I aimed for by a few miles, but I would have intentionally headed so far South or so far North of the point that I'd have known which way to turn when I'd got to Africa. And now I've let a kid navigator lose us out here."

I felt like crying; I could feel the tears in my eyes. I looked down at the water of the Atlantic, black below the clouds that we were flying under. Sometime soon, if we weren't on the right course, we were going to have to land in that water. And now that thought began to worry me too. Very few land-based airplanes—and the Flying Fortress of course was one of those not intended to land on water—had ever landed in the sea without injuring some of the crew.

A few minutes later, Jack frantically called up another course to fly and I changed to it, not knowing what else to do.

Then I came to a decision. If we had been on the course when we had been flying 81 degrees—and we must assume that we had been on the course—I was going to turn back now to that original heading. I told the co-pilot to go down and bring the chart up; we'd take a look at it.

Pretty soon Doug came back from the navigator's room with the chart of Africa's West coast. Now, if you'll look at the coast of Africa on the western side you'll note that we were heading for the big bulge North of the equator that stretches from up North of Bathhurst, South and East towards Lagos. Well, I took a ruler and drew a line from Bathhurst down through Accra. I drew a perpendicular bisecting that line, and assumed that we were out in the Atlantic on that bisector. When you're lost you've got to assume something definitely. Then I measured the angle of that line in toward Africa and found it to be 60 degrees. Looking over at Doug Sharp, I said:

"Well, Doug, there's only one thing and I'm going to do it. If I'd been flying two or three hundred hours, I might start searching around out here for land. I'm not going to do that. I've been flying long enough to know that the only way to get any place is to fly in a straight line, and that's the way we're going to fly."

I set my gyro on that sixty-degree course, called down to the bombardier—that tall, lanky bombardier named George—and told him to set and turn it over to the AFCE—it would be a straight course now, for that was our only hope. Then I looked around to see if I couldn't build up a little morale among the crew, most of whom had gathered up forward. They sensed what was wrong. The radio man was back there now, trying to get a radio bearing on Bathhurst, and some of the others were trying to get another place. I smiled at them all and I said, "If any of you try to take it off this course, I'm going to hit you over the head with this gun." And even with the smile they knew, and I knew, that I meant it. We might have to paddle around to get to Africa, but we were going to know just about where to head for land.

The farthest we could have been from the hump of Africa was around two or three hours' flying time. Giving the elements the benefit of the doubt, giving us in fact the worst of everything, I knew that three hours would tell the story. I looked over at the co-pilot again and asked him what was the best thing to do—throttle the engines far back to save fuel, or go on as we were? "Throttle them back," he said. I asked him then if it would be best to cut off some of the engines, and he advised doing it later; maybe we could try one and later cut two.

We went down as low as five hundred feet to be able to see under the clouds. As we watched we flew into more rain. At first that made me feel good; we're getting close to land, I thought—it's raining, and it's always raining around Africa. Just the mind making me think what I wanted to think—that was all.

Then I saw a freighter down below and by studying the direction in which the wake pointed, I tried to figure out where it had come from. We swung around it, so that we wouldn't scare the crew and also so that they wouldn't be tempted to shoot at us. I could just imagine those sailors down there having pretty itchy fingers—especially when four-engined bombers passed over far out to sea.

An hour passed. I looked at the fuel gauges, pulled back on the throttles a little more, and further reduced the manifold pressure in order to use less gasoline. We were now indicating about 165 miles an hour. I felt my throat kind of choke up. Looking at the other men, I know their thoughts were about the same as mine. The one that I pitied most was the poor boy down below who was the navigator. He had made a mistake—but all of us have made mistakes. I would be aware of hating him one minute, then of being sorry for him the next.

But we held to that course of 60 degrees, and I reached the state of looking in any direction and seeing the land of islands that I knew weren't there. Low clouds on the water would appear to be islands. Everywhere we looked there was land, but we kept going straight ahead. I knew what mirages were, and we were not going to roam in circles over that ocean until we ran out of gas and didn't know where we were. I thought constantly of this expensive plane ready with bristling guns to blast the Japs, but whenever I shut my eyes to rest them, I would see it slowly sinking in the water, no good to anybody.

I mechanically eased back on the throttles some more, and another hour went by. I looked over and checked the fuel gauges again, and the co-pilot said calmly:

"Well, Colonel, we can stay in the air about two hours more. We have to get there in two hours."

I don't know whether I throttled back more then or not—by that time we were flying just fast enough to keep the big ship in the air. The minutes dragged by, and every time I looked at the fuel gauges they seemed to be going towards the empty mark so fast that I thought there must be holes in the tanks.

Two hours and fifty-five minutes from the time that we had begun to doubt ourselves, something lurched through the rain clouds. At first it looked like a big black funnel, and I grabbed the controls and prepared to turn out of the way, for this was the latitude of water-spouts. Then with a start, I recognized— or thought I recognized—the object. This time it looked like real land. I felt the "gooseflesh" of excitement break out all over me, a shiver of pure thanksgiving run down my spine. For I could see trees on the black object and I knew there were no trees on water-spouts.

It was a hill, and this was Africa! I could have kissed that hill—I could have reached out my arms and hugged that ragged hill! Land Ho!

We didn't know exactly what part of the country it was and it didn't much matter. I heard the loudest yells I've ever heard in my life. Doug let out one, and then Sergeant Aaltonen behind him; I even heard the navigator cheering. I felt like looping the ship, and it wouldn't have been very difficult to do with the light gas load we were carrying.

I looked at the chart of Africa, and at the area we were probably over. The contours showed only two outstanding hills along the coast, from a hundred miles North of our destination to a hundred miles South. There was one near Freetown about 835 feet above sea-level, and there was one at Fisher's Lake, Liberia, where the mark indicated nearly four hundred feet above sea-level. It seemed too good to be true that we could have hit Fisher's Lake, Liberia, for that is very near the point we were heading for. There was a quick way to check on that. I dove down about a hundred feet. We went over the hill—and we were slightly over four hundred feet. And then I said "This, I believe, is Fisher's Lake. If it is, we're just too good or we're too lucky, or somebody has taken us by the hand and brought

53

us in here. But there's another check we can use. The town is supposed to be over there to the left."

So we circled over, and there was a town right where it showed on the map. I felt better and better; confidence was beginning to grow within me—even if we did have less than one hour's fuel remaining.

Then the possibility of another check occurred to me. Two nights earlier, a classmate of mine had left Natal piloting one of the B-17's in our flight. Reaching Africa too early in the morning, he had encountered thick haze, and rather than mill around and run out of gas, he had set down on a level beach. The radio that had come back from that ship via the Army radio at our destination had stated that this officer had gotten down safely at Fisher's Lake, Liberia. With the help of the natives, he had pulled the plane back along the sand, letting out part of the air from his big tires to make them sink less deeply into the sand. Later in the day he had taken off and flown to destination.

The last test, then, would be to go down low and look for the marks of this other Fortress's wheels in the sand. As I dove over the long beach near Robertsport I saw them, long before I expected them. They were distinct, and I could even see the cloth markers that Col. Torgils Wold had got the natives to put up on sticks, so that he could steer down the beach for the difficult take-off. I yelled again—for this had absolutely identified our position. We were only minutes from our goal.

Something else impressed itself upon me here, something that I shall think about many times in the years to come. I remembered a night long ago, when we were carrying the airmail through the snow and ice of the Great Lakes region—the night when I had been lost in a bomber loaded with mail. I have told how, finding myself on the Kalamazoo-Chicago lane of lighted beacons, I had finally got down on the proper course and had landed at what I hoped and prayed was Toledo. I've told how, to avoid giving myself away, I asked the sergeant a question about a friend of mine at the Toledo field. That man had been Lieutenant Wold, the same man who as Colonel Wold had made the forced landing on the beach at Fisher's Lake. Coincidence? Accident? I don't know. Many years had gone by, the world had changed greatly—and yet, at this point halfway round the globe, the same man had enabled me once again to locate my position.

No one can imagine the thrill of relief that ran through all our crew of nine as I turned that ship Southeast for the short run to our landing field. We had been out in the ocean in such a position that if we had flown a wrong course, such as the course of the ninety-degree change that we had made, we might easily have paralleled the coast below the bulge of West Africa for some twelve hundred miles, finally running out of fuel far out to sea, knowing only that any land would be roughly Northeast or East.

Now I took the ship down so low on the water that the props were almost touching the waves. We moved the throttles back to normal cruising position and hedge-hopped the beach. I dipped the wings in between the palm trees—I dove at dusky natives sleeping in front of their huts. I waved at them and they waved back. A feeling of friendliness came over me as I saw the flash of their white teeth. At that minute we loved everybody. All of us felt too good; all that crew knew we'd had a close squeeze, and now the tension was off. This great ship was still intact, ready to strike at the enemy—and not back there somewhere in the Atlantic, sinking. There weren't two rubber boats floating around with nine of us in them— good combat men perhaps now broken in body by an ocean "crash" landing. I was the pilot of that ship. The ship's loss would not have been my fault any more than it would have been the fault of the tail gunner or the radioman; it was the navigator who had lost us, for I had trusted him all the way until the trouble. Just the same, I knew that the pilot was the man upon whom the responsibility would rest—and in this moment I was bound to be the happiest in the crew.

Down in front appeared the river that led into the field. We followed the "corridor," that mythical line that we had to fly exactly in order to identify ourselves. Now there was the field —thousands of black natives working on the long runway, pulling stone rollers and carrying small baskets of earth on their kinky heads. I yielded to another childish temptation and dove to buzz the airdrome. In a dive just like a single-seater's, I pulled up at some three hundred miles an hour and chandelled off the runway as the native workers got out of the way. I almost looped the next pass, then slipped into a landing on our first stop in Africa.

10

Across Africa

WE CLIMBED OUT of the Fortress and stepped upon Africa at 11:05 G.M.T. Our crossing from Natal had been made in thirteen hours. Leaving the natives at work under Royal Air Force bosses, we hurried on to Operations, where we arranged for clearance down the coast. Then we were led into a thatch-roofed dining hall for good hot food. If I hadn't been so hungry and tired from the extra tension I had been subjected to, I think I'd have "gawked" at those wild-looking tribesmen who were serving us. In one night we'd left the hotels of South America, and here we were, having our plates brought by jet-black bush negroes with rings in their ears and noses, jabbering away in a West Coast dialect. To them we were "Bwana," the food was "chop," and dessert was "sweet."

Maybe the meal was really good—I've forgotten. But later we were to have some meals which were definitely on the rugged side. Some time just try a breakfast at three A.M. composed of warmed-over, mouldy, then re-warmed toast, with slightly sour canned tomatoes. After this year and more, I can close my eyes and see Col. C. V. Haynes sitting there looking at that delicacy—thinking, no doubt, about Carolina country ham, with brown gravy making a little puddle in the grits.

Well fed but on the tired side, we left the base at 13:35, for our next destination farther down the coast. For more than two hundred miles we were over friendly territory as we hugged the beaches, but later, along the Ivory Coast, we had to fly out to sea to avoid the prying eyes that were Vichy French.

We passed a fighter base at 17:00 G.M.T., and one hour later we landed at another West Coast base. The sun was setting back to the West in the Atlantic—towards home. Easter Sunday was fast coming to a close. I remembered then, from "hearsay evidence," that I had been born exactly thirty-four years before. From personal experience I would be able to recall this Easter as a memorable one.

Back through a great part of my hectic life, I had been the "timehog" when it came to chiselling airplanes from every station in the U.S.A. I had often stated that I had never had, and never would have, enough flying time. Right now, the way my head and eyes ached and the way my body fairly yearned for a place to stretch out, I almost resolved to eat those statements of the past. For during the last twenty-eight hours we had been in the air, for twenty-five of them under terrific tension. In that one day we had not only been lost in the South Atlantic, but we had covered nearly four thousand miles, from Belem to Natal to our stop near Fisher's Lake, and on to destination. I remember looking over at Doug and saying rather sadly that for once in my life I had had enough flying for one day.

As we rode out to our billets in a British lorry with a barefoot bush-boy chauffeur, I contemplated the completed trip. I firmly believe that had I been a confirmed ground soldier, wholly unconverted to air power, I would have realized that the airplane had grown up and was definitely here to stay.

Next day, while the crew worked on the tired airplane, some of us drove into the bush country. With a guide we made about a ten-hour trip into the interior, to Togoland. Entering a typical dirty village we heard jazz music and picked our way towards the source. I imagine all of us were expecting to find a radio or a victrola; instead we found that we were really in the land that had "birthed" jazz. Grouped about an earthen crock of palm wine was the population of the village, and the more they dipped the gourd cups into the stagnant-looking liquor, the hotter the music became and the more the sweating black bodies swayed to the beat of the drums. Their bare feet were moving to the rhythm in the dust, and their naturally musical voices, added to the syncopated rumble that came from black hands thumping many kinds of drums, made us wonder whether some orchestra like Cab Calloway's hadn't come to Africa with us on a USO project.

On April 7 we left the Gold Coast for Kano, in Nigeria. Off at 08:00 G.M.T., we flew a course of 90 degrees to miss more of Vichy France. Over Lagos, in the clammy heat of the equatorial jungle, we turned into the continent to a course of 58 degrees and continued over very thick country until we crossed the Niger. From there on East, the land that was Africa seemed to dry up, and my boyhood conception of how the Dark Continent should look faded away. Instead of constant jungle we now saw dry desert, like the lower hump of Brazil near Natal, or places in our own West.

We landed at the old walled city of Kano that afternoon. Our next take-off, for Khartoum, would best be made at nightfall, in order that we might land in the Sudan early in the morning before the dust storms had impaired the visibility. To waste time we walked into town to see the ancient city of Biblical days. Soon we found ourselves dodging camels, lepers, and Ali Baba—with his more than forty thieves.

None of us ever determined whether or not this Ali Baba was a descendant of the Arabian Nights original. But we did learn of a great decision that he had lost in a financial battle with some ferry pilots from the AVG. These men were members of the famous First American Volunteer Group under General Chennault, who were fighting the Japs in Burma.

General Chennault's AVG was composed of three squadrons, functioning under the supreme command of China's Generalissimo Chiang Kai-shek. About seventy pilots and three hundred ground crew personnel made up this organization, which for nearly four months had been in combat against the Japanese Air Force from Rangoon up to Lashio, Burma. These American boys had come from the air services of the American Army, Navy and Marine Corps.

The General was an old pilot, and through many years of single-seater flying in the noise of open cockpits had become moderately deaf, a circumstance that had helped to bring about his retirement. Knowing that war with Japan was more than probable, after his retirement he had gone to China, and there he had not only persuaded the Generalissimo to build the air-warning net within China, but had worked to train China's Air Force as well. Growing out of this, when the brave Chinese Air Force was virtually destroyed by the overwhelming odds of the Japanese juggernaut, Chennault had long cherished a volunteer force of American airmen, flying American equipment in China against the Jap.

The purpose was fourfold: to test American equipment, to train a nucleus of American pilots in actual combat, to furnish air support for the Chinese land forces, and to fight a delaying action against the Japanese until the Chinese armies could be equipped with modern sinews of war for offensive action against the stranglehold of Japan.

Finally, in the late summer of 1941, the Army, Navy, and Marine Corps permitted a few reserve officer pilots to resign their commissions and accept jobs as instructors with Central Aircraft Manufacturing Company, or Camco, as it was called. These seventy-odd pilots and some three hundred ground-crewmen proceeded in small numbers on ships of various nations—Dutch, British, Indian, American, and some unregistered—West from San Francisco to Java, then Singapore, and thence to Rangoon, Burma.

These "instructors" for Camco were carried on the passenger lists as acrobats, doctors, lawyers, and probably even Indian chiefs. I imagine that after they made their great record —with never more than fifty-five airplanes they shot down two hundred and eighty-six Japanese planes, losing only eight in combat—the complaining Japanese would have been disposed to add the remainder of the nursery rhyme, "Rich man, poor man, beggarman, thief."

Many times I had heard Radio Tokyo complain of the "cruelty" of these American guerrilla pilots. Under General Chennault's clever leadership and tactical genius they had virtually driven the Imperial Japanese Air Force from the skies of Burma, and held the Burma Road for months after it should have fallen. Against odds of more than twenty to one, they had "saved face" for America and the white race, in this battle against a much-belittled enemy.

When one considers that the AVG fought in what the British called obsolete tactical combat aircraft—the P-40B's and P-40C's—their deeds and scores become truly legendary. Throughout China today, General Chennault's AVG are regarded as "Saviors of Free China Skies." The Chinese sentry on the gate to the "Fijichan" or airfield may shake his head when you show him your pass; he may not understand your hard-won Chinese; but when you smile and call, "A-V-G," his face lights up in turn, and he calls, "Ding-hao—you are 'number one.'" He holds his thumb up in the old familiar signal, and you enter. Then, to show his high regard for Americans and his vivid memory of General Chennault's Flying Tigers, he calls after you, "A-V-G mean American Very Good—ding-hao, ding-hao."

But to get back to Kano and Ali Baba:

We had begun to meet members of the AVG on the West Coast. They were still fighting in Burma, but we found that some had been sent by Army transport plane to a base on the African West Coast to ferry new P-40E's or Kittyhawks back to General Chennault. In their travels they had passed through Kano and had made the acquaintance of Ali Baba, the rug, ivory, and snakeskin merchant. They were going to be remembered by Ali Baba for a long, long time, for when we met him he was diligently searching the faces of every American, trying to recognize someone. Ali Baba definitely agreed with the Japs about the AVG. He did not like them, and I'm sure if he had been able to speak Chinese he'd have held his thumb down at them and called, "Bu-hao," which is a Chinese Bronx Cheer, or literally, "You are very bad—you are not 'number one.'"

Some of the AVG had come through Kano with their new Kittyhawks, en route to China and Burma. They had priced Ali Baba's ivory and other commodities, and had not been able to resist the temptation to use their Chinese money as American dollars. After all, it was plainly printed on the Chinese national currency in English: "Made in U.S.A." Besides, there was a picture on the bills, just as on a five, ten, or hundred dollar Federal Reserve banknote. Of course it didn't matter that the Chinese money was called "CN," and was worth, on a rapidly fluctuating black market, anywhere from one-twentieth to one-fiftieth as much as U.S. or "gold" currency. Anyway, in business with an Arab it was first come, first served—when it came to who was going to be "gypped."

So the AVG pilots bought their souvenirs, and then presented Ali Baba with stacks of CN in tens, fifties, and hundreds. The old merchant took the new Chinese bills, looked at them questioningly, held them up to the light, and slowly shook his head.

"American, eh? But the picture is strange. George Washington I know, Abraham I know, but this picture I do not know."

Now the picture on the Chinese CN was that of Dr. Sun Yat Sen, but one of the AVG quickly said:

"Aw, good gracious, Ali Baba—that's our old President. He's already been President longer than George Washington and Abraham Lincoln put together. That's Franklin D. Roosevelt—and that's a brand new fifty-dollar bill."

Ali Baba took the money, and when he found out his mistake he probably tried to bite himself. But even at that, the AVG had not cheated him more than a bare ten per cent, for his prices had jumped about twenty times when he saw they were Americans. If they got their CN at near forty to one, the loss was about equal. Right now, though, as we walked through town, I could not resist picking up a snakeskin and offering Ali Baba my one souvenir Chinese bill in exchange. He almost had apoplexy. He had learned quickly enough that President Roosevelt did not look like Dr. Sun Yat Sen—and after all, an Arab trader is not the world's best loser.

We caught up with three more of our thirteen bombers at Kano, and all our crew had begun to feel confident that we could not be called back from the mission against Tokyo. To insure this to a greater degree, we were trying hard, without appearing to be too anxious, to be the first to reach our initial point—Karachi, India. So long as we were the first of the B-17's, we could claim a moral victory. For after all, Colonel Haynes was boss, and in a ship with longer range than the Fortress, and we wanted him ahead.

With full service aboard, and the temperature hot and stifling, even after nightfall, we threaded our way through the dust for the take-off. I remember that the heavy ship used the entire runway and some of the sagebrush prairie land too, for there seemed to be no lift whatever to the hot, dead air. Finally reaching a comfortable cruising altitude at twelve thousand, Doug and I breathed the old familiar sigh of relief at having once again gotten a loaded bomber in the air, and the sigh echoed around the ship.

Down in the dust haze not a light showed as we crossed equatorial Africa where Sergeant Aaltonen and Cobb wanted so much to land for a look at the big-lipped Ubangi women. Then Lake Chad and Fort Lamy went by. Just before dawn we crossed North of the mountain of El-Fasher. At six o'clock the White Nile appeared—we had crossed the western part of the Sudan. Our landing was made at Khartoum, where the Blue Nile and the White Nile meet.

On April 8, we left Khartoum for an easy run to Aden, on a course which was almost due East over the mountains of Eritrea. We went on over Gura and Massaua to the Red Sea. On our left we could see Yemen, and farther South and to our right, Somaliland. Reaching the South end of the Red Sea and the Gulf of Aden, the well-known landmarks, the Rocks of Aden, appeared about noon. Next day we'd make the run on to India.

The British garrison commander took care of us that night. But around the dinner table there suddenly dropped a blanket of despair. The London radio announced that Bataan had fallen. After the first comment we settled down to worry. Part of our mission was to bomb Jap concentrations around Bataan and Corregidor. Would this development cause that part of the attack to be called off? Again the fear of being frustrated in our effort to take the offensive clutched my heart. It seemed that once again help had been started too late.

We had caught the last of the B-17's at Aden, and next morning we got up an extra hour early for the take-off. Our Fortress was straining to get to the initial point just behind the B-24. Success was in sight.

At 5:50 we were climbing over the beach of southern Arabia, and as the light improved we all agreed that Arabia was a rugged-looking land. After the terrible stories about the mutilation of forced-down flyers at the hands of the tribesmen, we all were glad that we had the little cards written in Arabic, promising high payment to the Arabs if we were delivered unharmed to the nearest British outpost.

We followed the Arabian coast over the blue waters of the Arabian Sea to the Gulf of Oman, and then crossed to Karachi.

Colonel Haynes, with the B-24, had gone to Delhi. Our orders were to wait at Karachi. And now for two weeks we anxiously waited, while the rumors flew.

11
Burma-Roadsters

I THINK I SHALL always associate India with my first impression on getting out of my ship. No one seemed to know anything. Behind us lay twelve thousand miles, which we had made in eight days—for what? No one stood there with orders to expedite our departure. Instead they appeared to think we had ferried this ship for them to use in training. Training, mind you—here, halfway round the world and in a country that faced attack any moment! When we explained as much as we could about our secret orders, smiles came to the officers' faces. Bets were laid that we would never leave Karachi with those ships. But we were volunteers, and our combat spirit was still there. I remember that all my crew took the bets, as fast as they were offered.

But we lost.

Once again we had been frustrated in our effort to go to war on the offensive. Now, four months after Pearl Harbor, the stencilled word on a B-17 in our flight, SNAFU—meaning roughly, in Air Corps slang, "Snarled-up"—seemed to fit the situation. We learned the worst when Haynes came back from Delhi with a face a yard long. Sadly he told us the truth. Due to the fall of Bataan and the loss of other fields in eastern China—our secret bases—coupled with other factors beyond his control, our "dream mission" had come to the end of the line.

During the fourteen days in Karachi, when we had been waiting for Colonel Haynes, it had been a difficult job of finesse to hang on to the ships. All twelve of the B-17's were lined up to be turned over to Base Units on the field. But the personnel responsible for the conflicting orders had reckoned without the extreme loyalty of the volunteer crewmen to the flight commander and the pilot of each ship. The men stood guard twenty-four hours a day in and around the bombers. This was logical, too, because each ship contained not only the secret bomb-sight but full complements of loaded fifty-calibre guns, as well as the personal effects of the bomber crews. At first the crews appeared bewildered; but then their attitude seemed to imply stubbornly that they had been ordered to attack Japanese territory, and no matter if Bataan and all of eastern China fell, that's what they were going to do.

One day the General in charge of the Air Base sent a crew down to my ship with orders for them to take over and search out a Japanese Task Force far out in the Arabian Sea. They were met with the ready Tommy guns of my men and roughly told that no one except members of the crew could get aboard. A Major in the new crew showed his orders. My crew chief replied: "I'm sorry, Sir, but I have mine, too; we are on our way to bomb an enemy objective. No one gets aboard this ship except the regular crew."

Well, the Air Base General had to ask us to carry out the mission, and to ease the monotony we were glad to comply. Taking the bomb-bay tanks from the ship, we loaded with five-hundred-pound bombs and off we went, eight hundred miles into the Arabian Sea, looking for a Jap naval force composed of three warships, five destroyers, five cruisers, and two aircraft carriers—with our one bomber. Due to the low weather we had to fly beneath the cloud base at seven thousand feet. Reaching our patrol area, we searched until it was necessary to return to base for fuel. I have often wondered what we would have done had we had the fortune or misfortune to find that task force—if it existed. After all, from seven thousand feet we could have done very little damage with a single ship. Somehow I'm glad we did not engage the enemy—I always hated to be a clay pigeon, and though the future looked dark, there were interesting days ahead.

Slowly, though, through days in which some of the others took their ships to bomb Rangoon and the Andaman Islands, and finally when Haynes returned from Delhi, the realization sank in that our mission was cancelled. I have never seen thirteen crews of bombers carrying so many broken hearts. Morale dropped like a stone. On April 21, when the base took our ships, I think we would have been justified in getting stinking drunk.

New orders came for Colonel Haynes and most of us in the ill-fated "dream mission" to report to a remote base in eastern Assam, on the India-Burma border, to run the A. B. C. Ferrying Command. This Assam-Burma-China transport command was for the purpose of carrying supplies to China and Burma, to make up as much as possible for the fall of the Burma Road.

When Colonel Haynes and I arrived in Assam we both considered ourselves "shanghaied." I could tell, as we faced each other across the breakfast table that first morning, that we both knew that things were going to be bad. Our status had changed from participating in what we considered the "greatest mission in the world," to the insignificant task of running a ferry command from India to Burma. Once again combat duty seemed far away.

All around us now were the tea gardens of Assam. Our landing field was an RAF base. Our homes were mud and bamboo huts called "bashas." Through the jungle that surrounded our base, wild animals roamed; every night we could hear the jackals scream. We knew that cobras were everywhere. On flights over the Brahmaputra River, I would see rhinos, elephants and other animals which made me realize vividly that we were far from civilization.

Our base was situated in a horseshoe formed by the Himalaya Mountains to the North and West and by the Naga Hills to the East and Southwest. The altitude of our field was 600 feet above sea level, and all around us in three directions rose mountains—the lower Himalayas being 25,500 feet, just 150 miles to the North. These great peaks reached their ceiling, of course, at Mt. Everest, 29,002 feet above sea level—the highest mountain in the world. This was 300 miles from us.

Our first job was to begin the construction of other fields in the area—this was to permit us to have more than one base from which to work. For our job was that of being ferry pilots for both the Chinese Army and General Chennault's AVG down in Burma. We were to carry high octane gas, ammunition, and food into Burma, and later into China. We were soon to find ourselves returning from Burma with our ships completely filled and overflowing with wounded British soldiers. Col. C. V. Haynes was boss; he was Commanding Officer of the A. B. C. Ferrying Command, and I was his Executive Officer.

We began our work the day after we arrived in Assam. This was April 21. We had thirteen transports manned by the Army and Pan-American pilots. Our job in flying supplies into Burma was a tough one with unarmed transports, for by this time the Japanese had crossed the Sittang and the Irrawaddy and had taken Rangoon. They now had columns moving towards Mandalay. Their Air Force was all over Central Burma, and the only thing that stood between them and the capture of all of Burma was the few American pilots of the First American Volunteer Group, who had been forced now to base at Lashio. These were truly the dark days of Burma.

On April 24, Colonel Haynes and Colonel Cooper transported a load of ammunition and aviation fuel to Lashio for the Flying Tigers, and on their way back an enemy fighter plane made an attack on their transport. Recognizing the ship as an enemy Zero, Haynes and Cooper left the flying of the plane to the co-pilot and went back into the fuselage, to ward off the attack as best they could with Tommy guns. Don Old, the co-pilot, dove the transport until they were actually skimming over the jungle trees. These evasive tactics kept the Jap ship from coming up under the vulnerable transport. Just one of the Jap tracers in that Douglas would have set it afire.

As the Jap dived towards them, Cooper and Haynes and their crew chief, Sergeant Bonner, fired magazine after magazine at the Jap. This either discouraged him or the enemy ship lost the transport in a turn, for they got away. But even considering the bravery of these flyers in using their meager armament against a fighter ship, it is a poor policy to shoot Zeros with Tommy guns; 45-caliber ammunition is not very effective against aircraft, but, as usual in a case like this, if you have only a pop-gun to point at the enemy, it helps the morale.

Most of our pilots had been chosen from the crews of the thirteen ships of our original mission. Even with the loss in morale they had suffered when the attack on Tokyo was called off, they were still the best transport pilots I had ever seen.

Colonel Haynes was a veteran big-ship pilot, and for the last ten years he had worked in four-engine bombers. The records that he had set with the giant B-15 will inspire the Air Force forever. Here was a big, cheerful master pilot who never asked another man to do a job he wouldn't do himself. We of the A. B. C. Ferrying Command looked upon him as the best, and Haynes will always stand out in my mind as one of the greatest officers of our army. This jovial veteran was ready to do anything to help win the war, but we all knew he preferred to kill Japs rather than rustle freight across to Burma. I lived with Colonel Haynes on one of the tea plantations in Assam, where we were billeted with a Scotsman, Josh Reynolds of Sealkotte Tea Estate.

Major Joplin, whom we called "Jop," was another of our pilots. This man claimed that he had been born in a DC-2 and weaned in a C-47. One of the Pan-American pilots had made a forced landing with one of the transports, putting it down with the wheels up in a rice paddy near the Brahmaputra. Jop took a crew to the transport, took the bent propellers off and roughly straightened them. With his crew and some volunteer natives, he dug holes under the folded-up landing-gear and then let the gear down until it was fully extended, with the wheels down, to the bottom of the holes. Now he placed heavy timbers from the wheels to the surface of the rice paddy, putting them in at a small angle to form an inclined plane. Next he had about a hundred natives pull on ropes that were tied to the wheels, and dragged the Douglas transport up the inclined plane until it rested on the more or less level ground of the rice paddy. Then Jop demonstrated that he could justify all his claims of having been born in a Douglas transport. He gave the ship the guns, and in a flurry of mud and water and rice stalks, bounced it from the field and flew it home to base.

All the pilots were good, and they were eager. The weather never became too bad or the trip too dangerous for men like Tex Carleton, Bob Sexton, or the others to get through. The enlisted men were the best. There in Assam they fought a constant battle against boredom, malaria, and every form of tropical disease. They ate and slept in the mud and didn't grumble, more than the average soldier gripes, about the native food. The stringy buffalo meat was fairly tough; the mouthful used to get bigger and bigger as you chewed it.

Even with the hardships, we enjoyed the assignment—for after all, Burma was just over the Naga Hills and they said a war was going on over there. Down in his heart, each man really wanted to do something to stop the Japs from their rapid movement to the North through Burma. But we had no fighters and no bombers. I often heard of plots among the crewmen for going back to Karachi and stealing the thirteen four-engined bombers, but of course they were just soldier rumors. The small amount of good that we figured we were doing by flying ammunition, aviation gasoline, and bombs to the AVG was barely enough to keep our morale above the sinking point. Personally I made a trip almost every day over into Lashio and Loiwing, and some days I went on farther East to Kunming, China.

One day, during the last of April, two Chinese pilots landed with two P-43A's. These were good, fast-climbing, little fighter ships, the forerunner of the "Thunderbolts." But their fuel tanks had developed leaks, and when you added to that the fact that the turbo was underneath the rear of the fuselage, the greatest fire hazard in the world was born. So far had their ill fame spread that the ships were grounded until the faults could be remedied. So the Chinese left the P-43A's with us and went on back to China. Colonel Haynes and I fell heir to the two little fighters.

Sergeant Bonner worked diligently with everything from chewing gum to cement and finally repaired the leaks, at least to a point where they didn't catch fire right away on the take-off, as some of them had done. I took one of these ships and decided to use it to protect the ferry route. Even one lone fighter that could fire back at the Japs would be a good morale element for the crews of the unarmed transports.

12
Two Miles Above Everest

FOR SEVERAL DAYS I tested the single-seater around the field for fuel consumption, and got the guns working pretty steadily by shooting at crocodiles in the Brahmaputra. Every time I climbed above the heat haze of Assam, I'd observe the high peaks of the Himalayas to the North and Northwest, and the longing began to grow within me to fly up over the highest mountains in the world. But we had lots to do with the transports, and the days passed without my chance to fly into Tibet. Besides, we were getting more and more reports about the Japanese air activity a few hundred miles to the Southeast.

And yet, after each of my convoy flights above the transports, I'd look longingly at the snow-capped tops of Everest and Kanchenjunga. Every day that I put the trip off, I'd look at the P-43A with its turbo supercharger, all ready to take me into the stratosphere, and I'd try to plan some excuse for seeing how high that little fighter would climb. It got so bad that even when I'd run across passages in books referring to altitude and hills I'd feel more and more keenly the urge to tackle Everest and the Himalayas. Finally I saw one night that even Ruskin had read my thoughts, for he'd written: "Out from between the cloudy pillars as they pass, emerge forever the great battlements of the memorable and perpetual hills."

That must have made up my mind for me. I was a creature of opportunity, and here I was—right beneath those great battlements with just the little ship to climb entirely over them and fly the good old star insigne of the Army Air Force a lot higher than the highest bit of land in the world.

One morning, when the approaching monsoon period made it impossible to carry ammunition to the AVG in Burma, I kept seeing the tops of the greatest mountains in the world as I tested my little interceptor over Assam. I knew I could just as easily test this ship for maximum altitude by heading out over that mountain range, whose lowest valley was as high as Mount Whitney, as by what I was doing here over the safety of my home field in Assam. So I landed and filled all the fuel tanks of the Republic, got my movie camera and plenty of oxygen, and took off from the tea estates of Assam for the hills of Tibet, via the sacred city of Lhasa. My decision was well timed, too, for within two weeks we received specific instructions not to fly over the country of Tibet or Nepal.

Going out over the Brahmaputra River, I began to follow it as I climbed. I soon came to our auxiliary field of Sadiya, and turned North with the river and watched the thick jungle of northeastern India move higher and higher as the hills rose and the stream grew narrow. To my right were the Naga Hills separating India from Burma. To my left and rear was the densest jungle I had ever seen—a jungle for which unofficial reports claim a record rainfall of 980 inches a year. Ahead I could see the peak of Namsha Barwa, and I knew that I had suddenly begun my flight from the six-hundred-foot elevation of our base to as high as I could make the little plane go.

As I gained altitude to the North and entered Tibet, I kept looking down at the Brahmaputra and marvelling. Here was a stream that flowed for more than a thousand miles at an altitude that must average 13,000 feet; in Tibet, I realized, even the rivers were nearly as high as our highest mountain in America. From my map I saw that the Brahmaputra rose on the side of a peak far over in the West of India and flowed straight East near the city of Lhasa, then made an "S" turn between these two peaks that were directly ahead of me, then turned South and entered India, again turning Southwest at Sadiya, and keeping that course until it joined the Padna or Ganges and emptied into the Bay of Bengal. I had heard that this great gorge formed by the river's cutting into the mountains, this "S" turn which I was nearing, was one of the least known parts of the world, and I was approaching the Great Himalayas from this direction in order to look at that canyon.

In less than a hundred miles, the country below changed as if by magic from the rain-swept paddy fields, the dark green tea acres, the wide river flowing through relatively flat country, to jagged mountains. I pointed the fighter ship, still climbing, in between the two peaks that formed the gorge of the Brahmaputra. The mountain to my left was named Namsha Barwa on my map; the one to my right was unnamed. They were both about 25,500 feet above sea level. To the North the map showed a whole area unmarked with contour lines, an area listed as "unexplored and unadministered."

My altitude with the P-43A was now 20,000 feet. Under me I could see white clouds in the canyon. I had made about 175 miles. Continuing through the gorge, I turned with the river in its "S" through the mountains. Below me now, the mountains almost made the river reverse its course, but finally it came out seemingly in the clouds, and from my vantage point it appeared to me that I was looking into the greatest canyon in the world.

I continued climbing toward the Southwest, following the gorge. About ninety miles from the turn I reached a smaller river that came down from the North into the Brahmaputra. Turning up this, in forty miles I came to Lhasa, the city of the Dalai Lama. The forbidden city lay North of the little, unnamed river; it was made up of sprawling, dun-colored houses, and was built on an open plain. From Lhasa and its listed altitude of 12,555 feet, the land rose rapidly to the North, and in less than thirty miles the mountains were over twenty thousand feet. The maps are inaccurate, and the distances in that clear air are deceiving, but that was the impression I gained.

Circling Lhasa, I photographed the city and the Dalai Lama's palace in color. The most noteworthy thing was the plume of dust rising along the road through the town, a plume that was not so much rising as being blown horizontally by a very strong wind. Even from over twenty thousand feet, I could perceive that Tibet was a rugged country.

To the North of Lhasa I identified the peak of Tengri-Nor, and remembered that near that one mountain peak there rose five big rivers of Asia: The Irrawaddy, the Salween, the Mekong, the Yangtse, and the Yellow. Here were five rivers whose sources were almost within sight of one another—yet their mouths were separated by thousands of miles of Asia, from the China Sea to the Bay of Bengal.

As I turned from Lhasa and once more flew West, a farewell look showed me a white road leading East from the sacred city, and I knew it was the Yak trail that led across to northern China. The dust was being blown in all directions by winds that swept down from those lofty pinnacles to make the harshest climate on earth—icy winds that had climbed over these twenty-odd-thousand-foot peaks from the plains of Mongolia. I had read that this trail to the East crossed the gorges of the upper Salween, Mekong, and Yangtse to Chengtu, and that in summer a good pack train could make it in ninety days.

Leaving Lhasa, I also left the Brahmaputra, which continued westward to its source some five hundred miles away in the mountain of Gurla Mandhata, over 25,000 feet high. Across that same mountain, on its western slope, rose the Indus. Two rivers that almost encircled the borders of India in all her vast area rose on one mountain—yet one of them emptied into the Bay of Bengal near Calcutta, while the other flowed West and entered the Arabian Sea.

My course was away from the river as I pointed the nose of the fighter towards the great peaks that were now coming up over the curve of the earth. Even at the high altitude I had reached—over 25,000 feet—I could only gasp at their greatness. Now, as I swept my head around and made my pictures, in one glance I took in an area that must have had more than a thousand-mile diameter. In one sweep my eye passed from the steamy depths of the Assamese jungle, to the Naga Hills, ten to twelve thousand feet high; then from these mere foothills to the distant snows of the Himalayas—the roof of the world.

Now, straight ahead, I saw Kanchenjunga, with three of its five peaks visible. On ahead to the West, summit after summit pointed into the purpling sky. There was Makalu, rearing up to 27,790 feet on the other side of Kanchenjunga. Kanchenjau and Chamo Lhani were between Makalu and the great one—Everest. The greatest of mountains was still muddled together in its multitude of spires; so that from my distance I could not yet pick out the highest point of land on this earth.

With the turbo on full we climbed on, above twenty-six thousand feet now. Far to the West, I saw where the Himalayas end, and above the heat haze of India there appeared other peaks in other mountain ranges far away in the Punjab. One of these I recognized as Badrinath, itself nearly 28,000 feet high. The entire range of the Great Himalayas now appeared like the giant vertebrae of some greatest of animals from which during countless centuries the flesh had gone. Below me it stretched, from Burma, some four hundred miles behind me to the East, to that peak near Badrinath far out to the West. Approaching Kanchenjunga, I circled that impressive 28,150-foot pyramid and then wove in between it and the slightly lower peaks to the West. Continuing my color photography as the sky darkened in the substratosphere, I silhouetted the snow-covered pinnacles against the purpling sky.

On I went, to the peaks of Makalu and Chamo Lhani, keeping the little fighter climbing steadily, winding in among the saddles between the mighty hills. Even in the lethargy that comes with oxygen starvation—or aëroembolism, as the flight surgeons call it—I was proud of the loud American engine that was pulling me on and on to the top of the world. Looking at those massive, snow-covered spires, I respected the magnitude of nature and magnificence of the Himalayas, and I perceived the insignificance of man. Then, as my position above it all impressed itself on me, I realized that, after all, man had perfected that steadily purring engine which was carrying me on and on

70

above the greatest of mountains. Perhaps, then, man in all his insignificance deserved a little credit too.

Rising alone, without the proximity of lofty lesser peaks, Kanchenjunga is truly the most beautiful of mountains. Though a full thousand feet lower than Everest, it sweeps up in isolation from a fourteen-thousand-foot plain for another fourteen thousand feet in a graceful pyramid, commanding the chain of the highest mountains in the world.

The little fighter and I "topped out" over Makalu. On the other side, towards Everest, I saw Kamet. Then peak after peak met my gaze. There was Chamo Lhani, Chomiomo, Kanchenjau, Cho-oyu at 26,870 feet, Gyachung Kang, Lhotse (the South peak of Everest)—until finally and with reverence, as though I had saved the greatest for last, my eyes centered on Everest, in Tibet called Chamolang, the Sacred One.

I guess my real reason for finally yielding my eyes to the great mountain alone was that by now it was the only summit above me—the others had gradually sunk beneath the mounting altitude of the little fighter plane. Now even Everest was slowly giving way, and I headed directly for that mass of reddish yellow rock, all of it covered with snow and ice except where the everlasting winds of the upper air had torn the covering away. At 30,000 feet and just South of the center pyramid, I saw the "plume" of Everest, formed by snow being blown from the summit. On this day it pointed to the South, borne by a North wind, and the sun shining through it made a rainbow that was beautiful.

Above Everest now, I withstood my temptation to fly close to the big peak on the down-wind side—there were bound to be terrible down-drafts there, and I had respected lesser down-drafts of lesser peaks in lower parts of the world. Passing directly over the South peak, Lhotse, I photographed Everest against the sky, and as I opened the glass canopy of the plane I felt the chilling blast of the wind. I noted then that my thermometer registered 22 degrees below zero, which though cold is nowhere near the temperature one would experience at an equal altitude anywhere else than in the Himalayan region. For there the warm monsoon winds out of the Indian Ocean are raised rapidly by the slope of the earth, and thus the troposphere is evidently higher.

On we climbed, with my turbo moaning its din among the Himalayas. Everest fell farther below, and there came the feeling of exhilaration that I was higher than the highest of mountains—and still climbing. Circling, I set my course toward the peaks forming the northern Tibetan border—the hills of

Arma Dreme (according to my map) and the distant Kwenlun Mountains. My effort was to get that ship as high as it would climb and yet leave me sufficient oxygen to get me back to a safe free-breathing level—and at the same time have enough fuel to reach my selected refueling field to the South, in Cooch Behar. Finally at 37,000 feet as indicated on my altimeter—which is over forty thousand, probably 44,400 feet true, calibrated from temperature and pressure corrections—passed the point where for the sake of my heart and lungs it was best that I go home.

Already I could feel the aëroembolism symptoms to such a degree that I wanted to yell at myself one minute, beat myself over the head the next, and pat myself on the back in another. It's a peculiar kind of "jag" the high altitude flyer gets on, and it's best to be careful. I surely didn't want to fall suddenly asleep and dive down to be a permanent resident among the Lamas in Tibet. Anyway my eyes could no longer see well enough to appreciate the beauties of the mountains, and the reduced pressure was causing extreme discomfort in my stomach. Even with the oxygen regulator on "full" I gasped frequently, and when I raised my camera it seemed to weigh tons. Then I got to where I couldn't remember whether or not I had heard the camera mechanism run. You see, at that altitude the oxygen that we carry in the ship, even if you get it to your lungs, is only partially absorbed by the blood. Anyway, as I opened the canopy the cold air hit me in the face and revived me enough to enable me to make my decision to go down.

The temperature gauge on the dashboard was now minus fifty and on the peg. It had to be lower than fifty below, and that is cold anywhere. Though my camera had been hung over the cockpit heater, I knew that it had been frozen at times and didn't run. Below me now were mountains marked on the map with the familiar phrase: "Territory unexplored and unadministered." Probably some peak in that chain would be higher than Everest—who knows?

I passed over Everest and took my last pictures from the highest altitude that I reached—approximately two miles above the great mountain. To the North I saw, five hundred miles away, the summit of Ulugh Muztagh, itself over 26,000 feet. Around it I could see the desert haze from the sands of Chinese Turkestan. To the West now, and behind the top of Aling Kangri (over 25,000 feet) and Kamet (26,500), the real Western Himalayas, I could see the summits of Saser Kangri and Distaghil Sar. One mountain of this range was the 28,240-foot bulk of Badrinath. To the North of these I saw the desert of

Kashgar, almost five hundred miles from me. To the South appeared the hills of Shilong, nearly four hundred miles away, and around them were the boiling clouds of the approaching monsoon season. Back in the East—the direction from which I had come—was the top of Namsha Barwa, another five hundred miles distant, where the Naga Hills met Burma. On this Spring day, as I spiralled down my eyes must have covered millions of square miles, from my vantage point above the highest peak.

Just to ease a brain that was rapidly growing "befuddled" from altitude, I tried to fire my guns, but they were frozen. Circling in a power dive to exactly thirty thousand feet, I passed directly over Everest and into the "plume." Immediately I was thankful that I had heeded my better judgment of the earlier hour and had not flown close to the down-wind side below the summit. For I was sucked down in the most violent down-draft I have ever experienced.

As the nose of the ship went into the "plume" area, it felt to me as though some gigantic hand had reached up from old Chamolang and was drawing us roughly towards Nepal, the country directly beneath. My camera cracked me in the chin. My maps from the map-case flew all over the cockpit. I got the nose pointed down towards Asia as quickly as I could, got the prop in low pitch, fought the maps out of my eyes—and almost before I realized it we were out of the down-draft, sailing smoothly along at 25,000 feet, at least five miles South of the big peak. Even in that time we had lost almost a mile of altitude.

Gaining complete control of the ship, I circled for more photography, and climbed once more for a view of the North Col, the point where the best efforts at climbing Everest had failed. Out there now I could see that place, at about 28,000 feet above sea level, where man had been forced to turn back, beaten by Nature and the elements. I thought of the months that those hardy men had worked to condition themselves and to fight that high-altitude walk over the 18,000-foot passes from Darjeeling across Sikkim, through these perpetual hills—to failures here in the very shadow of success, barely a thousand feet below the summit. Personally, I want to do all my Himalayan mountain climbing right behind the steady drone of a "A Loud American Engine."

Fuel, oxygen, and film about gone, I turned now through the saddle of Everest's main peaks—the West promontory and Chamolang—and saluted with reverence the highest point on the earth's surface. I tried to salute by firing the two fifty-calibre guns into the glacier, but once more they failed to discharge. So I just waggled my wings and dove for my refueling base to the South.

With an aching head but with real exhilaration, I buzzed the Maharaja's palace and landed at Cooch Behar. Then, with adequate hundred octane fuel, I went on back East to the Brahmaputra, up past Tezpur, with my glance going back occasionally on my old friends, the Himalayas. The great pile of snow-covered summits seemed closer to me now, for I seemed to know them. Everest, with its ocherish-brown color accentuating the yellow sandstone band that traversed it, was back there already over two hundred miles away, still commanding the horizon and in reality the rest of the world. Closer to me and over the saddles of the great ones, every now and then I could see the jagged Nyonna-Ri range and the snows of Arma Dreme. Appearing now as another great mass superimposed on Everest, was the pyramid of Makalu, and from there my eyes swept across a hundred lofty peaks. Looking them all over, I tried to name them without reference to my map. Last of all my gaze centered in admiration on the massif of Kanchenjunga.

I had covered the highest range in the world. I had made the trip of over a thousand miles from our base up the Brahmaputra by Lhasa and Everest to Cooch Behar in five hours and ten minutes. My route had been over territory which was probably the most inaccessible in existence. Certainly it was forbidden, not only by nature but, as I later found out to my sorrow, by the very religion of the people.

For shortly after I landed in Assam, came the usual letter that has dogged me throughout my military career. "You will explain by endorsement hereon why you flew over Everest and crossed the country of Nepal."

You see, on the thread of this "reply by endorsement" there hangs many a tale. To dodge the veiled girl back in Galata, I had crossed the Black Sea to Varna and from Rumania had entered Russia. That had precipitated a letter from the Adjutant General, who demanded a reply by endorsement telling why I, an officer in the American Army, had entered the USSR—a country then not recognized by the U. S. A. Later, in each year, I had had to make the same written reply explaining why I had exceeded the maximum flying time of five hundred hours a year.

There had been many letters, but this one in far-off India had me guessing. I had flown a routine test flight and could not understand why it had required an official answer. Later it came out that the British authorities in India had complained to the

U. S. Headquarters in Delhi about the flight for two reasons. First, that a plane flying over Nepal, from which independent country came the fine little Ghurka soldiers, offended the religion of the people. Secondly, the entire incident had been discovered from the fact that a Calcutta newspaper had published a story that had been given world-wide publicity. This correspondent had dwelt on the ease with which my little fighter had climbed the 29,002 feet to the top of Everest and on up two miles above the highest of peaks, but he had closed his article with what the British considered a slap at their ability. It was this classic ending:

"While it required the British Government many months of planning and the expenditure of some hundred thousands of pounds to fly over Everest in 1927, it merely required an American Aviator, Colonel Scott, about five hours of his morning on a routine test flight and the consumption of a few gallons of aviation gasoline."

Of course I blush when I think that my gallant newspaperman did not consider the difference in the advancement of aviation between the years 1927 and 1942. Oh, well, with the letter answered, apparently to the satisfaction of all concerned, I am still at large, and permitted to fly and to breathe a purer air on high. And there are some magnificent memories locked within me, memories of nature's rocky masterpiece there in the tops of the Himalayas.

13

The General Preferred to Walk

THE JOB of being a ferry pilot had to go on nevertheless. As the leaks developed again in the tanks of the P-43's, I went back to flying the Douglas transports into Burma and China. One day while I was acting as co-pilot for Colonel Haynes, we loaded two disassembled Ryan Trainers in the C-47 and headed for Kunming. Besides this cargo we had some ammunition and food for the AVG at Loiwing, especially a bottle of Scotch whiskey to be left as a present for General Chennault.

We landed at Loiwing and delivered the designated cargo. The air raid alert came just as we were talking with the General. He didn't even change expression, but calmly said, "Guess we're going to have some Japs—you-all had better get those transports off the field." The Flying Tigers were already taking off, their shark-painted noses gleaming in the sun. Lord, but my mouth watered as I saw them—I'd have given anything to trade my colonel's eagles and that "delivery wagon" that I flew for the gold bars of a second Lieutenant and one of those shark-nosed pieces of dynamite!

But we started the Douglas up and took off for China with the cargo of trainers. Even as we cleared the field and climbed towards the Salween, I heard the call "Tally-Ho" from the AVG, and then others more like "Here come the ——." A few seconds later the Jap bombers arrived over the field at Loiwing and we knew all the transports couldn't have gotten off. The AVG radio man, "Mickey" Mihalko, called, "They're bombing the field." Then, in lighter vein, he said the Japs were falling like leaves—or he hoped they were Japs, for he could see many smokes from burning planes. Every now and then we could hear one of the AVG say to some unlucky Jap, "Your mother was a turtle—your father was a snake,"—and then the rattle of fifty-calibre guns over the radio.

We stayed low in the gorge of the Salween until we got to the old bridge near Paoshan, then turned East for Yunnanyi. Behind us the Japs damaged the tail of one of our transports with a bomb, and also blew up the bottle of Scotch that I had brought General Chennault—it had been left in one of the jeeps that was hit. But they had paid heavily for the transport tail and the quart of whiskey. I believe that even the Woman's Christian Temperance Union would have approved of the trade—for the AVG had shot down thirteen of the Zeros and bombers, while as usual they lost none.

At Kunming, with the surprised Chinese looking on, we unloaded the two small training planes from the fuselage of the big Douglas. Then, after something to eat, when I had just about arranged with the AVG squadron commander to go along with them on the morning raid into Indo-China, we received a radiogram that changed all plans.

Colonel Haynes and I were ordered to leave immediately for Shwebo, Burma, down on the Mandalay-Rangoon Railway, and evacuate the staff of General Stilwell. It seemed that the Japs had crossed another place on the Irrawaddy and were about to capture the entire American Military Mission to China—the Ammisca. We didn't even know whether or not there was a landing field in Shwebo, but I found it on a map and in the late afternoon we took off for lower Burma.

We flew through black storms all the way to the Mekong; then, turning South, we found better weather, even if we were getting into Japanese-controlled skies. We landed at Myitkyina and while servicing (so that we would have plenty of fuel to take General Stilwell anywhere he wanted to go), we learned from a British pilot that we would find a small field to the Southeast of the town that was our destination.

Flying as low as we could without hitting the tops of the jungle trees, we followed the Myitkyina-Mandalay railroad to the South. We knew that all the British had evacuated the area about Shwebo except for a small detachment left with the wounded; so we were expecting trouble. I know that neither of us had ever before been so careful at watching the skies. I had my ever-ready movie camera right by my side, but in the excitement I forgot to take pictures as we flew over the burning towns of central Burma. Long afterwards, Colonel Haynes told everyone that I had missed the best pictures in the world, but I imagine he would have dumped me out of the ship if I had raised that movie camera instead of diligently watching the skies.

All the country ahead of us was marked with columns of black smoke, rising straight into the clear sky. We looked for hostile ships until our eyes ached—or for any ship at all, for we knew it would be a Jap, ours being the only Allied plane in the air. We had been flying these unarmed transports so long that both of us had become used to it. Behind us in the empty cargo space I could see the crew chief and the radio operator searching the skies on both sides, with their inadequate Tommy guns at "ready" position. We kept the transport low to the flat country now, so that it wouldn't be silhouetted against the sky. Moreover, the trees under us caused the olive-drab of the ship to blend in, making us harder to see. I thought many times that we couldn't get lower; but we kept going down until I know if the wheels had been extended we'd have been taxying.

I guess we were both a little bit nervous as we peered ahead for any little dot that would mean a Jap. Fly specks on the windshield—and you get lots of them when flying as low as we were—scared us many times. I could feel the palms of my hands sweating as the tension increased.

Finally, straight ahead, I saw a lone column of smoke and thought it was Shwebo. The Japs must already have bombed that too. We kept right on going, expecting any minute to see about eighteen Zeros on our tail. Bombs had started these fires, and where Jap bombers were, fighters could not be far away. The smoke plume grew larger and blacker as we came nearer, until we could see the glow of the fires and the licking flames. We both must have automatically concluded that the burning town was Shwebo, for without more than a glance to check the map we headed for the Southeast corner of the town, where the field was supposed to be.

Then I saw them, high overhead—three planes. But I almost sighed in relief, for they were only Jap bombers—no fighters yet. We kept on low, trying to find the field, while more bombs blasted the town. After searching for several minutes we realized that we were looking into the smoke of the wrong town, for farther South we saw another smoke column, and after checking our position by a canal to the West, we agreed that this town was Kinu and that Shwebo was ten miles South. Shwebo was burning too, and, as we learned later, had been bombed only minutes before we arrived. Jap fighters had accompanied the bombers. So once again some hand of Providence had intervened—had made us mistake Kinu for Shwebo and waste a little time circling.

Colonel Haynes saw the field at Shwebo and pulled the big transport around like a fighter, slipping her in and sitting her down like a feather-bed. We taxied over to the shade to try to partially hide the ship, and I stayed to guard the Douglas while he went to see General Stilwell. You could hear the staff officers and the soldiers yelling, and see them throwing their tin helmets in the air. Jack Belden of *Life* magazine told me later that they had never expected an American ship to get through, and that when the white star of the U. S. Army Air Force was identified, they had even sung "God Bless America." But to us right then, America seemed a very, very long way off.

While Colonel Haynes went for General Stilwell, I stationed the crew around the ship, and we watched the sky with Tommy guns. There was a dead feeling in the air—the smell of smoke and of human flesh from the burning town—and I expected any moment to see Jap Zeros diving on the transport. There we stood with our veritable pop-guns, waiting for Jap cannon.

Just a few minutes later a jeep drove up and C. V. Haynes jumped out, saying that most of the staff was on the way behind him but that General Stilwell wasn't going. At my look of surprise, he added that the General was going to walk out—that he refused to be evacuated by air. Well, for the life of me I couldn't see what face would be saved, for the British Army had gone up the road to the North, and most of the Chinese armies were also on the way out. Perhaps the General knew things that I didn't know. But I remember that Colonel Haynes and I talked it over during the minutes while we waited for the staff to get aboard. We wanted to take General Stilwell out if we had to use force; after all, he was the Commanding General of all American

78

forces in China, Burma, and India, and we knew he was to have a very slim chance of walking out to India through Burma.

I guess if we had captured General Stilwell and taken him back to Chungking we'd have been court-martialled and shot. But we didn't much care what happened then anyway. Burma was falling, and there seemed to be a never-ending stream of Japs coming North. I guess we thought we had a very slim chance of ever getting out alive. After all, we'd been flying around bombed Burmese towns all morning, and when you expect to see Jap fighters any minute for hours, with you in an unarmed ship, and then get to destination and the General won't go—things just don't much matter.

We loaded the anxious staff and took off for Calcutta, with over forty passengers. We could easily have taken from fifty to seventy, but the staff colonel whom we instructed to give the signal when the load was aboard evidently lost count, for he came up and told Colonel Haynes that all were inside.

As we crossed South-Central Burma towards the town of Chittagong, we planned to come back that night and take General Stilwell out if we had to trick him into getting aboard. We crossed the many mouths of the Ganges in one of the worst rains that I've ever seen, and soon landed in the humid heat of Calcutta. While we were reservicing for the second trip of some five hundred miles, Joplin landed from Assam, and Colonel Haynes had him unload his cargo and take off immediately for Shwebo. Once again we ourselves flew through black rain across the Ganges into Burma, but when we landed we found that all had been evacuated except wounded British and American soldiers. In the half darkness, for the night was lighted by the fires of the burning villages, we loaded them on and took them to Calcutta.

General Stilwell with a few of his staff, his ADC, Colonel Dorn, and Jack Belden, war correspondent, had gone on to the North on the long trek to India by way of the Uyu and Chindwin Rivers to the Manipur Road. For weeks no one knew where he was.

One of the officers in this last cargo handed me an itinerary that the General had given him, and I resolved to try to drop food and vitamin capsules to the party as it made its way to the West. The projected itinerary would lead them from Shwebo North to the Uyu River, down that stream to the Chindwin at Homalin, then down the Chindwin to Sittaung and Tamu, and thence on the Manipur Road to Imphal. Using it, I expected to be able to contact them and drop the necessary food; Joplin and I even figured we could land on a sand bar in the Chindwin and pick them up. We planned all this out the next day as we flew back home, four hundred miles to the Northeast, transporting our first jeep into Assam by plane.

But though we began next day to fly into Burma to contact General Stilwell's party, again we found that there was many a slip 'twixt the cup, etc., even when one had an itinerary. After I'd crossed the Naga Hills in my single P-43, I would follow the Chindwin South until I came to Homalin. Then I'd turn to the East up the river, flying right down in the canyon formed by the thick jungle trees. I carried a Very pistol to identify myself, but learned that we had no air-to-ground liaison code with which to establish our identity to General Stilwell. As a substitute I decided to fire a green light, figuring that anything but red would indicate that I was a friendly ship.

Though I saw party after party, there was no way of identifying that of the General. I marked their positions on my map, and we went back later in a transport plane and dropped food to all of them—food, medicines, and blankets. Later I dropped letters attempting to establish a code between his party and our ships, so that if he wanted us to land when he reached the Chindwin, he could signal us with a panel. We were never able to contact him, but we continued to drop food to every party of refugees we saw.

Later on Joplin and I took food and carried two war correspondents on the Chindwin-Uyu circuit. Though we fired Very lights in compliance with the color schemes that we had dropped in the letters, again we got no answers by panel.

With the passing days we began to get reports from the British agents near Homalin that Jap planes were patrolling the sector. From then on, Joplin or Colonel Haynes would fly the food transport and I'd escort them with my lone P-43. I've often laughed since then at my ego. For what could I alone have done, with one little fighter—sans self-sealing tanks, sans big guns, sans brains? I guess I actually thought then that if nine of eighteen little old Japs jumped on me that I'd shoot down that half of them at least, and the other half would run. Right soon I was to learn that I would have been shot down pretty fast. Such is the valor of ignorance.

As the days stretched into weeks and no news came of General Stilwell's party, we just dropped bags of rice and medicines to all parties, whether they were led by a General or by a British sergeant. On my single-ship escort trips I noted that burning barges were floating down the Chindwin, South of Tamu. One afternoon I saw four big river-boats burning at the docks of the town where the Manipur Road began. I reported this to the British.

Then, about three weeks from the day we had flown down to get the staff out of Shwebo, I met General Stilwell and his tired group at the little Tinsukia railroad station. I told him that practically all the Air Corps officers in Asia were waiting for him outside.

14
Situation Very Confused

THAT NIGHT, as we gathered at tea planter Josh Reynold's house, we had the greatest gathering of Generals' stars that all Assam had ever seen. There was Wavell, Alexander—who made on that occasion the classic statement: "The situation in Burma is very confused"—Brereton, Naiden, Bissell, Stilwell, Hearne, and Siebert. Just about everyone except General Chennault, and he was very busy getting the AVG out of Loiwing and up to Paoshan. Burma had at last fallen.

The evacuation of these Chinese armies from Burma to India and China now gave us more adventures in the A. B. C. Ferrying Command. They were scattered all over northern Burma, from West of Myitkyina, North to Shimbyang and Putao. It was our job now to drop rice, salt, and medicines to these thousands of starving soldiers. I remember that as I first saw Burma it used to look to me like the greatest hunting country in all the world, completely wild and unspoiled. And it was just that—but there was nothing to hunt, for evidently there wasn't anything for even the animals to eat.

We'd fill a smaller burlap bag with rice or salt and sew that into another bag twice the size of the first. When these were dropped from an airplane, the inner bag broke but the rice was saved by the second bag. All we had to do was to fly through the monsoon rains of Burma, dodge the mountains, and find the places to drop the food to the waiting Chinese. Then, dodging the jungle trees, we'd go down as low as we dared and shove the bags out the door. We learned to hit the targets pretty accurately, and by the way the soldiers went after the sacks of food they were plenty hungry.

Once when it was clear enough to see the surrounding country, I was aware of a strange sight. We'd been dropping rice at Shimbyang when I saw some villages, and there again I noticed something that I realized now I'd been seeing through all the Burmese towns—white cattle, the bullocks of the East. It started me to thinking: How could people starve when there were hundreds and thousands of cattle in northern Burma?

That afternoon I got to talking over the food situation with one of the best of the ferry pilots, Capt. John Payne. He said he'd looked the field over at Putao—or Fort Hertz, as the British called it—and although it had been condemned by the British for the landing of aircraft, he could land a transport on the short runway. The entire length of that field was slightly less than one thousand feet, and if any other pilot than Joplin or Payne had made that statement I would have ignored the offer; but I knew that Payne knew what he was talking about.

We loaded on 4200 pounds of rice to land at Fort Hertz and went over the Naga Hills to Burma. As I sat there being Long John Payne's co-pilot, my thoughts were on this happy-go-lucky flyer. He had been an Eastern Airlines pilot for nine years before coming into the Air Corps. As he said, he'd let down into Atlanta so many times in the smoke and fog that the bad weather of Burma didn't worry him much. When Johnny first joined the ferry command he came into prominence by originating a saying that to us exemplified our feelings about the whole affair in Burma. Johnny had said, "If at first you don't succeed, give up, for no one in this country gives a damn anyway."

We got over Fort Hertz pretty quickly and circled the little cleared place on top of a hill. The single runway, if you could call it that, was just nine hundred feet long. There were tracks where ships had landed, but we found later that they had been slow RAF biplanes. There was a makeshift bridge at one end—two trees across a stream—and four markers made from dead trees which showed the other end of the "runway." Everything else was jungle. As Payne throttled the engines for the landing, he let down the wheels and said in his nonchalant way:

"When I say okay, give me full flaps—then if I don't hit the first ten feet of that field, spill 'em, for we'll go around again."

Well, Johnny Payne brought that heavy ship in like a master. He didn't hit the first ten feet—I honestly think he put those wheels down on the first foot of the available runway, and we had stopped at least fifty feet before we got to the other end. You ask a transport pilot if eight hundred feet isn't a damn good landing.

Johnny stayed back to unload the ship and guard it, for the Japs were supposed to be fairly close and we had learned that when people are in the panic of evacuation and starvation you can trust no one. I walked down the trail to contact the General of the Fifth Chinese Army. I wanted to ask him if he was getting the rice, and find out why he needed rice when there were bullocks all around; I guess I really wanted to see for myself if the stories of sickness and starvation were true. What I saw and found was proof enough.

General Ho took me about three miles down the road that led to Suprabum, and I counted fifty-five bodies of soldiers who had died either of cholera or from starvation. As I walked among them, with the harsh smell of death in the air, this Chinese General told me that his soldiers had been killed trying to get bullocks from the Burmese. You see, the Burmese are Buddhists, and it is against their religion to eat meat or to see the sacred bullocks slaughtered. We must keep on dropping rice or the entire army would starve, said the General. And we kept it up, dropping over two million pounds into Burma before the armies were evacuated into India for re-equipment.

Back at the field I found that Payne had loaded the transport with forty sick or wounded Ghurkas. In fact, we had to keep more from getting aboard by threatening them with our guns, for after all, we had the same small field for taking off we'd had for landing. Johnny swung the ship into the wind and we were off in some six hundred feet. We went in many times again, after the Ghurkas had lengthened the runway slightly, and we finally moved out most of the soldiers before the monsoon rains ran us out. But I'll never forget Captain Payne's feat in that first landing of a transport at Fort Hertz.

Following the defeat of the Allied armies down in southern and central Burma, the refugees poured to the North and to the Northwest. Those to the Northwest tried to walk out by the Lido Road, which was nothing more than a game trail. Many of them died, and of those who came out many died after entering India. I heard stories of bodies by the hundreds, almost buried in the mud, all along the trail from Burma to India. Those who kept coming North from Shwebo up the railroad to Myitkyina finally wound up on Myitkyina's small field, anxiously waiting for aerial transportation over the remaining one hundred and ninety miles to Dinjan.

Some of the loads that ferry pilots packed into those DC-3's would have curdled the blood of the aeronautical engineers who designed the ship. The C-47, or DC-3, as the airlines called the Douglas transport, was constructed to carry a full load of twenty-four passengers or six thousand pounds. The maximum altitude was expected to be about 12,000 feet—but we later went a minimum of 18,000 across the hump, and sometimes we had to go to 21,500 to miss the storms and ice. Carrying the refugees, we broke all the rules and regulations because we had to. There were women and children, pregnant women, and women so old that they presumably couldn't have gone to the altitude that was necessary to cross into India. There were hundreds of wounded British soldiers with the most terrible gangrenous infections. At the beginning we used to load the wounded first, those who were worst off; but later, when we realized that with our few transports we'd never get them all out, we took only the able-bodied.

That was a hard decision to make, but we looked at it finally from the theory that those must be saved who could some day fight again.

But as I say, at first we carried the terribly wounded, piling them in until the ship groaned and the door would hardly close. I always carried out fifty or more in this ship that had been designed for twenty-four, and one day I counted seventy-three getting out of one ship. A young pilot by the name of Lieutenant Sartz broke all records, as far as I know. One morning he took off with seventy-three, and on landing the British Customs counted seventy-four. En route over the Naga Hills a baby had been born, and now Sartz holds the world's record.

It was plenty hot flying the loaded transport off the fields in Burma. We'd try to fly with the windows open in the cockpit, but that created a suction that drew the air from the cabin up to where we pilots were. With those filthy bodies and the terrible stench of gangrenous wounds we couldn't bear it, and would have to close the side windows and just sweat. Sometimes the poor devils couldn't stand the trip and we'd have dead men aboard when we landed in India.

I remember one of the bravest men I have ever seen, who helped us load and control the refugees on the field at Myitkyina. He was a big, bearded Sikh officer, one of the aristocratic British colonials. He must have been six-feet-two, a fine looking man. He worked religiously with the refugees and soldiers, always efficient, always trying to send those out who should have gone. I can see him now, standing there in his tattered uniform, with his turban perfectly placed on his dark head, his beard waving in the wind from the idling propellers. He would patiently herd the passengers into the transport, sometimes holding hysterical people back physically, and in more crucial times pulling his pistol, but never becoming flustered or excited. I sometimes think he was the greatest soldier I have ever seen. Day after day, as the Japs moved North and ever closer to Myitkyina, he would be there, doing his thankless job.

When the end came, and I knew that the field would be taken in the next few hours, I went to him and explained the situation.

I found, however, that he knew more about it than I knew myself. The refugees had told him, he said, and he knew this was the last day we could land there. So I asked him to get aboard my ship and leave for India; after all, he was an officer and could best be used when once again the British entered Burma.

The Sikh officer refused with majestic pride. His orders had been to stay there and supervise the evacuation of those refugees, and he considered that trust sacred. We had to leave him, and when I last saw him he was herding the ever-increasing numbers of stricken people on to the North, towards Fort Hertz and the blind valley that led inevitably to the impassable mountains towards Tibet. I guess the Japs finally got him. But I know how he must have died, with that pistol in his hand, and finally just the knife—and I know that several Japs died before they killed him.

The Japs strafed Myitkyina the next day with heavy force and got two British transports that were on the ground. We had luckily decided that with the Japs eighteen miles to the South we could not risk our few planes, for they were needed for the run into China. From then on Myitkyina was an enemy-occupied field, but I managed later on to give it lots of trouble with a fighter.

15

Too Much Tin

THE WINDS from the Indian Ocean grew stronger, and the monsoon season began. And oh boy, the rains came! The clouds built up so black and high and thick that you could no longer go around them or over them—you had to just get on instruments and bore through. In some ways, though, it was a relief —for there in the safety of God's elements the Japs couldn't bother our unarmed ships. Many times I heard the remark that there was always something good in everything—even bad weather. I can hear still some of those pilots griping, saying they never thought the day would come when they'd be out looking for bad weather. But it was the truth. With the Jap fighter ships all over Burma now, it was comforting to know that there were rain clouds to dodge into with the transports.

One adventure with the monsoon still gives me nightmares. Lieutenant Sartz and I had taken a load of gasoline to Kunming, and as the day looked good—there being clear weather in China, terrible weather in Burma, and fairly good weather in India —we decided to take on six thousand pounds of tin ingots rather than the usual four thousand pounds. We knew that we could fly low and South of the course, thereby dodging the higher mountains until we had used enough fuel to compensate for the extra weight of tin. Then, if we met the Japanese air force we could duck into the friendly clouds in Burma, climb out over the top, and go on to India.

The theory sounds good. But as you'll see, it didn't work too well. As usual we were late in getting loaded and serviced, and there was some argument among the Service and Supply as to whether or not tin, tungsten, tung oil, or hog bristles were first priority that day. We were taking in fuel, ammunition, and food to China and leaving with lend-lease exchange products of the above strategic materials. Incidentally, the Chinese hog bristles are quite an item. It seems that the Chinese razor-back pig grows a square bristle, which may be split more readily than the round or spiral type, and the Navy must have the square kind for paint brushes.

Anyway, we were finally serviced, and were off with the load and a half of tin ingots for India, following the Burma Road towards Yunnanyi and western Yunnan. This slightly southerly course would keep us in lower country while we became lighter and lighter with the diminishing fuel load.

In the first two hundred miles we passed over Yunnanyi and had climbed to 13,000 feet. Everything was going well as we approached Paoshan, near the Salween, where China and Burma meet. Suddenly, ahead and to the South, I saw two black specks and above them two others. Zeros! We slipped the transport into the clouds to the North with no more than a short look. In the time that it took us to get into the rain clouds, we definitely identified them as enemy fighters. Then the gray friendliness of the monsoon clouds closed about us.

Now unforeseen circumstances began to operate. I set our course for Assam and tried to climb, but with the heavy load of tin the ship answered the controls very sluggishly. We gained barely a few hundred feet, and on this straight course to Assam we knew that the country rose quickly to over 15,000 feet. We were of course on instruments and could not see the threatening mountains.

Instantly I went back into the cabin, leaving Sartz to hold the ship on course. The tin ingots were lashed to the floor of the ship at intervals, in positions where passengers would have been. Going back to the tail, I untied the ingot that was farthest aft; each one weighed 112 pounds. As I unlashed the first one, I felt the turbulence of the air begin as we entered the storm center, or neared the convection currents caused by the approaching mountains. Hurrying, I crawled with the ingot to the door, while the swaying of the tail became more intense as the turbulence increased. The door came open slightly against the pressure of the outside slipstream, and I tried to drop the ingot out. My idea of course was to jettison about one-third of the cargo, so that we could climb to a safe altitude.

Try as I might, the roughness of the air kept me from getting the first ingot overboard. In fact, several times it threw me so violently to the side that I thought the ingot would break my arms or my ribs. Finally I realized I could not do it, and headed for the cockpit and the controls, dropping the ingot where it was.

Sartz was holding the transport on course, but the air was definitely getting rougher. Hastily now we made another decision: we turned South, for the valleys ran practically North and South, and I put the mixtures to full rich and the throttles wide open. I continued to try to climb, but my main purpose now was to use up the fuel in two of the tanks as fast as possible, and that was why I had gone to full power. This would lighten the load some 1800 pounds, and just about compensate for the 2000-pound overload of tin. It was of course impossible to jettison part of the fuel of a ship such as this transport.

We'd fly South for five minutes, then turn North for five. Gradually the ship lightened and climbed above 15,000 feet. We knew that if we didn't hit a mountain first, some time we'd get light enough to climb to the 18,000-foot altitude that was necessary to get over the hump and back to Assam. In the meantime we continued to cruise on instruments up and down the imaginary valley—we certainly hoped there was a valley there. But as the turbulence increased in some areas, many times we were sure that we were heading right into the side of the high mountains near the Mekong and Irrawaddy.

The minutes stretched into an hour of this hard instrument flying. Three hours after we had taken off from Kunming, we gained the welcome altitude of 18,000 feet.

Now we were temporarily safe from the tops of mountains. But where were we? If we were where we should be—on course for Assam—we were clearing the mountains by a cool thousand feet. If, however, the wind in the storm was from the South, as it more than likely was in this monsoon season, we could have been blown sixty to seventy miles North of our course in the hour that we had seen nothing but wet clouds. I know that Sartz and I were thinking the same things. We were very probably North of the safe 18,000-foot course and heading right for the 20,000 to 25,000-foot peaks of the Himalaya range to the North.

Then our öxygen gave out, and if possible I felt worse. It was just as Colonel Haynes used to say: "Some days you can't make a nickel." Everything was going wrong.

We just assumed that we were over where we should have been. We set our gyro on the straight course for home and turned the ship over to the automatic pilot—Old Iron George, we call it. When the air would get too turbulent in the storm we'd help the auto-pilot—the servos—steady the controls. For nearly another hour we went on. Then the weather got too rough for the servos and we started hand-flying the transport again. It's usually just a three-hour trip from Kunming to our base, and we'd already been out three hours and forty-five minutes.

Sartz's job was to keep the gyro on zero with the rudder; mine was to keep those wings level—and with the aëroembolism that was coming over us from the lack of oxygen, we had all we could do. Periodically I would look over at him, and I remember that I yelled at him for not keeping the course on zero. He'd correct it momentarily, then it would drift off again. I realized, though, that I wasn't doing so well myself at holding the wings level in the rough air, but I guess Sartz wouldn't fuss at me because I was a poor old Colonel.

For almost another hour we sat there glaring at one another, expecting every second that the jagged top of one of the Himalayas was coming through the clouds and into the cockpit. Try that some time while you are making two hundred miles an hour, when you can't see your wing tips—and just see if your hairs don't get grayer and grayer. Mine did.

Four hours and thirty minutes from take-off, I decided we had to let down now, mountains or no mountains. Night was closing in fast, and our fuel was running low in the tanks. I began then to wonder whether or not I'd done the right thing in making the engines drink up those first two tanks of gas.

We tensed a little more, if that was possible, as we throttled back slightly and started for the let-down. If we were on course, everything was fine—we'd break out in that horseshoe that our base was in. Just think of the mountains making a horseshoe, with the curved or closed end towards us—Oh well, in our position it was comforting to think of horseshoes anyway.

If we were off course, we'd know it pretty soon anyway, and it wouldn't make much difference. Just think of yourself as driving at sixty miles an hour through a tunnel, in a fog that's so thick you can't see your radiator cap. You don't know where the sides of the tunnel are, you don't know when you'll hit another car travelling as fast as you are, you don't even know when you're in the tunnel. We were that way, only a thousand times worse, for we were travelling over two hundred miles an hour and didn't know whether we were in Burma, Tibet, or India. As Sartz said later, if we had come out over Chicago or London we wouldn't have been too surprised—it had been so long since we had seen a check-point.

Every now and then I'd correct the course two or three degrees, as I recalled slight changes we had made just after we entered the clouds near Paoshan. The minutes passed. We went lower and lower, but still the top of a mountain failed to crash through. Sometimes the rain and sleet beat so heavily on the metal skin of the Douglas that I'd flinch, feeling certain that here it was at last.

Just then I saw a lighter spot to the right of our course. That lighter spot meant that the last rays of the setting sun were shining on the top of one of these clouds. There was a hole somewhere, and my heart skipped a beat. Both Sartz and I had turned instantly for the lighter sky. We had been without oxygen for nearly three hours, and we felt pretty low. Now we hurtled through another lighter spot, and I thought I caught a glimmer of the ground below. I know we were hoping strongly that we could see down and make sure that we were over a valley rather than over high mountains.

Suddenly I almost felt good again—down below I had seen a patch of green. Then we went into the soup once more. Immediately, however, I had started a turn to the left, with the gyro set to zero. Turning exactly ninety degrees, I flew this course for exactly sixty seconds. Then I turned another ninety degrees and flew on again for one minute. We did this four times with the aid of the minute hand and the gyro—the turn indicator. This was supposed to bring us back to the same spot where we had begun the square that we were flying.

As the fourth 60-second period passed, we came out into the light of our hole again and we were both looking down. There below us was land, and by its distance from us and its appearance I knew that it was the valley! Sartz knew it too, for he let out a nice football yell, and we cocked the ship over to spiral down, keeping as nearly in the hole as possible. As we got down to twelve thousand feet the hole in the clouds grew larger, and to the North I saw a river—it was a very large river and it had to be the Brahmaputra, and we were then fairly close to home. But no matter what we were near, we felt good, for we could set the ship down even in one of the rice paddies—safely down with that load of damnable tin that I hadn't been able to jetti-son.

I looked over at Sartz. There was the indication of a smile breaking out on his face, and he yelled: "That's the Brahma-putra and there's Sadiya—we're just about in—I can almost smell supper cooking."

And that's just where we were, and we both let out the loud-est cheers that the jungle beasts had ever heard. It would be good even to sleep in the wet "bashas" of Assam this night.

We went on down to a thousand feet, and out to the island in the river that we had to fly over in order to enter the military corridor. But we couldn't see the field, though we were within several miles of it, and as we came down low over the river we saw why. There, over the place where our base should be, was the blackest cumulo-nimbus rain cloud there's ever been. Boy, we were being put through our paces by the elements today! We set our course from the island, just on the treetops, and flew toward the field, but even right over it we couldn't see it in the black rain. For it was raining bucketfuls, and darkness had just about come. We had to go back to the island and try over.

This time we found the field but lost it while I put the wheels down. Sartz had set the gyro again, and we worked out a prob-lem, just as we had done up there with the hole in the clouds. For a minute we flew out parallel to the runway, then we turned a right angle to the left. Now we had done four of these and were coming in towards the runway with the wheels and flaps down, looking for the first sign of the field, the trees of the As-samese jungle almost brushing against our wings. With the gyro reading zero we came on for where the runway should be, the engines at fifteen hundred RPM's. We both had the side win-dows open now and were peering ahead through the tropical rain. Then we saw the paved strip. "It's over here," called Sartz, and I felt him slip the ship to the right. Down we plunked right in the center, in about a foot of water. We both landed the ship and held it straight by keeping the ball of the turn-and-bank in-strument dead in the center.

Well, it looked just as if we had landed in a lake. Getting the flaps up, we taxied slowly in to our parking place, following Sergeants Bonner and Creach, who were guiding us in their jeep. Out of the ship we got, and into the rain—looking as-kance at the fifty-odd little tin ingots that we'd brought safely through. Our trip from Kunming, which usually required three hours, had taken over five hours. Sergeant Bonner said that one ship had taken nearly eight, some others had turned back, and one was feared lost.

From the time we had entered the clouds, we hadn't seen the ground. Taking everything into consideration—luck, experience, and all that—I guess the Lord just got sorry for us, took us by the hands, and led us to that one hole in the overcast.

But incidents like that happened often in the Ferry Command, and there were probably many pilots who had similar experiences, going over and coming back. I know of some who got so much ice that the ships dropped thousands of feet before vibration and the temperature of lower levels either shook it off or melted it. There were pilots who made instrument flights from Assam to Kunming, back to Assam, and then back to Kunming, all in one day, over fifteen hundred miles at 18,000 feet or better, mostly over enemy territory—and without seeing the ground except at points of departure and destination.

You can't keep up flights like that without learning things. It develops some men, it breaks others. Those pilots suffer from a fatigue that is as bad as combat fatigue, if not worse. For there is no combat in the world that for strain can compare with instrument flying over country 18,000 feet high, where any moment a Jap Zero might pounce on your unarmed ship. Those pilots of the Ferry Command did it not only the three months that I was there—they kept on, and they're flying the hump today.

It's the life-line of China. Yes, the Burma Road is gone—that is, for the use of Chinese supply; but this airline takes its place. Over the route of the hump are coming the aviation gasoline that should have come from Yenanyaung down in Burma, the ammunition that should have come from Rangoon, and the clothes, food, and soldiers with equipment that would have come from America anyway. They are coming by air over this aerial Burma Road, that leads across the Naga Hills from Assam to the snowy heights along the Mekong and the Salween, over Lake Talifu and down to Kunming on the plateau of Yunnan.

16
No Hits, No Runs, One Error

ON APRIL 27, the AVG finally had to leave Loiwing, due to the failure of the air-warning net to the South. They moved on back to Paoshan by Mengshih, and finally to Kunming. One day about that time I went over to see General Chennault, for I had a question I wanted to ask him—one that I'd carried on my mind ever since I'd been shanghaied off the "dream mission." I still wanted to fight. Though this Ferry Command was important, I'd been trained for a fighter pilot. And here I was, just sitting up there in a transport, like a clay pigeon for the Japanese.

I still remembered that for nine years I had been too young; then when war came I was suddenly told I was too old to be a fighter pilot. When had I been the right age? I wanted to tell General Chennault that story. At the great age of thirty-four, I just didn't consider that I was too old to fly fighter planes and with his help I meant to prove it. Even with only one fighter ship in the sky with our transports, I knew I could give the boys in the transports just a little more confidence. Besides, I kind of thought I had a date with destiny, so to speak—or at least a date with a Jap somewhere over there in Burma. I desperately wanted to slide in behind one of those enemy bombers or fighters and shoot him down.

Finally I had my chance to tell the story of my ambitions to General Chennault. Busy as he was, he listened to my case, and even as I talked I admired the great man more and more. Here, I knew, was a great officer and leader as well as a great pilot. Here was an American who was a General in the Chinese Army, held by the Chinese in admiration and respect—a soldier who could see the problems that this modern war imposed on land armies as well as on navies and air power. Here, I knew, was genius.

I told the General that I wanted one single P-40 to use in India and Burma. I knew they were scarce, but I would promise him that nothing would happen to it, and the instant he needed the ship I would fly it back to him in China. The General smiled. I'm sure he was thinking back and wondering whether, if he were in my position, he wouldn't have begged for the same chance. He didn't give me some excuse that he well might have used—that the P-40's belonged to the Chinese Government, that it would have been against regulations, and so forth. General Chennault knew that I would use that "shark," as we called the P-40's, against the Japs. He made his own regulations then; what did it matter who killed the Japs and who used the P-40's so long as they were being used for China?

By the twinkle in his eyes I knew that I had won my case. The General said, "Some Forties are on the way from Africa now. You take the next one that comes through. Use it as long as you want to." That's the way I got the single fighter plane that was to work out of Assam.

With anxious eyes I waited, looking to the West for the next "sharks" to come to India.

Three P-40E's or Kittyhawks came to us from Africa on April 29. Two went on to Kunming for the AVG, but Number 41-1456 stayed with me. It was mine, and I was as proud of it as of the first bicycle my father had given me. All through the night I read the technical files and learned every little item about the Allison engine and the engine controls. I memorized the armament section of the book, and by morning I was ready to put theory into practice.

That morning I found a painter. Buying red and white paint from the village, I had him paint the shark's mouth on the lower nose of the Curtiss Kittyhawk. On that afternoon of April 30, I remember that as I waited for the paint to dry I walked round and round my ship, admiring the graceful lines, a feeling of pride in my heart. I gloried in the slender fuselage, in the knife-like edges of the little wings. The sharp nose of the spinner looked like an arrow to me—the nose that sloped back to the leering shark's mouth. At sight of the wicked-looking blast tubes of the six fifty-calibre guns in the wings, I felt my chest expand another inch. This was shark-nosed dynamite, all right —but even then I did not quite realize what a weapon this fighter ship could be when properly handled.

I don't know how long I walked around the fighter admiring it and caressing its wicked-looking body. I know the paint on the shark's mouth hadn't dried yet—but I'd held the suspense as long as I could. This was as if I were rolling old sherry around on my tongue; sometime I had to really taste it. Now, stepping on the walkway of the left wing, I threw first one leg and then the other over the side of the fuselage and slid into the little cockpit of the fighter. As I adjusted the rudder pedals and fastened my safety belt, I primed the engine a few shots. Turning on the toggle switches, I energized and engaged the starter with my foot, and now I heard the Allison break into a steady roar as I moved the mixture control from "idle cutoff." Out in front of me—a long distance, it seemed—the heavy, eleven-foot, three-bladed prop became a gray blur in my vision. An Allison, or any high-powered engine, doesn't have to warm up, and idling will soon foul the plugs. I was taxying almost as soon as the engine settled down to the steady roar.

Very proudly I taxied out for my first take-off in the new Kittyhawk. All around me on the airdrome I could feel the jealous eyes of every American and British pilot, even those of the earth-bound coolies—or at least my ego thought it felt their looks.

During the test flight over the dark green acres of Assam tea gardens, sweeping low over the Brahmaputra and then climbing steeply for the Naga Hills, I contemplated with keen anticipation the wonderful days that lay ahead. Here was no defenseless transport, no lumbering and unwieldly four-engine bomber —here was a fighting weapon, with a heart and a soul like the other combat ships. But more than that, here was an instrument of war with a distinct individuality, a temperamental devil of the skies. Truly like a beautiful woman, it went smoothly and sweetly at times; and then, as speed increased, it might yaw dangerously as the pressure built up. Again, it could become completely unstable. It had to be flown every second of the time; ignore it for one second and there was no automatic pilot to keep it on course, no co-pilot to help you—it would fall away and very soon would be out of control. Yes, like a beautiful woman, it demanded constant attention. There were no extra members in the crew to worry about, and here in Assam there were no other fighter ships to worry about. We were both isolated individuals.

When I had landed and had taxied back to my niche in the heavy jungle trees surrounding the field, I climbed out and reverently patted the ship on the cowling. The P-40 was fast becoming a personality to me.

Next day I tested my guns and dropped aluminum-powder practice bombs, bombs that leave a splash of aluminum paint on the ground or an aluminum slick on the water where they hit, in order to show the pilot how near he has come to the target. I aimed at the black snags in the river with the guns, then came around again and tried to dive and glide-bomb the snags with the little bombs. I was trying to train myself, trying to make up for the four years that I had been away from pursuit aviation and from tactical training in the art of killing. I needed a lot of this gunnery and bombing, for my life was very soon to depend on it.

I'll never forget the first time I pressed the trigger of my guns and heard the co-ordinated roar of the six fifty-calibre machine guns. Just by pressing a small black button below the rubber grip on my stick I could make three lines of orange tracers from each wing converge out ahead of my fast-moving fighter and meet on the snags in the Brahmaputra. Nearly a hundred shots a second those six Fifties threw out, and the muddy river turned to foam near the targets. The sense of their power impressed me as the recoil slowed me many miles per hour in my dive; I could feel my head snap forward from the deceleration. Sometimes when the guns on only one side would fire, the unequal kicks from the recoil would almost turn the ship.

I couldn't waste much time in practice, for after all Burma was just over the Naga Hills and the Japs were coming towards Myitkyina from the South and up the Chindwin and the Irrawaddy. It was open season and I needed no hunting license. Now I definitely knew that adventure was near.

On that afternoon of April 30, 1942, with a full load of ammunition and the shark-mouth seeming to drip saliva, it was so eager, I waited by my ship for an alert. Jap observation planes had been coming over at high altitude very regularly. If they came today I hoped to surprise them.

At two o'clock the alert came, but it was not observation. Many unidentified aircraft were reported by a British radio somewhere over the Naga Hills. I didn't ask for more than that scanty information—I was in my fighter and climbing over the "tea ranches," as Colonel Haynes called them.

High over the field at 22,000 feet, I cuddled my oxygen mask and circled, watching for enemy ships to the East, South, and Southeast—down in the direction of a course to Mandalay. I searched until my eyes hurt, but saw nothing. After about an hour, turning to a course that would take me in the direction from which an enemy had to come, I flew off to intercept—I now had barely two hours' fuel, and the farther away from my base I met them, the more successful my attack would be. Lord! the ego that I possessed! I honestly believe I thought I could shoot down any number of Japs with my single fighter. Again I say, more of the valor of ignorance.

After forty-five minutes I turned for home and began to let down to eighteen thousand. Thirty miles from the field I suddenly tensed to the alert. Off ahead of me was a dark column of smoke, rising high in the air right in the position on the world's surface that the home field should be. My tortured mind flashed back to other results of bombings that I had seen.

I nosed over and dove for the Zeros that should be strafing the field. (Later I was to learn a lot about this method too.) The smoke was from base all right, but I could see no enemy planes. The only thing in the sky was a single Douglas transport, making a normal landing on the runway. Calling "NR-Zero—NR-Zero," I asked what the fire was. The reply was muddled, but everything seemed to be in order, for I noticed two other transports clearing the field for China. I circled, then dove on the smoking ruins of the RAF operations "basha." That building had been the casualty, and it was a total loss. I could see the operations officer sitting out in the open, some hundred feet from the charred ruins, calmly carrying on his duties.

When I'd gotten my fighter parked again I went over and heard the story. No Jap attack had come, and I felt relieved— my single-ship war and I had not let the station down. But as I heard the embarrassed operations man tell his story I remember choking discreetly and leaving before I laughed myself to death.

When the alert sounded, "Opps"—the operations officer— had hurried to the window of the thatch and bamboo "basha" to see me take off in the "bloody kite—that Kittyhawk." Seeing a transport from China about to land, and fearing that the Japs would bomb it on the field, he had then fired a Very pistol out of the operations window: the red Very light would be the signal for the transport not to land but to fly in the "stand-by" area. The Very light had gone nonchalantly out of the operations window, into the wind, had curved gracefully back into another window, and had burned the bloody building in five minutes. Operations was being carried on as usual from operations desk, which was located in front of the site of the former office. Bloody shame, wasn't it?

Well, it was tragic, but I guess it was better than a bombing. And so my first mission ended. No hits, no runs, one error.

17

Rats on the Burma Road

THE NEXT DAY was May Day, and I began the greatest month in my life. I flew every day in that long month, sometimes as many as four missions a day. By putting in a total of 214 hours and 45 minutes, I averaged over seven hours a day for the month. Most of this was in fighter ships—my little old Kittyhawk and I learned a lot, and we were very, very lucky. When I had come in from my first sortie, the day operations burned down, my pal Col. Gerry Mason kidded me a bit. Since the next day started a new month, I vowed then on the sacred relics of my great-grandmother that during those thirty-one days I would destroy a Japanese plane if I had to go all the way to Rangoon.

We got pretty confident, the transport boys and I, for I used to go with them across Burma, and Joplin and some of the other daredevils would try to lure the Jap in to attack them. Jop would call over the radio, in the clear: "NR-o from transport one three four—I'm lost near Bhamo—give me a bearing."

Up there, some three thousand feet above them, I'd be sitting with my fighter, just praying that my "decoy" would work and some luckless Jap would come in for the kill. Then I'd imagine myself diving on his tail, my six guns blazing. But the ruse never worked. Sometimes I think the "Great Flying Boss in the Sky" was giving me a little more practice before he put me to the supreme test.

May the fifth was one of the big days in my life. Waving goodbye to Gerry Mason as I taxied out, I saw him hold his thumb up to me to wish me good hunting. I waved back and was in the air on a sweep towards central Burma. I went straight to Myitkyina; then, seeing nothing, I swung South along the Irrawaddy over Bhamo. Continuing South I went right down on the Burma Road, North of Lashio, and searched for enemy columns. North of the airport at Lashio I saw two groups of troops in marching order. I would have strafed them immediately, but I was afraid they might be Chinese; after all, there were two Chinese armies coming North somewhere in Burma. I made as though to ignore them and they partially scattered to the sides of the road. Twelve trucks in the column kept rolling to the North.

Then I momentarily forgot about the troops—for in the north-western corner of the field at Lashio was a ship. From my altitude of 2500 feet I saw at once that it was a twin-engined enemy bomber, later identified as a Mitsubishi, Army 97. It was being serviced, for there were four gasoline drums in front of it and a truck that had evidently unloaded the fuel. My gun switches were already on, and had been since I had seen the troop column. Now I was diving for the grounded bomber and getting my "Christmas Tree" sight lighted properly.

Hurriedly I began to shoot. I saw men running from the truck and jumping into the bushes to the side. My first shots hit in front of the plane, probably striking the fuel drums, for heavy dust covered the enemy ship. I released my trigger as I pulled out of my dive, just clearing the trees behind my target. As I looked back I saw the red circle on one wing, but the other was covered by the body of a man who either had been shot or was trying to hide the identifying insignia.

Keeping the ship very low, I turned 180 degrees for the second attack. This time I did better. I saw my tracers go into the thin fuselage and then into the engines. At first I thought that what I was seeing was more dust; then I realized it was smoke pouring from under the ship. It was on fire. Foolishly then, I pulled up to about six hundred feet; if there had been anti-aircraft fire, I know now they would have shot me down. Again I turned and shot at the truck and the gasoline drums, and once more I saw the tracers converge on the enemy ship. Smoke was floating high in the sky—I could smell it over the odor of cordite that came from my own guns.

Keeping very low again, I turned East and found the Burma Road, turned up it and started looking for the columns which I now knew were Japanese. I approached them from the rear, fired from about a thousand yards, and the road seemed to pulverize. The closely packed troops appeared to rush back towards me as my speed cut the distance between us. I held the six guns on while I went the length of the troop column and caught the trucks. There were only six now, but I fired into all of them and two I saw burn immediately. On my second pass, as I "S'ed" across the road, I shot at each truck individually, then turned for the troops again. The road was so dusty that I could barely see the bodies of those I had hit on the first pass. I suppose the others were hidden in the brush to the side. As I pulled up, I could see the black plume of smoke to the South— my first enemy ship was burning fiercely.

I made as though to leave the area, then came in again from the South on the troops after the dust had settled. They had reformed but were not as closely packed as before. Again I strafed them, but this time I saw that they were firing at me. The trucks couldn't get off the road, and I exhausted my ammunition on them in two more passes. One truck that I caught dead center with a full two-second burst seemed to blow up. When I left, I knew that four of the trucks were burning, and farther to the South I could still see the smoke of my first Jap plane rising high above the trees of Burma.

Straight back to the base I went, feeling very intoxicated with success. At last I'd been able to see Japs and draw blood. In this case they had been treated just as they had been treating Allied ground troops, and I was happy.

That afternoon I went back on the second mission. I found the wrecks of four trucks and baggage, and objects that could have been men, scattered all over the road. The place where I had caught the troop column showed about forty dead men. The grounded plane had burned, and with it had burned about ten acres of the jungle. I fired a long burst into the truck and into the four fuel drums in front of the debris of the enemy bomber, but they didn't burn; I guess the morning fire had finished them. I searched the country to the North for more troops, but didn't intercept any.

I went back home highly elated—I had drawn my first blood. I felt that the world was good again. With pride I radioed General Chennault that his "shark" had been in use, that I had caught lots of rats walking along the Burma Road, and that one Army 97 bomber would fly no more for the Japs.

Well, at last I'd seen an enemy ship. It was a grounded bomber—but after all, I've learned since then that these planes on the ground are sometimes pretty rugged business to get when you're flying down on them with all the anti-aircraft fire in the world seeming to converge on you. You've got to worry about small-arms fire from every soldier, too, and it takes only one little slug in the prestone radiator or the oil-cooler to stop you mighty sudden.

The next day I went to Lashio again and strafed the hangar that had once been used by China National Airways Corporation—CNAC—but I couldn't burn it. There were no ships on the field except an RAF Blenheim that had been strafed by the Japs on the ground on the North end of the runway.

I turned back to the North to look for the gasoline stores that I knew had been at Myitkyina. I was determined they were not going to fall into Jap hands. Not finding them, I spent the rest of my time flying low on the Irrawaddy, looking for enemy barges. It was a pretty unprofitable day.

When Myitkyina fell, I went over there every day to burn the gasoline that had been stored in tins in the woods to the Northeast of the end of the runway. I had found out its location from British Intelligence, but the RAF Group Captain had exacted from me a promise that I would not fire into it until he gave me the word.

It seems that he was afraid that the firing and the burning of the fuel would excite the native Burmese who were in the village. I couldn't see what difference that would make, for after all the Japs would capture the thousands of gallons of aviation gasoline, and the natives were more than likely helping them anyway. Though I held off, every time I saw the shiny four-gallon cans in the trees my finger itched to burn the cache before the enemy could use it. I passed the three days of waiting in burning three barges on the Irrawaddy, South of Bhamo, and in setting a fuel barge on fire down on the Chindwin. In this last raid my ship picked up a few small holes; evidently some Jap sympathizers had managed to get my range.

Later in the week, the RAF Group Captain told me that his Commandos in Myitkyina were going to knock holes in all the fuel tins with picks before they left the field to the Japs.

Nevertheless I kept watching the gasoline stores while the Japs moved to the North. On May 8, when I got in my ship and started the Allison, my friend the Group Captain ran across the field to tell me that the Japs could not get the gasoline—it had been destroyed without fire, and thus the villagers would not be panicked. Over the roar of the engine I yelled that in that case it would not burn when I fired into it. For I had waited long enough; the Japs were in Myitkyina and I wasn't taking any chances on their acquiring over 100,000 gallons of aviation fuel less than two hundred miles from our base.

When I came over the field at Myitkyina, the enemy fired at me while I was yet ten miles away; I could see the black bursts of the 37mm AA in front and below me. I started "jinking" and moved to the Northeast, so that I could come from out of the sun and be as far as I could get from the field. With my first burst the whole woods seemed to blow up—I have never seen such a flash as that which came when that veritable powder-train of high octane fuel caught fire from the tracers. I also fired at two of the gun installations on the field. But the bursts from the Jap guns were so close to me that I decided to let well enough alone, and turned for home in Assam. Many times on the way home I looked over my shoulder, and the smoke from the thousands of gallons of gasoline was visible when I was sixty miles from Myitkyina.

Next day, May 9, I made four raids into Burma. On the first of these I escorted two transports piloted by Sartz and Sexton to Paoshan, where they were going to land to pick up the baggage of the AVG, who were going on to Kunming. I waited for them to land and take off again, and then called good-bye. They were going on East within the air controlled by the AVG, and I wanted to look for Japs to the South anyway. Two hours later Paoshan was badly bombed by the Japs; and so I missed a good party by not staying around.

After following the Salween to the South until I could see Lashio, I turned West for the field and came in right on the tree-tops, strafing the anti-aircraft guns in two passes. On the second run across the field I felt and heard bullets hitting my ship, but didn't see their origin until nearly too late. Down close to the West end of the field, almost under the trees, were Japanese ground soldiers. They were grouped into two squares like the old Macedonian phalanx, and were firing rifles at me. I turned my guns on them and could see the fifty-calibre fire taking good toll from the Jap ranks. But even after I had made three runs on them, I noted that they continued to hold their positions, an excellent demonstration of perfect battle discipline. Later on one of the AVG aces, Tex Hill, told me that he had seen the same thing down in Thailand, and that after he'd strafed one of the squares of about a hundred men and there were only two or three on their feet, those few still were shooting at him when he left the field.

Leaving Lashio, I went to Katha looking for a Jap train on the railway, but succeeded only in gathering a little more ground-fire. From there I went back North to Bhamo, and seeing no barges, continued on to Myitkyina, keeping very close to the surface of the Irrawaddy, and strafed the gun positions of the enemy on the field with the last of my ammunition. When I landed I had made almost eight hundred miles, which is just about the limit for a fighter ship, especially since I had strafed at full throttle for several minutes. There were a few holes in my ship, but mostly in the fabric of the rudder and the flippers. The Japs couldn't learn to lead me enough; I guess they'd never hunted game birds.

In less than an hour I took off again and made a shorter trip to Mogaung and Katha, searching without success for a train. After getting more fuel I went back and strafed Myitkyina, turned South, and caught a barge of enemy equipment at Bhamo. Though I didn't sink this river boat, I put at least eight hundred rounds of ammunition in it, and left it settling in the water and drifting slowly with the current. The crew either were killed or jumped into the river.

And now, to close the big day, I got in the air again and set my course for the bridge on the Salween about twenty miles West of Paoshan. I had received a radio report that the AVG under Tom Jones, Bishop, and Tex Hill were dive-bombing the Japs who were constructing a pontoon bridge there. Reaching the rendezvous point, I couldn't see a thing except some burning trucks that the AVG had strafed on the Jap side of the Salween; evidently I had got to the battle too late.

I had turned South towards Lashio and was flying through a moderate rain when, down below on the Burma Road, I saw a troop column marching South, probably towards Chefang. At this point the Burma Road is about eight thousand feet above sea level, rising nearby to its ceiling, just over nine thousand feet.

The troops below me were Japanese soldiers, evidently retreating from the mauling they had taken back there on the river, when the AVG had bombed them with five-hundred-pound bombs. I turned to the side, to watch them—they were in heavy rain, and from the standpoint of their own safety they were in the worst possible place on the road. The Burma Road was cut out of red Yunnan clay, and there were steep banks on both sides of the column—besides I don't think they had heard me over the roar of the rain, and I know they hadn't seen my ship.

I turned my gun switches on and dove for the kill, sighting carefully through my lighted sight. My tracers struck the target dead center, for I had held my fire until the last moment. There was no need of doing this job at high speed, for if I merely cruised I'd have longer to shoot at them and could also look out for the hills hidden in the rain and the clouds. This time there was no dust, but the red, muddy water went up like a geyser. The six Fifties seemed to cut the column to bits. As I passed over, I could see those who hadn't been hit trying desperately to crawl up the muddy bank to the safety of the trees and slipping back.

Turning very close to the hills, I came back over. Every now and then I'd lose them, for the rain was heavy and it was dark in the clouds, so dark that my tracers burned brilliant to the ground and then ricocheted away into the air again, still burning. I think it was in my third pass, as the Japs seemed to be giving up the effort to climb off the road, that I decided my ship would be called "Old Exterminator."

Their officers must have called double-time, for they spread out as much as they could and ran South on the road through the rain. I kept on cutting them to pieces until my ammunition was gone; I fired 1890 rounds into those three or four hundred Japanese, and I don't think more than a handful escaped.

Rather tired from ten hours' flying that day, all combat, I went back home but somewhat on the thoughtful side. It had taken me about two weeks of flying this ship to realize what a weapon it really was. I had just seen it cut a Japanese battalion to bits, had seen the firepower of one American airplane leave three or four hundred dead and dying enemy soldiers in the mud of the Burma Road. As I listened to the roar of that Allison engine and patted the gun-sight affectionately, "Old Exterminator" was more than ever a character to me—it was an institution. I knew right then that this ship was almost a human being.

As the May days drifted into weeks, I made up little schemes to fool the Japs. Perhaps the schemes worked, perhaps they didn't—anyway they eased the disappointment of not getting letters from my wife and little girl and from the other folks back home.

I'd make my two, three, or four mission flights a day with the fighter. But I'd go early in the morning with the spinner on the "shark's" nose painted white, and I'd attack Lashio or Mo-gaung from the South. Later in the morning I'd strike from the West, with the spinner painted blue. After lunch the eager painters or my drafted crewmen would have the spinner another color for my flight. By the time I made the fourth sortie, with the spinner a fourth color and my approach from a fourth direction, I'm sure the Japs didn't know where I came from—and most certainly they didn't guess that the American fighter force in Assam was composed of one single Kittyhawk. If they had, they would have been forced to do something to "save face." For at the moment, with me drunk with the wine of my first combat, the Jap was losing face.

During this month I went to China as much as possible to talk to members of the AVG. Some of these pilots I had taught to fly in the Army Schools back home. I had checked quite a few of them and I was older, but I'm glad I realized then that these younger pilots knew a million times more about combat than I did. I'd corner some of these Flying Tigers and ask them questions, for I longed for the day when I'd get to fly on attacking missions with them.

18
Salute to the AVG

AT FIRST they were hard to know. The men they had met as representing our Army in China had been pretty harsh with these high-strung flyers, who after all had done the greatest job in the war against the enemy. In the beginning they were reluctant to answer my questions or tell me the secrets of their success in combat. They couldn't understand why a Colonel in the Army Air Corps had to know anything. As George Paxton put it: Didn't the Army know everything? "Seems like to me," he said, "every army officer we've seen out here knows all the answers."

When he found out that I was serious, and that my ambition was to get over there and fly with them, and learn combat from them, so that in the end I might teach it to our younger pilots who would be coming out, he told me things that I would never have learned otherwise.

"First," he said, leading me off under the wing of one of the P-40's, "first, the Old Man says, never turn with one of the Zeros. He says that's bad."

I learned that the Jap ship would outmaneuver anything and would outclimb the P-40 four to one. "But that doesn't matter,"

Paxton said. "The P-40 is the strongest ship in the world. It's heavy as hell, but that makes it out-dive just about anything, and it'll out-dive the Jap two to one. With the two Fifties and the four thirty-calibre guns in the B's we have done pretty good. Now with the six Fifties in the new Kittyhawks we out-gun anything."

He told me that Hill, Rector, Bond, Neal, Lawler, and other aces had seen Zeros disintegrate in front of their six Fifties, and went on to advise that I use the good qualities of the P-40's against the bad qualities of the Jap, but never try to beat him at his own game—climbing and maneuverability.

Paxton did me a lot of good—he got me my first flight with the AVG on the Emperor's birthday. But the Jap didn't come in. We were the most griped bunch you've ever seen. Everyone up and waiting at three A.M.—and then the dirty so-and-so's didn't have the guts to come in!

I heard a story on George Paxton that will show you the kind of tough Texan he was. It was down over Rangoon, near Mingaladon airdrome, in the early days of the Burma war. Doctor Gentry, who told me the story, said that the squadron George was in was aloft and engaging the Japanese over the field. Looking upstairs, you could see the condensation streamers criss-crossing the sky, and every now and then a trail of smoke as a Jap Zero burned and plunged towards the earth.

Finally eight or nine Zeros ganged up on George Paxton. They got on his tail and they got all over him. He fought his way partially out of the trap, but two of them right on his tail literally shot him to pieces. George's ship was seen to trail smoke and dive straight down, from about fifteen thousand feet. Doctor Gentry said they watched the stricken Forty and knew who it was by the number. As it disappeared behind the trees they mentally crossed the boy Paxton off their list of living men.

But George and the sturdy P-40 were not through. There was the surging scream of an Allison engine's last boost, and the ship skimmed over the trees and made a belly landing on the soft part of the field. Even then, considering the number of Japs who had been using George for target practice and the way the ship looked, with big holes in the tail, wings, and fuselage, as they drove out for him in the jeep they expected to find just a body.

Instead, they found George Paxton standing by the side of his ship, swearing and shaking his fist at the sky.

Doctor Gentry said he looked into the cockpit. The instrument panel was just about shot away, the rudder pedals were partly shot to pieces, the armor of the pilot's seat was badly bent—but Paxton was out there yelling:

"I still say those little ————— can't shoot!"

Even his Texas boots were practically shot off. Two doctors picked rivets from George's back all the afternoon, and Jap explosive particles from his feet, legs, and hands. The worst injuries had been caused by the Japanese explosive bullets hitting the seat armor and driving the rivets through into George's back. But for the armor, those explosives would have been in Paxton's back, instead of just the rivets.

On May 17, I flew with the AVG on a mission from Kunming into Indo-China. Squadron Leader Bishop led the attack. I flew the wing position with R. T. Smith, one of the aces of the Flying Tigers and one of the pilots I remembered checking during his training days at Santa Maria, California.

We got off the Kunming field with our fighters and headed South over the lakes at twelve thousand feet. In a few minutes we passed Mengtze and the clouds thinned out and the weather got pretty clear. We went just about over Laokay, on the Chinese-Indo-China border. Then we followed the River Rouge through the very crooked gorge in the mountains, on South towards Hanoi.

Just about halfway between the border and Hanoi we saw a train coming North on the railroad. Bishop led four of us down to strafe it while the other four stayed at twelve thousand for top-cover. We circled over the train as we spiralled down to attack, and while the speed of the dive built up I got my gun-switch on and tried to trim the ship for the increasing speed.

As we levelled off and went in for the kill, I saw Bishop's tracers hitting the engine. By the time I got there—in number two position, on Bishop's wing now—the white steam was spraying from the punctured boiler. I saw the engineer and fireman jump from the locomotive, and as we went on down the cars, shooting into them, I saw Jap soldiers and probably Vichy French civilians jumping off too. We came back and set some of the cars on fire. It was a cinch now, for the train had stopped and was no longer weaving through the narrow curves of the gorge.

While the boys talked to one another, we re-formed and I heard Bishop say, "Let's bomb the railroad yards at Laokay with our frags*." I thought then that was wrong, for we had alerted

---

* Fragmentation bombs.

Laokay as we flew over and they were probably listening to us and would be waiting for us. That didn't matter, though; we'd get the railroad yards and some of the anti-aircraft crews too, if they didn't look out.

We spiralled down to bomb the target and I saw Bishop's bombs hit dead center on the round-house. Then I dropped mine. Just at that instant Bishop's fighter belched fire and smoke, and I saw him slide his canopy open and jump. His chute opened so close in front of my ship that I pulled up for fear I'd run into it. I hung there for what seemed like hours, with my air speed indicating three hundred miles an hour, while black bursts of anti-aircraft fire broke all around me. The ship just seemed to stand still, but I saw Bishop floating towards the river that was the boundary between China and Indo-China. At the very last moment, as I got my nose down and got out of the center of the anti-aircraft, I saw an unlucky wind blow the chute back to the Indo-Chinese side of the river, and Bishop was captured. We heard from him later that he was really a prisoner of the French and was getting along all right.

We re-formed North of Laokay and went back to Kunming. General Chennault said that the train wasn't worth Bishop—we should have left Laokay alone.

Word had come now that the AVG, with General Chennault as Commander, was to be inducted into the Army Air Corps. Chennault, then a General in the Chinese Army but a retired Captain in the U. S. Army, was to be given the rank of Brigadier General to head the China Air Task Force. But from what I had gathered from the few newspapers we had received and from rumors that filtered through, I knew that not many of the AVG were going to accept induction.

There were officious men around the China-Burma-India theater who thought the AVG were unruly and undisciplined. To these statements I always remarked that I wished we had ten such undisciplined groups—for they would have destroyed some three to four thousand enemy airplanes, and that would certainly have hindered the Japanese. There were others who claimed that the fighters of the AVG fought for the high salaries and the extra bonus of five hundred dollars for each enemy plane they shot down. That made me laugh, for I had seen the AVG fight, and later on I was to fly with them against the enemy. I knew those great pilots—I knew that they were great American adventurers who would have fought just as hard for peanuts or Confederate money—as long as they were fighting for General Chennault and were flying those beloved P-40's.

As it stood now: after long hours of combat the men were tired; they had been out of the United States under the most trying conditions for nearly a year. They were all showing combat fatigue and needed a rest. Some of them were combat-weary and ought never to be risked in combat again.

Furthermore, the induction of the AVG had hit a snag, from poor judgment on the part of one man. It seems that some one had lined the boys up for a fight-talk on the glamour of induction into the Army, and had used very little tact. He recited newspaper stories intimating that the AVG fought for the high pay of Camco—between $600 to $750 a month, depending on whether or not the pilot was a wing man or a squadron leader. This salesman went on to state that he sincerely hoped the AVG would accept induction, because if they didn't, and when their contracts with Camco expired, they would probably find their draft boards waiting for them when they stepped off the boat that carried them back to the United States. In that case, they would of course be inducted as privates rather than commissioned as officers.

A large percentage of the AVG are reported to have got up and walked out on the speech. After all, they were high-strung fighter pilots who had fought one of the greatest battles against superior odds that has ever been reported. In this case, they were being threatened without complete knowledge of all the facts involved. I know that from that day on they taught the Chinese coolie boy on the refueling truck jokes about that reverse sales-speech. One involved an expression that of course was never permitted to reach its destination. The boy was trained by some of the AVG—who were leaving China—to run up to every transport that landed, and, as the passengers got out, to repeat for their benefit an unprintable American expression aimed at the speech-maker. The gas-truck coolie would religiously meet every C-47 and with bland countenance would repeat the sentence. Most of the AVG used to make sure that he never reached the transport unloading the right man, but several times it took the best of American flying tackles to stop him in time.

Handled in another way, I believe that every one of the AVG who was physically able would have stayed. As it was, only five pilots remained, and some thirty ground-crew men. We had wanted to divide them into two groups—those who from a physical standpoint badly needed rest in the United States, and those who could stay out in China for six months longer without impairing their health. We were to permit the first group to go home on July Fourth (the day their contracts

107

with Camco terminated) and to remain there on leave for no less than a month, after which they were to come back to China. It is my opinion that at least ninety per cent of the AVG would have accepted this offer. But as it was, five of the greatest pilots in the world stayed with the group when their contracts expired. And those five were enough.

19
You've Got to Shoot at People

I WENT back to India and continued my single-ship raids on the Japs. After my flights with the AVG, the burning of the train in Indo-China, and the news of my one-man war in Burma, the story got to the war correspondents. I began to hear from home in the States that I had been written up as "The One-Man Air Force." From an egotistical standpoint I felt the thrill that a normal person would, but by this time I was beginning to realize that one man and one ship in this type of warfare meant very little.

In the days that followed I sank barges filled with enemy soldiers, bombed enemy columns, and strafed enemy soldiers swimming in the water from the barges I had sunk. But when I went back next day there were more and more Japs surging northward into upper Burma towards India. No, the title was an empty one—for even I, with my egotism of success in combat, knew by now that one man could make no real mark on this enemy that we were fighting. I had the satisfaction, however, of knowing that I was learning things. I had the experience of ten years of military flying, and I knew I was a good pilot. The day was going to come when that knowledge of mine, learned the hard way, would help train the new units that would come from home. There is no substitute for combat. You've got to shoot at people while you're being shot at yourself.

For the time being, though, there was just the one ship, and I nursed it like a baby. Flying it constantly, I had begun to feel a part of it. Sometimes at night I'd think of my wife and little girl, but never in combat. Sometimes, coming home after striking the enemy, I'd think of them and they seemed far, far away. Towards the last of May, after I'd flown just about two hundred hours in combat and had gathered about a hundred holes in my ship, I think I must have wondered if I'd ever see them again. I carried a Tommy gun with me in the cockpit of the

108

ship, for at strafing altitude there would probably be no time to bail out with the chute anyway, and I knew that prisoners taken by the Japs received very harsh treatment, especially those who had been strafing the capturing troops when shot down. With that gun, after my crash landing I'd have one more crack at the Japs—I certainly didn't intend to be captured.

When my imagination failed to supply new tricks like painting the nose different colors and changing the number on the fuselage, I got Sergeant Bonner and my armorer to attach a five-hundred-pound demolition bomb under the little fighter, for I was planning some real damage to the Japs. This bomb was hooked on to the belly-tank release of the Kittyhawk and overloaded the ship somewhat, but I was to become used to that. With eighteen-hundred-odd rounds of fifty-calibre ammunition, three tanks of fuel, the pilot's weight, and this 500-pound bomb, I was taking off with over 2500 pounds in the little single-seater. Later we were to increase even this load; but for the time being my wing loading was enough.

Well do I remember the first time I took off with this five hundred pounds of steel and TNT down under my ship. I pulled the heavy little plane off the last few yards of the runway and tried to climb. The straining ship mushed along just over the tea bushes, and I told Sergeant Bonner when I got back that even ten miles from the field I was going along through the tea planters' breakfast rooms, getting my wheels up.

My greatest bombing day came late in the month of May, when I dropped four 500-pound bombs at Homalin, down on the Chindwin, where the Japs seemed to be concentrating. Early in the morning I headed South with the heavy yellow bomb, slowly climbing over the Naga Hills and through the overcast, topping out at 15,000 feet. As I continued South on the course to where the Uyu met the Chindwin River, the clouds lowered but the overcast remained solid. In one hour, computing that I had made the 180 miles to Homalin, I let down through the overcast, hoping that the mountains were behind me. Luck was with me, as it usually was in my single-ship war, and I found the overcast barely a hundred feet thick. I couldn't see Homalin and my target area, but I kept right up against the cloud ceiling and circled warily. I knew that I was in luck: I could drop the bomb and then climb right back into the overcast, no matter how many Jap fighters came to intercept.

Soon I saw my target—and sure enough, there were loaded barges coming out of the broad Chindwin and heading for the docks of Homalin. I continued circling against the clouds at 11,000 feet.

For I had a plan. Dive-bombing from a P-40 is not the most accurate in the world: you can't dive very steeply or the bomb might hit the propeller, and also in too steep a dive it's hard to recover in the high speeds that are built up. It seemed to me that the type of bombing one had to do in order to keep the speed under control and to miss the prop, was more in the nature of glide-bombing. Most beginners, however, are always short with their bombs. That is to say, the projectile strikes before it gets to the target on the line of approach, rather than over it. From my practice bombings on the Brahmaputra, I had developed a rule of thumb: I would dive at some forty-five degrees; then, as the target in my gun-sight passed under the nose of my ship, I would begin to pull out slowly and count— one count for every thousand feet of my elevation above the target. Then as the ship came almost level, if I was at two thousand feet when I reached the count of "two," I'd drop the bomb.

I let the four barges get almost to the makeshift wharf; then I dove from my cloud cover. As I got the middle two barges on my gun-sight, I made a mental resolution not to be short—for even if I went over I'd hit the Japs in the town. As I passed three thousand feet the nearest barge went under me, and I began to pull out and count: "One—two—three—pull"—putting in the extra count to insure me against being short. I felt the bomb let go as I jerked the belly-tank release, and I turned to get the wing out of the way so that I could see the bomb hit.

The five hundred pounds of TNT exploded either right beside the leading barge or between the barge closest to shore and the docks. As the black smoke cleared, I saw pieces of the barge splashing into the river a hundred yards from the explosion. I went down and strafed, but the black smoke was so thick that I could see very little to concentrate on; so I climbed to three thousand feet and waited for the smoke to clear. Then I dove for the two barges that were drifting down the river. I must have put two hundred rounds into each of them. I got one to burning, and from the black smoke it must have been loaded with gasoline. The other would not burn, but I'm sure I left enough holes in it to sink it. Coming back over the target again, I strafed the Japs in the water who were either floating dead or swimming towards shore.

On my second raid I dropped a five-hundred-pound bomb on the largest building in Homalin, which the British Intelligence reported the next day had been the police station. They said that two hundred Japanese were killed in that bombing, and that between six hundred and a thousand were killed in the series of bombings. Many bodies were picked up about thirty miles down the Chindwin at Tamu and Sittiang. All four of my bombs had done some damage, and I was quite satisfied.

In British Intelligence reports I read that Radio Tokyo had mentioned Homalin. One bombing had taken place, it seems, with very slight damage, and that only to the innocent Burmese villagers, but the Imperial Japanese Army had evacuated Homalin because of the serious malaria that was prevalent there. Anyway, I always like to think that my four trips to Homalin with four 500-pound packages of good old American Picatinny TNT had something to do with the monkey-men's deciding that the malaria was too bad along the Chindwin.

My raids with "Old Exterminator" continued through May and into June. Some days I'd climb out of India through the rain clouds of the monsoon and fly on into Burma. The trip back would then be one to worry me, for I never knew exactly when to let down. Almost every day, however, if I worked my take-off time properly I'd get back from the mission as the storm clouds were breaking, and I'd have a nice, welcome hole to dive through. On other days when I wasn't lucky, I'd just have to roll over and dive for the valley of the Brahmaputra— and that's where I always came out, or I wouldn't be here to tell about it.

Some of the flights into Burma were just a waste of gasoline; I would see nothing. It follows that I have written of the more exciting ones. There's nothing so monotonous as to fly for four hundred miles with plenty of ammunition, or sometimes for two hundred to three hundred miles with a heavy bomb attached, and find no place to drop it. I'd have to come back then, and gingerly letting down through the dark monsoon clouds, land the 500 pounds of TNT as if I had a crate of eggs aboard. After all, we didn't have bombs to waste.

Early in June I did have one exciting trip. From reports of the ferry pilots I heard that the Japs were building a bridge over the river N'umzup, some forty miles North of Myitkyina. The very afternoon the report reached me, I went over and strafed the engineers at work on the bridge. And I nearly got shot down, for the efficient Japanese had moved in their antiaircraft with the bridge crew. When I landed at the base I helped the ground crew count the thirty small-calibre holes in my ship. My cap had one hole in it, though luckily it had not been on my head but back in the small baggage compartment

111

of the Kittyhawk. That was pretty bad, though, for it was the only cap I had, and for months I had to wear it with all the felt torn from the crown by the Jap ground-fire. I remember that later one of the young bomber crew men asked Maj. Butch Morgan—it was when we stepped from our ships after bombing Hongkong—whether or not I'd had that cap on when the bullet went through.

I cussed about the cap and loaded the ship for another run on the bridge. As I came in from another direction this time, and very low, I saw bodies of the enemy from my first strafing, but the Japs were still working on the bridge. I strafed the working-party in two passes from different directions, so low that the anti-aircraft couldn't shoot at me effectively.

But I had seen enough. Even though this bridge was being built of bamboo, they were making it very strong, for the abutments were of heavier lumber and of stone. The Japanese were evidently planning to transport trucks, tanks, or some other heavier equipment North. I went right back to Dinjan and had Sergeant Bonner strap on a nice 500-pound bomb with a delayed action fuse. At any rate the armament men told him it was a ten-second delay fuse. This type of target had to be hit exactly, and if I were to glide in for a dead shot I'd surely get shot down by all the anti-aircraft. So I made up my mind long before I got there to turn it loose just as low as I could fly. Even if I missed the bridge by only fifty yards, which is close for dive-bombing in ships not made for that type of work, I'd knock a lot of leaves off the trees, make a big noise, and maybe kill some gunners. But the abutments of that bridge had to be hit just about dead center if I was to make the Japs stop work.

I came in to the target from the West, with the sun right at my back. I flew so low that I was afraid the little windmill on the nose of the bomb would get knocked off by the bushes. And then, as I saw the bridge, I let the bomb go.

It was a direct hit!

When I got back home I looked at "Old Exterminator" and I couldn't see why it hadn't spun in right there over the N'um-zup. There were holes as big as footballs in the fabric flippers and in the metal stabilizers of the tail section. There was a hole in the fuselage and five holes in the wing. But I guess the hill just East of the target had saved me. You see, the bomb hadn't waited ten seconds to go off—which would have given me just that long to get out of the way of the explosion. It had gone off almost immediately, and as a result I'd been just about blown out of the sky. The one-tenth second of grace, with me travelling at some three hundred miles an hour, had let me go

112

only about fifty feet across the target, but even that had been enough to permit a small knoll to shield me from the main explosion.

When I could get my breath again I asked Sergeant Bonner to find out from the armament men what in hell was the matter with the bomb. He brought them back with him, and the ordnance expert told me that he hadn't said ten-seconds delay but one-tenth second delay. Just one hundred times less delay than I had expected! But "Old Exterminator" lived through it, and as soon as they'd patched the holes I went back over the bridge. We'd blown the abutments, all the timber, and all the Japs from off the N'umzup. A five-hundred-pound bomb with either a ten-second delay fuse or a tenth-second delay fuse will discourage even the most persistent people.

As the June days passed, Colonel Haynes was moved to China to head the Bomber Command under General Chennault, and I was left alone as Commanding Officer of the Ferrying Command. On the day the cheerful Haynes left, I felt as if I had lost my best and last friend. For this meant that I'd have to stay on the ground more, and work the administration as well as the operations of the ABC, which was getting tougher and tougher with all the rice we were having to drop and the passengers we were having to haul.

On the one day that I stayed on the ground, it seemed to me that every time I looked up from the desk that I was "flying," some long, lanky tea planter would be standing there in the door in sun-helmet and shorts. With his bony knees sticking out, he'd ask me in cold clipped accents: "I say old chap—do you have transportation for Calcutta?"

My morale got pretty low. And the rains got worse; some days we'd have a foot of water in the "basha" that was Operations, and the men were sleeping almost in the water. I remember most of the Southern boys would argue with the Northerners on the old familiar subject of the whys and wherefores of the War Between the States. As the Southerners were in greater numbers, they of course won most of the friendly arguments.

From over near Sadiya, we had gotten eight elephants, tame ones, and were working them to move some heavy timbers to be used on the warehouses of the new field. There was an old Southern sergeant who took good care of the pachyderms. He must have been a mule-skinner in either the first World War or the border war with Mexico, for he did everything in his power to keep the eight elephants dry and well-fed and content. Even when he tied the chains to their legs at night, he would wrap the links with cloth to keep them from chafing the thick skin of the big beasts.

Another sergeant, from about the same section of the country that the old elephant caretaker hailed from, came by one day and looked the stalls over with a quizzical eye.

"Say, Micky," he called back as he left, "you're taking too good care of those elephants. You're going to get 'em so comfortable that the Yankees will come down here and free 'em."

20
Great Day

BOB LAYHER, one of the AVG pilots, came over for several days, and we drank good Scotch whiskey at night and flew our planes across into Burma in the day—when I didn't have to get passengers on the freight ships. I learned a lot, flying on his wing. We'd go over for a look at Myitkyina, and it would amaze me how effortlessly, without apparent forethought, Bob would get our ships into the sun before we came within sight of the field we were to observe. I picked up little things like that as I flew with him, and they helped me later.

On the twentieth of June, members of the Army Board that had been appointed to induct the AVG passed through Assam, and my hopes faded of ever getting over to work under General Chennault. I knew that out of those Colonels, the powers-that-be had surely picked some lucky one to get the greatest job in the world. This was of course that of commanding the AVG after it came into the Army, with its nucleus of old AVG personnel and the new pilots as replacements from home in the States. General Chennault was to be the Task Force Commander and was to be over the Fighter Group and the Bomber Force.

If the Scotch hadn't given out, I would have got drunk that night. But instead I went on another strafing raid in the late afternoon, and had to land after dark.

So I took it out in action. I bombed Homalin and the railroad yards at Mogaung the next day, and strafed the field at Myitkyina coming back. During the ensuing days until the 26th of June, I carried out attacks on barges near Bhamo, and on one trip went to Shwebo and almost to Mandalay, making a round trip of nearly nine hundred miles. I strafed the field at Maymyo, caught a train on the railroad North of town, and set it on fire. It was anything for action—and the engine of "Old

Exterminator" got pretty rough at times, for by then I had three hundred and sixty hours on it and my mechanics had had little experience with Allisons.

That night, when I got home from my trip into Burma, I was handed a radiogram that saved my life. As I read it my face must have turned white; I know that tears came to my eyes, for I felt them burn. But I didn't care. I was ordered to report in Kunming, China, to General Chennault, as Commanding Officer of the 23rd Fighter Group which was to be activated from the AVG on July 4, 1942. I wiped the tears from my eyes and looked out on an improving world. I could hear the birds singing again, and people were laughing; I knew I was the luckiest man in all the world.

I carefully folded the radiogram to show my grandchildren when the war was over and went out to look at my ship. For I had something else on my mind too. I was going to go into Burma the next day on four of the damnedest strafing and bombing raids the Japs had ever seen. It would be my swansong from Assam and I had to celebrate.

I told my crew to load a 500-pound HE on "Old Exterminator," and I walked around looking the old ship over. Somehow I figured that Kittyhawk had had a lot to do with getting me the greatest job in the war. It's not every man who finally gets what he has always wanted in the Army—after being pulled out of fighters for being too old, after being an instructor for four years, after being shanghaied into being a Burma-roadster, important as the job had been. Well, I had got what I wanted and I felt as though I could jump over the moon. I patted the leering shark's mouth on old 41-1456, and caressed the prop that had taken me in and out of many messes. Then I left, while they pulled the belly tank and put the big, fat, yellow bomb under the belly, and tightened the sway braces.

Next morning before dawn I was in the air, my course set for Homalin. As I climbed out above the clouds I began to recite poetry in rhythm with the engine. To the verses of "Gunga Din" I dropped my first bomb of the day on the docks of Homalin. Then I flew back home with the words of the "Galley Slave" going out over the radio in a private broadcast to the world. On my next trip I dropped a five-hundred-pounder on a barge at Bhamo and came back and strafed the much-abused Myitkyina. My third attack was on the railroad station at Mogaung and I strafed the empty freight-cars in the yard. I had to use a belly tank on the fourth trip, and so I couldn't take a big bomb. But I loaded on six eighteen-pound frags and set sail for Lashio. I remembered to drop the belly tank before I went down into the anti-aircraft, and I dropped the six little frags in two of the big green warehouses by the railroad tracks. I shot up the field but saw no planes, and I finished my ammunition by strafing the main street of the town. I saw two plate-glass windows spatter across the street like artificial snow from a Christmas tree, and I laughed hysterically as two figures ran from a pagoda.

That day I landed back home tired and happy. More orders had come for me: I was to go to Delhi before I went to China. I went there the next morning with "Long Johnny" Payne.

When I had received my official instructions from headquarters in Delhi, and had been wined and dined by good friends—war correspondents like Berrigan, Magoffin, and Briggs—I came on back to pack my things in Assam. I tried to take the old fighter ship with me, but my crew had chiselled a new Allison engine from somewhere—had probably stolen it from some ship, but I didn't know where. So I went on over in a transport, expecting to come back later and ferry "Old Exterminator" to his new home.

As we came down into the rain over the lake South of Kunming, I never have felt so good. This was another step to the East, towards Japan, and when I got out and saw all those sleek-looking fighter ships that my Group was going to receive from the AVG in five days, my spirits soared another mile in the air. I was through with all that lonesome "one-man war" stuff. From now on we'd be fighting as a team, with bombers escorted by fighter ships in a proper force to represent America.

I had already met most of the members of the First American Volunteer Group, but it was an even greater pleasure to meet them now. Some of them were men who were going to stay with the 23rd Fighter Group and fight under me. Of all the honors that I ever have received or ever will receive, the greatest to me will always be the honor of being given command of that great group, under the Command of Gen. Claire L. Chennault.

During the four days that followed I took over the military equipment of the Group from the Commander of the squadron that was based at Kunming, and I got my headquarters staff organized. In this Army, Master Sergeants showing officers what to do have always been the backbone of a fighting force, and I will never forget Master Sergeant McNeven. I was certainly expecting to lead the group in its fights against the Japanese, and the administrative work that the Sergeant Major of the 23rd

Fighter Group accomplished so efficiently made it possible for me to fly and have the paper-work go on at the same time.

Later in the week I heard that "Old Exterminator" was ready with a new engine. But with the report came another that some other Group was moving into Assam, and that the engineering officer had stated he knew nothing about that ship 41-1456 belonging to the Chinese Government. It would stay in India, he said. I went on and flew back to India in one of the P-40E's that we had just received from the factory that repairs them in China.

Landing at my old base, I waited until dark, and then had the numbers on the ship that I had flown in exchanged with those of my old fighter. For morale purposes alone, we had to have that ship in the 23rd Group. All this change involved was a stencilling operation to put 41-1456 on the ship that I had flown from China, and another to put on "Old Exterminator" the serial number of the fighter that I was leaving in India.

So, early the next morning, July 3, 1942, "me and the old Kittyhawk" wended our happy way across the hills and jungles of Burma to Kunming and more adventures together. From that moment, we left the Air Corps number 41-1456 on that insignificant ship in India, and for all practical purposes the old P-40E that I had used for sixty-three days over Burma became another number, but it would always be "Old Exterminator" to me. In those two months we'd flown together 371 hours over enemy territory and we were more than friends. That is somewhat over eighty thousand miles, and in combat that's a long, long way.

Everything had happened fast in this war, and the organization of the 23rd Fighter Group was no exception. There was no holiday, even if it was activated on the Fourth of July. There was no time for celebration. Radio Tokyo started right off with a bang, and we definitely knew hard work was ahead. On the night of July 3, Radio Tokyo—the only program we could ever hear in China—warned the new American fighter group that they would quickly annihilate them, for it was common knowledge that the experienced AVG personnel were leaving for America. But Tokyo had reckoned without the strategic brain of the General, or the loyalty of those great pilots of the First American Volunteer Group.

The General was expecting an attack on Independence Day anyway, for the Japs had always shown an affinity for raids on our holidays. When the Japs arrived over Kweilin, expecting to find green and inexperienced fighter pilots, they found

117

many American boys who for weeks had been flying with the AVG. These were led by five of the most valuable of the AVG, and there was one great ace-in-the-hole that only the General and the AVG could have arranged: Two squadrons of these Flying Tigers had agreed to stay behind for a two weeks' period to help the newly formed 23rd Fighter Group. I think this gesture by those men such as Bob Neal, Charley Bond, George T. Burgard, Frank Lawlor, John E. Petack, Jim Howard, and others who were suffering from combat fatigue and ill health, was one of the bravest and most self-sacrificing incidents of this war. In the two weeks that they remained, two of them gave their lives, and their sacrifice was beyond the call of mere duty. These men, with those five who stayed with us to lead our squadrons—Hill, Rector, Schiel, Bright, and Sawyer—and the AVG radio, engineering, armament, and ground personnel, were our backbone and our inspiration. We of the 23rd Fighter Group salute you.

That Fourth of July, as the overconfident enemy ships came in over Kweilin, they brought a new twin-engine fighter that was supposed to murder us. They came in doing arrogant acrobatics, expecting to strafe the Chinese civilians in the city without opposition. General Chennault watched them with field glasses from outside the cave and called directions to Bob Neal, Ed Rector, and Tex Hill, who were sitting with their ships "in the sun" high overhead, at twenty-one thousand. At his radio order of "Take 'em," the newly formed 23rd with the AVG attached dropped down and massacred the Japs. There were soon thirteen wrecked Zeros and new twin-engined I-45's around the field for the Chinese to celebrate over.

Out of this initial air battle for the new Group came one of the best nicknames of the war. General Chennault told me that after the Jap attack had been broken he saw a lone Zero tear across the tops of the hills that jutted up all around Kweilin, and far behind it he heard the unmistakable rolling thunder of six fifty-calibre guns. The hurrying Jap kept going in the direction of Canton and home, and had just about disappeared in the Southeast when the General saw a shark-nosed P-40 roar out of the West, with its six guns going steadily, the tracers dropping far, far below and behind the fleeing Zero. Well, the Jap got away and when the American ship had finally gotten his guns stopped and cool enough to land, the pilot was found to be Lieutenant Dumas—just an eager American pilot who had seen the Jap at too great distance and had opened up.

Dumas laughingly told us, during the usual kidding that came that evening, that it had been the first time he had seen an enemy plane, and he had gotten so excited that he'd fired too soon. All he did was shoot—but when he got the trigger down and saw the tracers out in front he couldn't turn it loose. He felt about the same way that all of us feel in our first combat. But this escapade earned for him the title of "Long Burst Dumas."

Thus was the 23rd Fighter Group organized, initiated, and activated in combat. When I took over things at Kunming there were three fighter squadrons and one headquarters squadron. Major Tex Hill had one squadron at Hengyang, China, and with him were such deputy leaders as Maj. Gil Bright, Maj. Johnny Alison, and Capt. Ajax Baumler. Maj. Ed Rector had another squadron at Kweilin with Capt. Charlie Sawyer for his assistant in leadership. These outlying stations are about five hundred miles in the direction of Japan from our headquarters on the plateau of Yunnan at Kunming. The third unit was the squadron under Maj. Frank Schiel, who was very busy training the most junior members of this new fighter group in the way of fighter aviation. I got the Group headquarters to running and stood by for orders to begin leading the fighter forces in action to the East.

On July 10, Tex Hill led a small flight, including Baumler, Alison, Lieut. Lee Minor, and Lieutenant Elias, up on the Yangtse. Their prime job was to escort a few B-25 medium bombers against the docks of Hankow. This objective of mission with our China force was never all we considered to be the duty of our fighters, for if any other target presented itself after the bombers were on the way home, we'd have some fun. Tex Hill led his flight along with the bombers, who were led by Col. C. V. Haynes. After the bombs had been released and the B-25's were heading back for base with their bomb-bay doors closed, Tex called for an attack by the fighters on the enemy shipping in the river.

One of the bomber pilots said that Tex rolled his ship over from sixteen thousand feet and streaked down for the Jap gunboats below. The little gunboats were shooting everything they had at the American fighters—but that, I've learned since, was what Hill liked. Tex Hill's guns were firing even as he pulled out right on the water, and they swept the decks of the enemy gunboats. The bomber pilot said that as the fighter ships would turn low to the water and come in, each concentrating on one of the little Jap warships, he could see the six lines of fifty-calibre tracers cutting across the water. At long range they seemed to meet out in front of the fighter and then fan out and cover the deck of the target. Then, as the speed of the fighter narrowed the range, the point where the fire crossed—the zero or convergence point of the guns—was right at the waterline of the Jap boat, and it must have knocked in a hole that crippled the boat right away. On the second attack one of these gunboats was sinking and on fire. Hill's four fighters sank all four of the little metal gunboats.

Next day, on another flight such as this one, Hill led eight fighters, four with wing bombs, for dive-bombing Nanchang. While these four went down with their bombs, Hill was to stay aloft with the other four to act as top-cover—just in case some Zeros tried to surprise the dive-bombers. Ajax Baumler said that he was on Petack's wing for the bombing and that he saw the whole thing: Johnny Petack dove for his target, one of the gunboats on the lake, but as his bomb hit the boat the P-40 was seen to explode, evidently hit by ground-fire. Ajax followed the burning ship almost to the ground and saw it strike in a rice paddy near a Buddhist temple.

So Petack, one of the AVG who had stayed for the extra two weeks, was killed in action. It's peculiar how a man could fight all through those last nine months and then go down from a lucky anti-aircraft shot. John Petack had remained for the purpose of training the new pilots and his job was that of airdrome defense. He was killed on this offensive mission. It was one that he could have refused with honor; instead, he had volunteered for this dive-bombing flight and had been killed in carrying it out. It was the most inspiring thing he could have done.

I kept sweating out the organization of the Group, and finally on July 17, I received orders from the General to proceed to Kweilin area and take charge of fighter operations. I know my heart nearly beat my ribs to pieces, for I was at last being ordered to go out and lead the fighting. Just as I landed on this airdrome in the Kwansi province I saw the remainder of the AVG get into a transport to begin their long trip home to the U. S. A. They called to me as they got aboard and I saw Bob Neal, their greatest ace, wave from the door as he stepped in. We were on our own now, except for the five AVG veterans who had accepted induction in China, and the thirty-odd groundmen.

21
Some Good, Honest Lead-Poisoning

As the transport got away and the dust settled down, I climbed out of my fighter and looked around at the country. I could but marvel at the geographical situation. Colonel Cooper and I—Cooper had been in the movie production business—used to discuss the peculiar beauty of the place, and he'd say that it would make the greatest location in the world for a moving picture.

It was a flat, tableland country, and over the ages it must have been under water. From the level plain rose vertical, rocky hills, like stalagmites. These were honey-combed with caves where water, when they were submerged, must have dissolved the limestone that had been in the pockets. Evidently the glacier period had planed the valley flat as the glacier moved South, but the jagged rocks had withstood the pressure. Then, as the glacier melted, the caves had formed under water. Now the gray pinnacles of lava-like rock pointed straight towards the heavens. These one-thousand- to two-thousand-foot sentinels gave the valley an eery appearance that always subdued my general feeling of cheerfulness. As long as I went to Kweilin, I dreaded the extra nervous tenson that I knew it would produce. Add to this a summer temperature of over 100 degrees, a humidity of almost 100 per cent, and a fine powdery dust that gagged you, and you can realize that Kweilin was not a summer resort.

There was just the single runway for the planes, cut there between those silent needles of stone. We had the operations office in one of the natural caves, and the radio set in another. As I climbed out of my P-40, I could see neither.

Here in Kweilin I first had explained to me the air-raid warning system on which we depended. It was of course a working dream that General Chennault had developed. Many times it had saved our fighter force in China, and without it our chances there against the Japanese would have been hopeless.

It seems that the General had always known that Japan was our natural enemy. When he was retired from the Air Corps, instead of staying on his farm in Waterproof, Louisiana, for the rest of his life and living an easy life shooting ducks and fishing, he had gone to China. Here, in a rugged existence, he had told his story to the Generalissimo. With the approval of high Chinese officials he had built this air-warning net, had caused to be constructed many strategic airdromes in China, and had preached the doctrine of pursuit aviation.

The warning net is of course secret and cannot be discussed in detail. But if you imagine two concentric circles, one with a radius of one hundred kilometers and the other of two hundred kilometers, around each of most of the fields and large cities in Free China, you have a general picture. In these circles are thousands of reporting stations—some within the enemy lines, some right on the enemy fields themselves. There may be a coolie sitting on a city wall watching for airplanes or listening for engine noise and reporting it with a visual signal. There may be a mandarin in a watch tower; a soldier in a field with a walkie-talkie radio. All reports finally get in to the outer circle, where some of the information is filtered. Then by telephone it goes to the inner circle, where it is refiltered, and finally it goes to the plotting-board in our cave or operations shack. There Chinese interpreters get the reports and move little pin flags along the map of China—and we know where every enemy ship is in our territory and can see where ours are. The net works so efficiently in certain areas that we don't take off until the Japs are within the one-hundred-kilometer circle; this gives us more fuel with which to fight.

When the Japs come we know at what altitude they are approaching and from exactly what direction. We know their speed and their numbers. It's kind of a joke, too, that in several places we know when the Japanese roll their ships from their hangars or revetments, when they start their engines, and when they take off. Also it not only works for the obvious purpose of defense but has permitted us in many cases to locate lost pilots, for the navigation facilities in China are not the world's best.

Of course the locating of lost, friendly ships took another element besides the warning net. It required the existence of intelligent radio operators who knew the country and had common sense. These men, like Richardson, Mihalko, Miller, and Sasser, with others, stayed out there with us, and if you count the AVG aces as the first factor that permitted us to carry on in a manner that didn't discredit the Flying Tigers, then these men who helped us by radio were the close second factor.

Suppose that one of our pilots, returning from a flight, loses his position on his map because of a cross-wind, because of unfamiliarity with the country, because of his own stupidity—which we call a "short circuit between the head-phones"—or just because the maps of China are very inaccurate. In many such instances we would have lost an airplane worth virtually millions in our combat zone, and perhaps the pilot too.

The pilot who is lost calls the radio station that he thinks is closest to him, and in code tells the trouble. The radioman tells him to circle the next town he passes for a few minutes. Down in that town, marked on his map with an unknown Chinese character, some member of this warning net sees him and reports one P-40 circling. In a few minutes the radio operator gets the report and tells the pilot: "You're reported over Lufeng —fly fifty-eight degrees at two hundred miles an hour and we'll have supper ready—we've got grits tonight—yeah."

One amusing but near-tragic instance of this orientation by means of the air-warning net happened about the time the AVG induction board came to China. Another fighter group commander had waited for several days over in India to come into China with a large flight of P-40-E r's. He finally came over on a transport and eventually got tired of waiting for the fighters. He didn't know that the weather was very bad in Burma, and that the monsoon winds from the South could take them so far off course in a few minutes that the entire flight might easily get lost.

After a long wait he came back to Assam in the transport and led his pilots towards Kunming. First of all, he corrected too much for the southerly wind, and in a very short time he was fifty miles South of his course and near two Japanese fields. His unbashful deputy leaders herded him to the North. And then the monsoon wind from out the Indian Ocean began to work on his navigation, and in another hour he was lost far to the North of the course. Night was falling, and the hills of North China were rising threateningly.

Then the net, if it hadn't justified its existence long before, would have begun to pay for itself. The leader called Kunming, and the operator there, a tough old former Navy man, heard him and gave the instructions: "Circle the first town you see." The group commander began to argue at once—said he didn't have enough gas to waste circling; but the AVG radio-man talked him into doing it. Then the net reported, and Kunming operator said, "You're over Yangpi—fly 240 degrees for twenty minutes and you'll see the lake Kunming is on."

Well, the lost leader looked at his map and still couldn't see how he was North of the course and really past his destination. So he began to argue again. The old Navy operator stood the bickering as long as he could; then he "took over." With the initiative he had developed, he gave off some of the most classic advice that I've ever heard, and he gave it straight from the shoulder.

"Blast it," he called, "who the devil's lost, you or me? Now you fly the course I'm telling you and we'll meet you."

And so another man of the Occident failed to change the East, and in failing learned a little and became a little more like the East. It saved twenty-five airplanes.

People have asked me what made me able to shoot down my first Jap, and probably they expected me to say that I had practised on tow targets until I could put every shot in the black. Or that I had been to all the schools from Leavenworth to Mount Holyoke, and had learned tactics. Or perhaps that I was better at piloting than the Jap. I must have disappointed them. For if any one thing more than another enabled me to meet the Japanese fighter pilots in the air and shoot them down while I escaped, it was an American girl.

First of all, I don't know exactly what democracy is, or the real, common-sense meaning of a republic. But as we used to talk things over in China, we all used to agree that we were fighting for The American Girl. She to us was America, Democracy, Coca-Colas, Hamburgers, Clean Places to Sleep, or The American Way of Life.

To hurriedly explain this theory, let me say that I learned to fly as anybody else did—with an instructor in a flying school. That is, I learned to take a trainer off and to land it. But to correct this, I learned to be a combat pilot by flying all over the Western Hemisphere to see an American Girl. I went from every State in the Union to Georgia to see her. I went from South America to Panama to see the same girl. I went from Central America to the Canal Zone to see her. All on government missions certainly, but that mission was more to develop myself into being a pilot who could navigate over the world, or fly instruments when I had to, or fly at night, than it was to carry out the routine flight that I was on. I always imagined that my sole duty was to get through with the ship safely. I knew that if I could get through in peace-time I could get through in war. Then if I could fly the ship as an expert, I would only have to point the guns at the right place and the enemy would go down.

To prove this, I go on and answer the question further by saying, "No, ma'am, I didn't learn it in school. Why, my greatest victory in the air was on a cross-country—that's what we call a navigation flight." And here's the story.

124

Early one morning —July 31, 1942—I took off from Kunming headquarters to return to the eastern theatre at Kweilin and Hengyang. High mountains are on this five-hundred-mile route to the East, and I went on top of the overcast right away. From my twenty-thousand-foot altitude I kept looking down at the solid cloud layer just below me, and I guess that subconsciously I prayed there would be breaks at my destination. There were mountains at my destination too, and it's still not the best feeling to have to dive through overcast into hilly country with a fighter ship—or with any ship, for that matter.

As the minutes rolled by and the miles spun behind the P-40, I still didn't see the welcome shadow of a hole in the clouds. In just a little over two hours I arrived over the point above the clouds where Lingling should have been. You see this point was in flat country, and between Kweilin and Hengyang. By intentionally making an error to the North I knew at least what side of Kweilin I was on, and knew furthermore that I could go down much more safely there than farther South in the mountains that surround Kweilin.

I called Lingling over the radio, but before I could get a reply, Sasser, the operator at Kweilin, broke in with an "alert" warning. He said: "Chinese net reports noise of enemy airplanes coming up the Canton-Hengyang Railway at high altitude. Last report Section A-5." Looking at my map, which was marked off in squares with letter and numeral co-ordinates, I saw that I was very close to that section. But at the same time I was really not oriented as to position, and was into the last twenty or so gallons of my fuel. Here was a chance at last to intercept enemy planes; by the time the P-40's from our fighter stations could get there, the enemy would have gone on with their mission. What was I to do?

As I considered it for the second that was necessary to make up my mind, I remember thinking that my loss of this ship would be justified if I shot a Japanese ship down, and if I was out of fuel above the clouds I could dive down and land in a rice paddy. That would be an even trade. But I guess my ego thought I could shoot the whole formation down—and the exchange of the Japanese flight for my one ship would certainly be favorable to our side.

But my mind was already made up. Even then I was on my way towards the position that I thought was Section A-5, there on the pretty white tops of the overcast.

Calling to Sasser, I told him I thought I was just East of Lingling and very close to the Jap formation, and was going to try to intercept. I dove down until I was just over the tops of the clouds, at 17,600 feet. I dodged in among the tops of the fluffy cumulus, looking ahead for the first sign of the black silhouette of an airplane. As the enemy ships had been reported heading North, I estimated where they should now be and flew to intercept them.

I'll never forget. I had just looked at the fuel gauge for the hundredth time, and as my eyes left the instrument board to go back to my diligent search, I saw the clock, and the hour was 9:08. At that instant I saw an enemy airplane—one silhouette. From that second on, I know I moved automatically. I saw that on our courses we were going to meet head-on.

The other ship was now much nearer, and closing fast. It was a twin-engine bomber and was right down low over the clouds, just as I was. Down below now were holes in the overcast, and I imagine the bomber was trying to locate its position to go down through. He didn't see my ship, and I kept hidden by the clouds as much as possible. I felt my left hand go to the instrument panel to turn on the gun-switch. Then, as I looked at the red switch, I saw that I had evidently turned it on without being conscious of the act. I moved it off, then back on again, as a kind of test. I turned the gun-sight rheostat on and got the lighted sight reflected on my glass armor in front of my eyes. The enemy ship came on, "mushrooming" in my vision; our relative speed of approach was perhaps five hundred miles an hour. By now I had shoved everything forward on the throttle quadrant—the engine was pulling full power, and the prop pitch was set to high speed, low pitch.

Then, just before I pressed the trigger, I saw the other planes, two enemy fighters above and behind the bomber. I had evidently not been seen by any of the three ships, for after all I was coming on very close to the clouds. But I nearly stopped my aiming from the surprise of seeing them. They were about three thousand feet above the bomber, and were weaving back and forth in loose formation. I saw the square wing-tip that told they were Navy Zeros. There flashed in my mind the warning that I had heard from General Chennault about attacking bombers when there was fighter escort. Everyone in China had always neglected to consider odds on the side of the enemy— they were used to that. Personally, I just didn't know enough about aerial combat to worry much, or I might have gone on anyway. My six guns would neutralize their four; I could shoot the bomber down and dive into the clouds before the Zeros could get me.

I really don't know whether I thought it all out or not, for by now I was shooting. The tracers seemed to go towards the enemy all right, but now the Jap came into my sights so fast that I don't know whether they hit him then or not. I dove right under the nose of the twin-engine ship, and I'll bet he was one surprised pilot. I noted that he had started to turn and maybe that made me miss.

As the ship crossed over my head, I pulled around in the tightest turn I have ever made, mushing down in the clouds a good distance, and that must have hid me momentarily from the fighter escort. As I came out, the bomber was completing its turn opposite to the way I had turned, and I moved in for a full-deflection shot—a shot possible when the other ship is crossing your path, at 90 degrees. I had slowed down, however, and had to reef in and shoot at it from beneath and behind. I got a good burst in here.

But now I saw tracers all around me and felt a couple of hits: the Zeros were shooting at me. One of the enemy fighters dove in front of me and I got a snap shot at it from a hundred yards. I dove under the bomber again, and with the speed that I gained, tried to make a belly attack; I got in another shot burst and felt some more hits on my ship.

As I pulled up, the Zero that had been shooting at me made the mistake of rolling at the top of his climb, and I dove at him and gave him about two hundred rounds with a no-deflection shot: I know the burst hit him badly. I shot at the other fighter from long range as he tried a head-on run. But the clouds were worrying the Japs—they seemed to have trouble seeing me. As my dive at the Zero built my speed up, I turned towards the bomber again; it saw me and started a turn to the right. I snapped a short head-on shot, and before I got to the enemy ship, I tossed caution to the winds and made a hundred and eighty degree turn—the Jap was right in front of my guns and I was already shooting. I held the trigger down and saw the tracers hit the big wing, the fuselage, and saw the glass stream from the canopy. I just squeezed the trigger and "froze" as the bomber seemed to come back towards me.

As I drew up to less than a hundred yards the big red spots on the wing grew wider and wider apart, and I saw pieces come from the left engine. I nearly rammed the enemy—I still don't see how I missed the radio antenna pole behind the glass canopy; I could see the guns waving to and fro, and they shot at me.

But the bomber was going down. I didn't pull up as I went past him this time, but dove steeply. When I came out of the dive I looked back for the Zeros but they were not to be seen. Above and behind me, the bomber was spinning slowly in flames, the black smoke making a spiral above the clouds—I saw it go into the clouds as I mushed through in my pullout. I came out below the clouds, which were broken in a few places now, but I couldn't see the Jap ships. I made one half circle and didn't know where I was.

Finally remembering my fuel supply, I breathlessly glanced at the gauges, and they were all bouncing around on—EMPTY! I turned and headed West with my throttle retarded and the prop set back for cruising. Now I called Sasser, having forgotten to call him at the moment of contact with the enemy. I told him about the interception, that I knew I had shot down the bomber and had gotten some bursts on the fighters. Sasser told me that there was a flight on the way from Hengyang, led by Gil Bright.

My altitude was ten thousand now, and I held it while I just about glided with power to the West, where I should see the Hengyang-Kweilin railroad. As I finished my report over the radio, Sasser in Kweilin told me S-3, and Richardson at Hengyang said S-3 also. But Miller at Lingling told me I sounded close to his station, and gave me the report S-5. These mean, in radio technical language, that my volume was louder in Lingling than at either of the other two stations. More than likely I was closer to the middle town. I assumed this and flew West, letting down gradually.

Just then Miller must have received a report from a town that heard my engine, for he said, "You're Northeast of the field." I turned a little South and saw the welcome red clay of Lingling. I started feeling happy then—I'd been in the air on a cross-country for nearly four hours, and knew that I'd shot down at least one plane. I couldn't buzz the field though, for any minute I expected the engine to cough and the prop to start "windmilling"—out of gas. I put the wheels down and landed without even looking to see which way the wind was on the runway. I got the ship parked without the engine's dying, but the mechanics said they couldn't see any fuel in the tanks.

Rather excitedly I told my story. We counted the holes in my ship and then went over to count those in one of the fighters that had been in another battle that morning. Just then Miller came dashing up in a jeep to say that my air engagement had been reported over Leiyang, sixty miles to the East, and that confirmation had already come in on my bomber. It had crashed and burned eight miles from the town. That noon I was so excited that I couldn't eat my lunch—I just sat there and relived the battle. The sergeant came in to tell me there were seventeen holes in my ship, and two of them were from the cannon of the Zeros—they were all back near the tail; so maybe George Paxton had been right, and maybe they *couldn't* shoot. Well, we were to find out during the next ten days, very vividly.

I flew on to Hengyang that afternoon, and with Lieutenant Cluck in a jeep we drove to Leiyang. We had information that some of the crew or passengers had jumped from the bomber that morning and had been captured, and we needed the prisoners for information. With Chinese guides we climbed on foot over the rice paddies built on the hills, towards the scene of the crashed plane. Even before we'd covered the ten or more miles that we had to walk, I saw evidence of the airplane. It seemed as if every coolie that came towards us was carrying a piece of the Jap plane. Near the wreck I saw pieces of aluminum on the houses covering holes in the roofs, and saw some of the clothes from the Jap airmen. These we examined, and found a notebook, a map, and a pistol. Later the soldiers at the wreck gave us a chute and some other things of military value.

When we came to the burned bomber we found it pretty well scattered. The fabric was gone from the parts that hadn't burned, but the larger part was just a mass of burned metal. I noticed that the bodies of four Japs were lying where they had fallen, and several days later other visitors reported them still in the same positions. I looked in vain through the wreckage for a Samurai sword, which is the souvenir valued most from the Jap.

The surprise was that another plane had now been found several miles from the bomber. It was supposed to be a fighter, being smaller, and it had burned upon crashing. I therefore received credit for two enemy planes destroyed on July 31. It had been my first aerial combat, and I felt very proud indeed.

We found the reported prisoner, but he was dead. While being questioned he had tried to escape, had killed several Chinese, had wounded others, and in turn had been mortally wounded. Lieutenant Cluck got to him before he died, but was unable to get any valuable information.

My first aerial engagement started a story in Delhi—I found out about it four months later. The story told there was to the effect that I had engaged an enemy bomber over China, and regardless of its escort of two Zeros, had shot it down. It had crashed into the ground, and when they located it, they also found the two Zeros, which had dived into the rice paddies at the tail of the bomber, one on each side. Thus had the embarrassed pilots committed hara-kiri, for they had lost face by having the ship that they were escorting destroyed.

Well, it was a laugh. But I'm fairly certain the one Zero didn't commit suicide—I'm prone to believe that some good, honest lead-poisoning from six fifty-calibre American machine guns had a lot to do with it.

22

Too Busy to Remember

MAJOR TEX HILL was the Squadron commander of the outfit that I had come to live with at Hengyang. He was a blue-eyed Texan, lean and lanky, six-feet-two of fighting blood. I imagine if he had lived in the frontier days of the American West, he would have been a gunman over there around the Pecos River—but a gunman on the side of the Law. I used to shut my eyes out there, sitting on the alert in Hunan, and think about him. I could picture that drawling Texan walking slowly through a border town with two pearl-handled 45's swinging low at his hips. Walking with his arms stiff at his sides, and watching with his cold, blue eyes some "villian" that was approaching the other way. I could almost hear the hot lead spitting from those guns as the two shot it out, and I could always see the villian fall, with Tex standing there looking at his smoking guns. Tex would always have won, for he was the greatest fighter that I ever saw, the most loyal officer, and the best friend.

I'd seen Tex shoot down Japs in the sky, and I had followed on his wing to learn the tactics of the AVG. I know that if there is any man I owe my life to during the months I fought in China, it is Maj. Tex Hill. Seeing what he did in combat, and how he handled his ship; seeing his coolness on the alert, and his keen desire for action. I can hear Tex now, after he had studied the plotting board that the interpreters were covering with little red flags showing the positions of the approaching Jap fighter ships. I can hear him saying: "Well, gentlemen, I think we'll take off." And he would smile as he pulled on his helmet and goggles.

Tex was the son of the Chaplain of the Texas Rangers. Before the AVG days he had been a Navy pilot flying off carrier decks, and in the Flying Tigers he had been second only to Bob Neal as the leading ace. Tex was the most truthful man I ever met—even his subconscious thoughts were truthful. He used to tell me that one day after Madame Chiang Kai-shek had pinned a medal on him for shooting down some Japanese planes over Toungoo, she had asked him the next time he shot down one of those Japanese planes to please think of her and dedicate it to the people of China. Tex of course said, "Yes, Ma'am. . . ."

I imagine that most any man among us would have said "Yes" to the Madame, and the next time we shot down a Jap we would have told the great lady all about it. We would have remembered after the fight what we had promised her, and we would have gone in with a romantic story of how we had met the barbaric Japanese and had seen the Madame's face in the skies as we shot the enemy down . . . and had thought of her and the people of China. But not Tex Hill— he was too honest for that. He told me, "Colonel, I promised her that, and I really meant it. And I've shot down about twelve Japs since that promise four months ago. But you know I never can remember to think about her when I'm in a battle—I'm too busy."

Well now, you hold that picture of Tex Hill for a minute while I show him to you in another light.

One day over Hengyang, after we had broken the Japanese wave with our assault and support and there were some fifteen Zeros burning around among the pagodas of this Hunan capital, I saw an odd sight down below. There was one lone Jap, doubtless of the suicide Samurai school, for though his buddies had either been shot down in their attempted strafing attack or had turned for home, this arrogant follower of the Shinto Shrine was strafing the field—alone. Two of us rolled to go get him, but from the end of the field towards the river I saw a P-40 pull out of a dive and head for the Jap. It was Tex Hill.

As the two fighters drew together in this breath-taking, head-on attack, I saw their tracers meeting and for a second I didn't know whether the ships ran together or both exploded in the air. As the smoke thinned I saw the P-40 flash on through and out into the clear, but the Jap crashed and burned on the field of Hengyang. Hill and the Jap had shot it out nose to nose, and once again I thought of the days of Western gunplay.

We landed and waited for Tex to come over. As we stood around the burning enemy ship, I saw Hill striding across the field from his fighter. Hanging low on his right leg was his army forty-five. Subconsciously I looked at his other leg as if I expected to find the mate hanging there.

Tex's blond hair was blowing in the wind, his eyes were looking with venomous hate at the Jap, his jaw was set. I had opened my mouth to congratulate him, for he had shot down two enemy ships that day, when I had a closer look at his eyes. . . . Tex strode over close to the fire and looked at the mutilated Jap where he had been thrown from the cockpit. Then, without a change of expression, he kicked the largest piece of Jap—the head and one shoulder—into the fire. I heard his slow drawl: "All right, mister—if that's the way you want to fight it's all right with me."

Tex calmly left the group and walked back to his ship and into the alert shed for his cup of tea. None of us said anything. The Chinese coolies who usually yelled "Ding-hao—ding-hao" saw his eyes and the set of his jaw, too—and just waited until later to congratulate him.

Things kept right on happening at Hengyang, for after all there are Japanese bases fanning out in many directions—East, North, Northeast, South, and Southeast. Some of them were within an hour's flight of our field. Hankow was the one to the North on the Yangtse. The Japs sent their bombers to worry us from up there, and before we caught on how to do it, they made life miserable for us. They had gotten tired of sending their day bombers down, for they lost too many; so now they had resorted to a period of constant night attack.

Just when the full moon in the clear sky would begin to light the ground like daylight, the telephone would start ringing, the Chinese interpreters would begin to stick the little flags into the map, and we'd know that the Jap was on the way. We'd be just about to sit down to supper after a hard day's work on the alert. We'd leave the rice and fish and squash, amid the house-boys' calls of "Jin-bao—" (air raid), and we'd rush for our planes that had been assigned to night duty. Sometimes the attack was a harassing one only, and we'd return without seeing them and go wearily back in the moonlight to the hostel, get some tea and a cookie, and crawl in the bed.

Just about the time the head hit the pillow and the body felt a little comfortable the alert would go again. I'd hear the tinkle of a small dinner bell and the plaintive voice of one of the house-boys—"Jin-bao, Jin-bao—please get up, master—Jin-bao." Off we'd go again and into the sky. Sometimes the Jap would feint two or three times to make us use valuable gasoline. Sometimes he'd circle Hengyang by fifty miles and then go back to Hankow. We'd spend the night between the hostel and the alert shack; but after all, as we used to say, you weren't supposed to be comfortable in a war, and we were no exception.

Sometimes, though, the Jap didn't feint.

General Chennault got us to pick the best and most experienced pilots for the night interception missions. We'd use two to four ships and place them at different altitudes over the field, and wait for the Jap in the light of the moon, with our lights out. On this particular night Johnny Alison was at 13,000 feet, and a thousand feet lower we had Ajax Baumler. I'll tell you about Johnny now, but we'll take up more on Ajax later—for this was mostly Johnny's fight.

Alison was a superior airman, fighter pilot, and officer, and was the ideal combat leader. A Florida boy, he knew the Allison engine well enough to have designed it. He knew the P-40's better than anyone I have ever seen, for he had instructed the British in their use in the United Kingdom and then had gone over to show the Russians how to fly and repair them near Moscow. Tonight he was about to carve his name with his six fifty-calibre guns in such a manner that few of us would ever forget it, and certainly no Chinese in the city of Hengyang would ever forget the night.

We got our four ships into the air at staggered altitudes. We heard the radio reports from Richardson giving the latest positions of the Japs. Reported over Changsha. Then North of the field. Then all was silent while we waited. In our positions over the field we placed ourselves down-moon—that is, where the bombers would have to fly between us and the moon and thus silhouette themselves against the full orange light.

Then I saw the five bombers against the moon. They were at 13,000 feet. I know I swore because they were below me, and I could imagine the cursing of every one of the others who were at the wrong altitude, for we could not change altitude until the first attack. But they were at Johnny's height, and I listened for him to say that he saw them. Down the field they told us later that you could hear the moan of one Allison engine as a P-40 moved in for the attack, could hear it above the sound of the ten radial engines on the enemy bombers.

The seconds dragged, and then we heard Johnny say, "Okay, I see 'em." And now we saw their exhausts, looking like ten bushel-baskets of blue fire. For a full second, as the enemy bombers moved towards the target that was our field, all was quiet, and I wondered if Johnny had lost them in the darkness. Then I saw him, so close to the enemy ships that he seemed to be in formation with them—and clearly over my radio I heard Johnny Alison say, "Watch the fireworks."

133

Six lines of tracers went into one of the bombers and glowed brighter than the two bushel-baskets of exhaust fire. The first Jap bomber trailed fire, slowly turned on its back, and spun crazily towards Hengyang, right over the town. Below, I could see a few flashes from the exploding enemy bombs, but most of them seemed short of the target area and very scattered. Johnny's tracers were still going into the enemy ships and I could see their return fire now, but it seemed to go in no certain direction. I had moved in closer, trying to get to the altitude of the fight.

On the ground the mechanics and the Chinese interpreters had a grandstand seat for one of the best moving pictures that has ever been—except that this was real. They too had heard Johnny say, "Watch the fireworks," and had seen and heard the heavy guns of the P-40. They could see pieces of the bomber coming off and going back into the slipstream, reflecting the glow of the fire that came with the explosion. Then the whole sky lighted as the first one plunged to the earth, with the fire making a queer sound as the wreckage fell.

The lone fighter now was sliding over behind the other bombers, and the second one was exploding and turning over. The third one tried to turn, seemed to hang for seconds against the full moon, then dove in flames in a pitch that got steeper and steeper. Several thousand feet below our level it exploded and burning gasoline fell with it. The light of the three burning bombers combined with the brilliant moonlight to make the night like day.

The number four enemy ship had turned back now, with an engine shot out, but Ajax Baumler got it ten miles North of the field. The last enemy dove out and turned for home when he saw his three leaders burn, but Baumler followed him thirty miles North and shot him down in flames.

From the ground, the watchers told us later, they could hear the fifty-calibre guns above the noise of the smaller calibre Jap guns. Within seconds after the attack, there were three ships burning around the city walls, and none of the formation got home. The Chinese people in the town had been watching the battle in awe. They had always had to just sit and take Jap bombings, especially night attacks, and this was something they had dreamed of. They were cheering now, and were out looking for enemy survivors with hoes, scythes, knives, and any weapon they could find to cut the Japanese to pieces, if any of them should escape.

But something was the matter with Alison. We could see his ship and it was not flying normally. Every now and then it would stream fire that was more than just a backfire. On the ground they could hear his engine missing badly.

Alison called in that he was hit, but would try to land his ship on the field.

To land a crippled fighter in daylight is quite a feat but to attempt to land one at night, one that has been shot to pieces and may burst into flames any second, is more than that. We knew why Johnny was taking the chance: we needed that ship if he could get it on the field, and even if it was shot to bits we needed the parts that could be salvaged. It would have been perfectly all right if the pilot had gone over the side as soon as that engine began to fade out that night. Whether or not he had shot down three bombers, he could have "hit the silk" and floated to safety in his chute. But Johnny must have known we needed this ship—we always needed ships. To keep the old P-40's that we flew in flying condition we had to rob parts from every airplane that we could salvage after a crackup. This is called "cannibalizing" in the lingo of field depots in the Air Corps, and covers a multitude of sins.

So Johnny glided to the field with his missing engine, and then we heard him say that he couldn't make the field and was going to sit down in the river. The moon made it fairly bright, but even at that I knew that Johnny had to be mighty good and very lucky. Then I wondered whether or not he was wounded. Silhouetted against the light from the three bombers he had shot down, his fighter looked awfully low. He skimmed over the Chinese junks on the river, and I saw the splash as the P-40, with its wheels up, hit the Siang Kiang. Down on the ground they heard his engine give one more dying gasp, as with a surge of power—probably from full gun and a prop in low pitch—it lifted him over the last of the masts of the junks and let him level off to skid across the surface of the river.

We came in and landed now, for the ground crew had gotten the smudge-pot boundary lights set out to mark the runway as well as the bomb craters. We gathered together fast with the boys who had stayed on the ground, and talked about the great battle. I remember Tex Hill shaking his head and saying, "I'm afraid Johnny didn't make it. Dog-gone, he was a good boy." We all felt a sinking in our hearts. We waited and we kind of prayed too.

I sent Captain Wang, our salvage man, out to see if he could get any news of Major Alison. We made our reports out and kept waiting on the alert. Just when we had really given up hope, we heard the sound of sharp explosions. All of us ran out of the alert shack, to see the strangest sight that we ever saw, even in China.

A procession had entered the field. The Chinese sentry had passed the crowd of people and was himself holding his thumb in the air calling, "Ding-hao—ding-hao." In the midst of the procession and surrounded by children shooting Chinese firecrackers in celebration, was a sedan chair carried on the backs of the villagers of Hengyang. And Johnny Alison was in the sedan chair—smiling.

While we cheered too and some of us even got some firecrackers from the kids and shot them off, we helped Johnny out and heard his story. He'd hit the river like a feather-bed, he said, and had swum ashore, having to kick off his good American shoes to make it. As he crawled up the bank of the river the Chinese had rushed upon him, thinking he was a Jap out of one of the bombers. Johnny said it looked as if they were going to cut him up, until he remembered the one word of Chinese that he'd picked up. He yelled this—one that sounded like "Merugay," which means "American." And when they read the Chinese sign that each of us carried on the back of his flying suit, which asks aid and protection for the American who has come to help China fight, they realized who he was. Just the man who had shot down the three enemy ships. And from then on he was the hero of the town.

Johnny Alison had a couple of burns on his hands and legs where some bits of the Japs' explosive bullets had hit him. He'd been slightly cut on the forehead when, on landing in the river, his head had hit the heavy metal of the gun-sight. But the scar that would leave would be a common one after the war, for every fighter pilot flies along with his head just inches behind that hunk of steel that contains the lights and prisms of the modern gunsights. Just the slightest accident and it is out there to split your head.

I asked Johnny why he went so close to the bomber formation, and he grinned and said, "I was scared I'd miss one of them."

23
The Chinese Really Know How

OUR SALVAGE crew worked and worked at the job of raising the P-40 from the bottom of the Siang-Kiang. But with the fourteen-foot depth and the swift current, they had more than modern engineering with the limitations of our floating equipment could accomplish. Under Captain Wang—Chinese-American and in our Army—they floated barges out to the spot and tried to tow it ashore with lines. Then they lowered steel drums, tied them to the ship, tried to pump the water from the submerged drums and thus float the P-40—but everything failed.

During all the work of the Americans with windlass and block-and-tackle, the Chinese villagers, who had offered their services long before, smiled and stood by. We asked ourselves: What in hell could the Chinese coolies and rivermen do if we, with our general knowledge and advanced civilization, couldn't raise the ship? We went on and failed for three days, and then to the persistent Chinese we said, "Okay, go ahead."

We watched them float raft after raft of long thick bamboo poles to the buoy that now marked the spot where Johnny's fighter had sunk. Mentally we set down the raising of the ship as impossible and got ready to mark it off the list. But the Chinese went on cheerfully with their work. I saw them pull themselves down into the river with ropes tied to the fighter, taking with them an eighteen-foot length of bamboo. They would slide this under the wing of the ship and lash it into place with grass rope. Hundreds of times they did this, until a perfect mat of bamboo was under the entire wing of the little P-40. Then they lashed the mat to the fuselage and started another row under the wing. Through it all we smiled at the wasted effort, and I heard men say, "Oh well, there are lots of Chinese anyway. Let them work."

But towards the second day's close, I began to wonder, and that evening as darkness settled over the river I went out to watch their tireless labor. Suddenly there was a movement among the rivermen to tighten the four cables that tied the fighter to the barge, and I saw the canopy and the prop of Johnny's fighter ship rise above the surface of the river. Involuntarily I cheered, and I felt a lump in my throat as if I had swallowed something; as I tried to talk to the officer with me I felt my lip tremble with emotion. But the Chinese never cheered or got excited; they remained as stoical as ever. They seemed to know that they were going to be successful, and had merely been waiting for the crazy Americans to quit playing around with all the strange gadgets.

They had floated the 9100 pounds of P-40, and now they towed it to shore. Our salvage crew put the wheels down in the water, and with the aid of about a hundred coolies the ship was pulled up the river bank and then out to the field. We counted eleven bullet holes through the engine and in the cockpit. Next day the ground-crews began the work of repair. Days had to pass before an engine from another damaged fighter could be installed, and more time had to go by before we got it completely worked over. But in the end it flew again in combat against the Japanese—thanks to the bravery of a gallant officer, the labor of good mechanics, and the unswerving patience and devotion of those brave Chinese coolies and rivermen who had never heard of the word "impossible."

When I first went to China I think I imagined in my short stay that I would gradually change the simple Chinese. I used to rant and rave about this and that, and try to show the houseboys better and more efficient ways to do things. But they never changed, and finally I realized that they were changing me. Now in raising this ship they had used a method three thousand years old. I have read since how they had employed it in Burma, long years before, when the great temple bell weighing over thirty tons was thrown into the deep lake to save it from the heathen. When the heathen had occupied the land and had himself been beaten in due time, probably by the country and by time itself, they had come back to the lake, these Chinese, and with bamboo poles had raised the thirty tons of metal.

During my stay in China I have watched the Chinese being bombed, and have seen them go out and pick their dead from among the ruins of their cities. Then wait bravely for the Jap to come again, while they went on scratching out a road with their bare hands, stoically working and watching for material to come over that road with which to fight the enemy. Waiting patiently, as though they knew that some day they would have a chance to fight the Japanese who have tried to exterminate them.

I've seen a Chinese woman run into a bomb crater, pull the dismembered pieces of her child together, and wipe the dirt from the face of her dead husband, a look of misery on her face. Then, when she saw me staring, she stood there and smiled. When I glanced at General Chennault with a question on my face, he said, "Don't interpret that wrong now, Scotty. She's showing you she can still smile, no matter what happens."

Even with the small fighter and bomber force that we now had in China, the people had taken a new lease on life. Every time we had an air battle over Hengyang they would capture another town along the Yangtse or near the lakes around Nanchang. I think we realized then, as General Chennault had realized for a long time, that all these people needed was a chance, with air support for their ground armies and modern equipment for their soldiers.

Our small force had put new life into them. They had plaques embroidered in commemoration of the battles that we fought. These would sometimes represent the American eagle holding the flags of America, Britain, Russia, and China. In Chinese characters would be a poetic account of the battle that the pilot or the squadron had fought. As we drove along the roads in our jeeps to the field for the alert of the "Jin-bao," the little children would hold their thumbs up and call again and again, "Ding-hao."

More and more we asked ourselves, "What couldn't we do with plenty of equipment for the Chinese ground armies, and us over their heads with adequate air support?" Would the day ever come when we could make an attack with a force that was a credit to the greatest country in the world? Towards the middle of August, as our pilots died in the old ships that we had, we had begun to doubt it.

For no, we didn't win all the time. Sometimes we lost, even when we traded one for ten. We lost because the Jap could replace his lost planes; we could not. It was more than losing ships—sometimes our pilots died in the unequal battles.

One day in August, Johnny Alison was leading six P-40's to intercept a larger number of Japanese coming against Hengyang from both Hankow and Canton. When interception was made, the Japs had fifty-three planes. They were in three waves, so of course Johnny didn't get them all together and let them take shots at his little force. He circled in the sun, waiting for the opportunity to strike, and get away with all his ships. Then it came. He dove through nine of them, and his six planes shot down four of the enemy. In his second attack, after diving away and climbing back into the sun, he sent four of his six down against them and then came on with the other two, just in case the enemy should follow the small attacking force out of the familiar "circling movement" that the Jap with his ever superior numbers always went into.

The little force of fighters knocked down another Zero. But one of the P-40's was in trouble. Johnny said later that he had seen the enemy ships following the Forty, but thought the closest one was another P-40. Too late he realized the error and went to help the pilot, whom he knew by then to be a boy named Lee Minor. The Zero rode the American fighter's tail and shot it down with cannon, and the P-40 burned. Johnny watched for a chute to open, but nothing happened.

As we drove out along the highway that afternoon—Baumler and Alison, Jack Belden of *Life* magazine and I—we were hoping by some fluke that Minor had bailed out and that Johnny had failed to see him do it, but we suspected that we were merely being optimistic. The farther we drove down the road to the South, towards the battle area of the morning, the more we expected what we found. Finally we saw it.

Four Chinese coolies were walking towards the nearest village, carrying an object lashed to poles, and carrying it in the old way of the East, with the poles over their shoulders. The thing they were carrying was wrapped in grass matting, but I saw the bare feet sticking out. We stopped the jeep and called to the coolies. Jack Belden spoke to them in Chinese and took the cover from the face. It was Lieutenant Minor, and of course he was dead. His ship in exploding had evidently thrown him out and opened his chute, but the explosion had killed him. He had definitely not crashed with the ship, for there was hardly a mark on his body.

Wrapping Minor in his parachute, we took him back in a rickety Chinese bus that we commandeered. We knew we'd miss Minor and men like him. He'd been one of the up-and-coming younger pilots, and had already shot down one Japanese plane.

We took Minor's body to the Catholic mission across the river, and bought one of the old, ancient-looking Chinese coffins, made out of wood about six inches thick, with corners that turned up like a pagoda roof; they must weigh two hundred pounds. We put Minor's body inside and held a simple service; for you have to work fast in temperatures of a hundred and eight, when the humidity is just about a hundred. Then we filled the casket with quick-lime, sealed it up on our brother officer, covered it with ten layers of heavy bricks to protect it from robbers and rats, and left it there to wait for the next transport to Kunming.

The headquarters in Yunnan is the burial ground for all of our pilots killed fighting against the Japanese. There on the plateau in Yunnan is the only memorial ground the 23rd Fighter Group will ever have. Our pilots lie beneath a gray slate slab from the earth of Yunnan, under the wings of the Chinese and the American Air Forces. They lie there in the shadow of a little Buddhist temple which for all practical purposes is the Christian temple of our God.

24
We're Doing All Right

CAPTAIN A. J. BAUMLER was the best operations officer I ever saw. He could go out and shoot down Japs all day, then come in and read the combat reports of twenty pilots, digest them all, and write out the most comprehensive report in the world—one that would give higher headquarters a ringside picture of the fight that had taken place.

"Ajax" was from New Jersey. He had fought for nearly two years with the Loyalists in Spain, and had shot down seven Messerschmitts and Fiats in that war; when he became an ace in the 23rd Group he was the first man in the war who had shot down German, Italian, and Japanese aircraft. Ever since America had entered the war he had led a hectic existence. Months before December 7th, he had left America from California to join the AVG and General Chennault, as a Lieutenant in the Air Corps. He had been stopped in Hawaii for a month and then had received permission to continue on.

But on the day when he finally got out on his way to what he wanted to do most, the Japs struck at Pearl Harbor. Ajax had just landed at Wake Island, and, soldier that he was, he had reported to the Marine Commander for duty. He was having breakfast with the CO, Major Devereaux, when the Japanese attack came to Wake.

Ajax used to say that the unusual strength he demonstrated that morning was due to the heavy supply of vitamin pills he had taken. As the first bomb hit the runway of the field, he ran with the others for the door and the safety of the slit trenches on the outside. The door opened inward, but Ajax opened it outward, taking the screen, the door, and most of that end of the flimsy building with him. Part of the glass hit him in the face—and that cut was the only wound he received in the bombing. But he carried the scar with him when I last saw him in China.

Baumler got out of Wake Island the next day on the last clipper, but to join the AVG he was no longer going West. It was now necessary to go all the way back and around the other way, towards the East. Anyway he managed to go by way of Washington and got promoted to Captain. I believe if Ajax had stayed in Washington just one more day, he would have been a Major. After seeing Ajax Baumler in a few fights, I wish that he had gotten to be a Major before he came to China, for he certainly was a fighter pilot.

During the month of our battle of Hengyang, I saw Captain Baumler do some of the nerviest things I've ever seen any man accomplish. We had a few ships that had been strafed badly on the ground; some of them had been shot to pieces, and in others the engines or hydraulic systems had been damaged. In most cases these same ships couldn't be got off the ground when the Japs came over; sometimes they were caught three or four times by Zeros, and consequently they were in a continual state of repair.

One of these was old Number 104, the ship that Ajax had been flying. The ground crew had worked on it for days, but whenever they'd have it just about ready to be taken back to the factory in Kunming for overhaul, the Japs would catch it again. Finally one morning Ajax must have said, "The devil with it." For when the "Jin-bao" came he went and got into the crippled fighter to take off before the Japs could get there to strafe it again. He told me later that he was tired of seeing it sitting on the ground as a target; whether it would fly or not, he was going to get it taxying as fast as it would go and at least make it harder to hit than it had been in the revetment. Well, Ajax did better than taxy—he got off. But the story of it all reached me later on.

I was on the ground that day, and didn't see it. But I heard Ajax talking on the radio, and I heard his six guns when he caught one of the Zeros. Just a little later I saw the trail of black smoke that marked the enemy ship going down. I was glad to hear Ajax talking that morning; for a minute I'd thought that smoke might be he, going down in that luckless Number 104. All the time he'd been flying the ship he'd been having to pump the landing-gear up manually, for the hydraulic system had been shot up by the Jap strafer days before. Added to this, an exertion which is no pleasant task at fighting altitudes, was a more painful experience. The cards were stacked even more heavily against Ajax in this jinx ship, for his electrical system was shorting out.

On his take-off from Hengyang, as he gave the ship the gun Baumler had felt a terrible electrical shock through his sweaty hand on the stick control. He couldn't turn the stick loose or the ship would have crashed in the take-off run; so he grimly held on. Take hold of the spark plug of your car some time while the engine is running, and you'll feel just about what Ajax felt. But he kept holding it until he was at an altitude where it was safe to turn the stick loose, get out his handkerchief, and wrap it around the stick.

Even after he had been through the fight and came in to land at Lingling he had to take some more of the shock cure, for by that time the handkerchief was damp and the electricity was jumping through it. He couldn't stay long on this last field, for the Japs were on the way back in waves; so he reserviced and taxied out to take off. Though the engine was now missing badly, Ajax couldn't wait—the Japs would be there in a matter of minutes.

He tried a take-off with the current going through his arms again and the engine spitting and sputtering—and at the end of the runway he still hadn't enough speed to get in the air. He would swerve the ship about and try the other direction. Finally after three runs he got the fighter plane in the air, pumped the wheels up by hand and continued doing it for five hundred miles—and so flew back to Kunming. He told me later it didn't matter what he did now; when he got in jail they'd never be able to electrocute him in the chair if the old P-40 Number 104 had failed to do it that August morning.

But it wasn't all hard work and no play in China. Some evenings we used to sit in our cave down at Kweilin and listen to the Tokyo radio. They would give us reports on the missions that we flew to Hankow, Canton, and the cities near Lake Puyang Hu—Nanchang and Kukiang. They'd declare that we were using barbarous tactics and that we were going to be treated as guerrillas if we were captured.

One night while we sat there calmly listening to the news and playing gin rummy, Tokyo news-analysts announced they did not think the American fighter force in China was large. True enough, said the radio, they had struck weakly at several cities, in their barbaric way bombing innocent Chinese women and children, and for this the American pirates would pay when they were prisoners of the Imperial Japanese Government, now fighting to liberate Asia for the Asiatics.

We listened to the usual "blah" without raising an eyebrow, until Radio Tokyo continued: "We don't think the American fighter force in China is more than three hundred ships."

You could have knocked us over with a feather. We dropped our cards and I looked at General Chennault—he'd been acting as if he was taking a nap, but I knew he had been listening. We all laughed. We had thirty-two ships in

143

China at the time, and only sixteen of these were in first-class combat condition.

I remember that the General said, "Well, boys, if we're making them think we have three hundred—we're doing all right."

The General got up and called to his little black dachshund. "Come on, Joe," he said, and they walked out.

There was a squadron that came over from Assam to work with us, part of another group from India. In this squadron there were some fine fighter pilots, one of whom was Lieut. Dallas Clinger from old Wyoming. Clinger was another man who in years gone by in the West would have been a great gunman like Tex Hill. Only Clinger wouldn't have cared whether he was on the side of the Law, the Mormons, the Church, or Jesse James. He just wanted to fight.

One morning Clinger was one of a formation of three fighters over Hengyang. His combat report read like this:

"I was flying on my leader's wing—Lieutenant Lombard—at 23,000 feet when we saw three enemy planes down below circling. There were larger formations reported around. Just then I heard my flight leader say: 'There are three stragglers—let's attack 'em.' So we dove into them like mad. As I shot into the Zero on the right of the formation I saw that we were in the midst of twenty-four other Zeros, all shooting at us. I got mad and shot at every plane that I could get my sights on. I think I shot one down but I was so busy I didn't see it crash."

This was signed "DALLAS CLINGER—2nd Lieutenant—Almost Unemployed."

What Clinger had really done was the greatest piece of dare-devil flying that any of us had ever seen. Instead of diving away from the twenty-seven-ship circus as the others had done, he had stayed and fought the old-fashioned "dog-fight" until the Japs just about took him to pieces from sheer weight of numbers. When they straggled home they must have been the most surprised bunch of pilots in all Japan, for this crazy American with his heavy P-40 had done everything in or out of the book. He fought right side up and upside down, from 23,000 feet down to less than one thousand. As many Japs as could fill the air behind Clinger would get there and try to hang on while they shot; but Clinger wouldn't fight fair and stay there. In the end, he came right over the field, diving from the enemy until he had outdistanced them enough to turn; then he'd pull up into an

144

"Immelmann" and come back shooting at them head-on.

He was last seen after the unequal fight skimming out across the rice paddies, making just about 500 miles an hour, with some ten to twelve Zeros following. For some reason they seemed reluctant, as though they didn't know whether to run after Clinger or leave him alone. He came in for lunch with his ship badly shot up by their cannon. But he had shot one of them down and had got another "probable."

Down Lingling way on another morning, Clinger went into an attack with his engine acting up. After the first contact with the enemy, he was forced to land, followed by two enemy strafers. As Clinger maneuvered the failing fighter into a safe landing, the two Zeros came down shooting at his rolling P-40.

Dallas from Wyoming got out on the wing to jump onto the ground, with his ship still rolling. Just then one of the Jap bullets went right through his seat-pack chute, passing exactly between Clinger's pants and where he sat on the parachute. He got so mad he jumped back in the cockpit and shot at two Zeros as they passed over his nose. After all, air-cooled guns are made to shoot while the ship is going two or three hundred miles an hour—but Lieutenant Clinger said he got in a pretty good burst from his grounded fighter before the six Fifties froze.

It goes to show that a fighter pilot has got to be the most offensive-minded man in all the world. I think he's got to know he's better than any other pilot he'll ever meet in the air, and such a man was this one.

Johnny Alison had helped to train Clinger in the tactics of fighter pilots. In fact, Johnny used to fly with every man in his flight on his wing, at one time or another. In one training flight such as this he took Clinger up and they practised attacking one another—"dog-fighting," the "pea-shooter" pilots say. Up there at nearly 20,000 feet they came at one another head-on, time after time, until the moment when, as Johnny told me later, he was sure Clinger was going to run into him. Alison, who usually forced others to give way, had to dive under Clinger's P-40. They circled it and tried again, and again Clinger kept right on coming, until, as the ships drew together at well over six hundred miles an hour relative speed, once more Johnny had to dodge, and the Wild Man from Wyoming went on over his head.

They landed then, and by the time Johnny had climbed out of his ship he had calmed down. Clinger came nonchalantly over. Just in passing Alison said, "That was pretty good flying, Clinger; you fly formation well and you look around okay. But you want to watch these head-on runs—you nearly hit me up there. Did you know that?"

Clinger shifted the weight of his body back to both feet. With his chin out, he answered: "Yes, Sir, Major—I tried to. You see, you've been flying longer than I have and I know I'm not as good a pilot as you are. But, Sir, I knew I'd come closer to you than you would to me."

You can find the remains of a good many Japs in China, or somewhere down in the China Sea, who know that Clinger meant just what he said. He'd keep coming at them head-on and shoot them out of the sky before they got to him.

25
Stranger Than Fiction

THE BATTLE for the defense of Hengyang lasted through August, but we didn't just sit there on the defensive. We rapidly took the offensive as our best defense, and kept it up until higher headquarters sent us a very classic radio:

"You either did not understand or did not receive my last radiogram to remain on the defensive. Repeat quote on the defensive unquote. Signed, Chennault."

We knew that he had had to adopt defensive strategy because we were so short of equipment. But before the order came we really had the fun. We struck every Jap base we could make with our fuel range—along the Yangste, Hankow, Kukiang, Sienning, Yoyang—and strafed along the river. We bombed Nanchang five times in three days, and in six days we dropped 30,000 pounds of five-hundred pound bombs there from P-40's.

At Nanchang, on August 11, 1942, I shot down my fourth enemy plane that was confirmed. Though I hate the Japs with a passion, I felt sorry for that pilot, for he never saw me at all. But as I left his burning ship North of the runway that he had been taking off from, I thought of the boys in the Philippines and Java, and I wasn't so sorry.

I had dropped my five-hundred-pound bomb on the hangars, when in pulling out of the dive I saw Lieutenant Barnum, from Old Lyme, Connecticut, continue his dive on a Jap ship, and begin to fire on it. I looked below. There was dust at the far end of the Jap field where one enemy plane was taking off. I rolled over and dove, pulling out about a half mile behind the enemy at the moment that he got off the ground. His wheels had just begun to move to the "up" position as I got him dead in my sights and pressed the triggers. As the pilot died, his new 1-97-2 pulled straight up, then spun into the ground the few feet it had climbed. I passed over it as the flames belched from the wreckage. I climbed for an enemy observation plane higher over Lake Puyang Hu, but the Jap outclimbed me, and though I fired at him several times from long range he finally got away.

On this trip, Barnum had shot down one enemy ship, and Lieutenant Daniels, though unable to release his wing-rack fragmentation bombs, had strafed the field with his bombs hanging on. After the attack, this pilot had force-landed his plane in a rice paddy near Hengyang rather than bail out— and this decision to save the ship for spare parts had been made with the six frags still hanging from the faulty wing-racks. He got away with it, and Captain Wang was able to salvage the fighter.

When the P-40's got so shot up that we were afraid they'd quit running and we'd lose them over the enemy lines, we were called back to Kunming. There sitting around for two weeks while we worked on the ships and anxiously looked for mail from home, the war seemed far away. When strange things would happen, we talked about things of the sort which had once been told in story books. All of us agreed that when this war was over, there would be nothing that had ever happened in fiction that wouldn't have actually happened in this battle of the universe. For instance:

Likiang is a city in China far up on the big, northern loop of the Yangtse-Kiang. It is China, yes, but that part of China is as wild as Tibet and Arabia. The people are called "Lolos," and they must be descendants of Genghis Khan. I had flown over the place, for it was just North of the ferry route from Assam to Kunming, and I had seen the flat clearing South of the village that could have been an emergency landing field. I noted that it was close to nine thousand feet above sea level, and therefore not a field to use unless one had to.

Capt. Charlie Sawyer had crash-landed just South of there, closer to Talifu, and had been unable to identify himself. While the wild-looking Lolo tribesmen were getting set to execute him with ancient-looking flint-lock muskets, Sawyer said the holes in the barrels looked twice as big as fifty calibre bores. Just at the crucial moment, however, when his fate looked darkest, some new arrival in the party saw the identification card that Sawyer had been pointing to. It was inscribed in various languages, and with pictures. The new arrival didn't recognize the Chinese flag, or any of the languages, or the Generalissimo's signature "chop"—but he saw a star. As it happened, it was the star of India over the imprint in Hindustani. Then the tribesman pointed to the same star on the wing of Sawyer's ship—the insignia of the Army Air Force. Sawyer was saved, and later he was feasted on wild buffalo and rice wine.

But why? Here in the wilds of the Lolo country, where very few white men had ever been, the tribesmen were more familiar with the white star of the Air Force than with any written language. We learned the principal reason later.

A report had come in to General Chennault's headquarters that a native village in the Lolo country, between Lake Tali and Likiang, was under siege by the Burmese northern tribesmen who had crossed the Salween, perhaps under the direction of the Japanese. Two of us, Holloway and I, were sent to look the place over in two P-40's. We were told by the General that we could determine whether the town was under siege by noting whether or not the usual pedestrian traffic was passing in and out of the city gate. All the cities are walled, and are obviously very far from roads or from civilization.

We made our observation and returned to report. The village was besieged, and we had seen the horsemen encamped a half mile around the city wall. We loaded up and went back with six eighteen-kilogram frags on the wing racks and plenty of fifty-calibre ammunition. I also carried a Very pistol and all colors of shells.

As we circled the town, we could see the villagers watching us; then we dove on the besiegers and bombed them from a thousand feet. The lines of prehistoric cavalry broke and retreated towards the Salween and Burma. We machine-gunned them until they spread in panic. Then I used the Very pistol, shooting first green lights, then red. Holloway said it was the best display of fireworks he'd ever seen. We checked up for several days, but the raiders hadn't come back, and normal pedestrian traffic was passing through the city wall. Holloway and I, with two of the General's P-40's, had stopped a war.

The white star of the Air Force had been seen by those villagers, and they had told the surrounding country that we were friends. Perhaps the constant sight of transports from India to China and return had made the big white star a familiar symbol. At any rate, the Lolos who were about to execute Sawyer recognized it, and to them it meant more than written languages or sealed orders. Such is the strangeness of this global war.

More true fiction came out of the Lolo country during the autumn. A Ferry Command pilot, Lieutenant Aronson, "lost an engine"—which means that his engine failed—on his trip from Assam to Kunming. He barely made the big meadow that was South of the town of Likiang, in the hairpin loop of the Yangtse. After several days we went in there to look the improvised landing-field over, in the hope that we could fly another transport to him with a good engine, or carry in the mechanics and the tools with which to repair the bad one.

More romance of the war was in progress. When the transport had come down, the villagers were not hostile but merely indifferent. They were somewhat enlightened, for there was a Catholic priest in the town, but they offered very little help—there was no food to spare, and things were generally unfriendly.

Late the first night, word came to Aronson that a Lolo infant was dying with what the priest diagnosed as double pneumonia. Aronson began to think the situation over, and later in the night he went with the priest to the mud hut of the Lolo mother and received permission to spread over the child's bed the canvas engine-cover from one of the transport engines. Then, using the bottles of oxygen from the Douglas, he improvised an emergency oxygen-tent.

The baby lived. We hope the engine-cover and the oxygen saved it, but we don't know. Anyway, we of the Air Force, with Aronson as the messenger of good-will, received the credit.

We agree now that when the war is over, out in the world they won't even know that one had been going on there among the grandchildren of Genghis Khan. But the white star of the Army Air Force will be as well known among the savage tribesmen as are the symbols of the moon and the sun.

26
Morale-Builder

IN EVERY organization there is always one person who holds up the morale, some one who makes the darker moments brighter and who can bring a little sunshine into the tense reality of war. Out in the China theatre, and especially in the 23rd Fighter Group, my most unforgettable character was Lieut. Henry Elias. This pilot was a Southerner, like most of the others in the China skies. When I first reached Hengyang he was acting as assistant operations officer to Ajax Baumler. He had a reply for every person, and a come-back to every joke. He was definitely a morale builder, and you can ask anyone if they're not as valuable at the front as ammunition.

Elias had been on several raids and had shot down two Japanese when I heard the first joke about him. He'd been on an attack to Nanchang, and as the ships turned for home in the fading light of late afternoon, some one in the rear of the formation observed something peculiar. Up ahead there were five P-40's with their sleek silhouettes showing wheels up and everything in proper order. But off to the flank, in almost the position of the number-three man in a Vee formation, was one ship with its wheels extended. Some one called on the radio, "Hey, Elias, who's that flying in formation with you, with their wheels down?"

As the words sank into the consciousness of the flight, and of Elias especially, their ominous significance became apparent. Elias jerked his head around and looked at his wing man. Even to an inexperienced eye, the silhouette was unmistakable. It was a Jap Model 1-97, one of the old fixed landing-gear types. The entire formation tried at once to get it as they finally realized what it was. But they had the laugh on Elias. Just as he recognized the Jap, the enemy pilot evidently recognized the P-40's in the twilight before darkness—perhaps he saw the leering shark's mouths. For as Elias shoved the nose of his ship straight down and dove for him, the Jap pulled his ship straight up and climbed for the sky. Later, when our imaginations began to embroider the joke, Elias took the kidding in good part and always had a come-back.

A small two-seater biplane, a Fleet, came to Hengyang from Kweilin one day with a Chinese officer. We looked the little ship over as it came into the field wide open at some seventy-five miles an hour, and I told Elias that I saw his future destiny.

"We now have just the bait we need," I said. "Lieutenant Elias, I want you to borrow that Fleet from the Chinese. I know a trick to make the Japs lose lots of 'face' and airplanes."

Elias had laid down his Operations reports and was listening attentively. "This ought to get you promoted," I went on.

"Now you get that plane and service it tonight, then early in the morning you take off for Hankow. Alison, Baumler, and I will be along later, and will arrive over the Jap city before you do." Elias was looking at me in wonder. "Then, when you get there, fly over the enemy airport at thirty-five hundred feet—that'll keep you just above their small-calibre fire and they can't shoot accurately that low with the big stuff. Over the field you fly with one wing low, kind of skidding, cutting your switch on and off so the Japs will think you're either wounded or over there with a bad engine."

Elias was trying to figure out whether I was serious or not. Then I added: "We'll be up there in the sun, and as fast as the Zeros come up for you, we'll knock them down. After all, Elias, if they get you, a Fleet isn't worth much."

But by now Lieutenant Elias was walking out and calling over his shoulder: "No sir, Colonel, I just want to be a plain pilot—I don't want to be no ball of fire."

Well, we saw the value of Elias when we lost him, for in this second battle around Hunan he failed to return from the strafing raid of September 2, 1942. We had taken sixteen P-40's back to Hengyang when we had gotten them in shape to fight, and had landed there just about dark to surprise the Japs. That's the night the Fleet landed and the night I had been kidding Henry Elias.

Next morning we got into the air before daylight and went for Lake Puyang Hu, near Nanchang, where the Japs were moving the Chinese rice out by junks and barges—robbing the breadbasket of China in the yearly rape of the rice. Hill took eight of the P-40's and I took the other eight.

Elias was on Tex Hill's wing. We split at Nanchang and my eight went to the South to catch some gunboats that had been reported in Sintze-Hukow Strait, near Kukiang, coming from the Yangtse to the Lake. I heard Hill call that he had caught the rice ships and was burning them. Later he told me that he found twenty-six of them, junks and steel barges; he sank some and saw others with their sails on fire, floating for shore where the hungry Chinese coolies would salvage the rice.

Through the four passes at the Japs Elias was right on Tex's wing, but on the fourth pullout he dropped behind the formation, perhaps to shoot at something Hill hadn't seen. Maybe he'd seen a Jap fighter and had gone for it; we knew there were eight Zeros supposed to be over Nanchang. Elias didn't return with the flight, and for two days we carried him as "missing."

Then the Chinese net reported that a group of Chinese soldiers had seen a lone American P-40 engaged by four Japanese Zeros. The American had fought them but his ship had been shot down. The American had jumped out in his parachute and the four Japanese had strafed him on the way down.

The body had been found, with the identification flag number listed. The pilot's name was Lieutenant Elias. All of us watched for Japs bailing out, so that we could shoot one or two down for Elias, but we didn't get the chance.

We sent Captain Wang down to Kian to get Elias's body. Wang had to travel a hundred and sixty miles by buffalo cart, by alcohol bus, and on foot, but he finally got there. The trip took him twenty days. When the body of our lost pilot finally arrived at the field from which he had last taken off, it was in a Chinese coffin that Wang had gotten at Kian. We placed the flag over the grim reminder of war and sent it by transport to Kunming, to lie beside his other brother pilots in that Buddhist graveyard in Yunnan.

And so it went: tragedy—humor—tragedy. For on the same raid I had led the other eight ships, with elements led by Holloway, Schiel, and O'Connell, and had caught the Jap gunboats, ten of them, at Sintze-Hukow Strait. They were more than likely coming to Puyang Hu to convoy those rice barges—but we were going to interfere with their rendezvous.

Even as we circled them from sixteen thousand feet, I think they knew they were going to have lots of trouble. They had to stay almost in line, nose-to-stern, for they were going through the narrow strait. We circled warily for a minute, looking the sky over for enemy fighters, then spiraled down. As soon as we got close enough to the Jap ships to see distinctly, we noticed that the seamen were jumping over the side into the water. Only a few seemed to have remained to fire the anti-aircraft guns, and Schiel and Holloway silenced most of those with their initial pass. I saw two of the boats turn sharply off course and try to run aground.

I think most of the ammunition had been fired at us while we circled at sixteen thousand feet, for we were the whole show now. We'd rake the steel decks from stem to stern and then swing out low to the water and come back with quartering shots from the beam. We were so low that we were actually shooting up at the decks of the boats. I saw many human heads above the water as the Japs tried to swim from the boats, and I fired at them. Those bullets ricocheted from the water into the steel side of the gunboat and went on through. As my range would reach the "sweet spot" of some 287 yards, where the six lines of tracers and armor-piercing Fifties converged, it would appear as though an orange-colored hole the size of a flour barrel was being burned into the side of the Jap vessel at the water-line. Looking back at the next man in the column and observing his hits, I could see his tracer bullets coming through the boat and out the other side.

We S-ed along the ten-ship line and shot at them all from both sides. On the second pass, two of the vessels were listing, and others were smoking. On the fourth attack, seven out of the ten were smoking and burning and some of these were on the bottom with their masts barely out of water. Photographs taken later from an observation plane showed that seven had sunk immediately in the strait, and that the other three had sunk within a thousand yards of the battle area.

I was so happy, so excited and eager, that I tried to be glamorous that morning. After the fourth attack I had called to re-form and head for the rendezvous point to the Southwest. But as the ships left the target, I saw something I had to go back for. It was a Japanese flag, waving defiantly from the mast of one of the sunken gunboats. Forgetting caution, and with the other seven planes speeding away to the rendezvous point, I dove to strafe the flag in a gesture of hate.

When I finished the job and pulled up again, I could barely see the last of my flight several miles away. I gradually climbed after them, forgot to look around, and just sat there, "dumb and happy." Just sat there too long over enemy territory, without looking around every second. Without thinking about it, I had become a straggler.

In a high-powered engine, as soon as we go into combat we take military power from the engine—that is, we take as much boost as the engine will stand without "detonating," put the prop in low pitch, high speed position. As you leave the combat and the area, if you're not too excited the hand automatically pulls the prop controls to maximum cruising position to save fuel and to keep the engine from running hot. I began subconsciously to do this.

Just then, very dreamily, I heard—pop-pop-pop-pop-pop. I raised my head slightly, to try to see my other fighters ahead, and pulled the throttle back just a little more. That popping sounded like engine detonation to me. Then I tensed, for I had seen that my manifold pressure was barely 35 inches (on the manometer gauge), and therefore I could not be detonating from too much boost. At the same instant I heard again the pop-pop-pop, and became all attention in a flash; my nose went down—I had been climbing—my prop went back to low pitch and my throttle *really* went forward enough to cause the engine to detonate. A cold shiver went down my spine, there in that hot glass cage. I skidded the ship to the left and looked around as my speed built up fast.

What I saw in the sun, ahead and above me, chilled me more. I saw winking lights and the blurred outline of an airplane—and not so far away. Then I saw another, and I guess there were others. I could see the orange lights winking down at me even in the glare of the sun. They were Japs firing at me, and I had only slightly more than a thousand feet.

Cold turkey and a straggler!

While I fumbled with my mike button to my radio to call Holloway and Baumler for help, I realized the futility of it. I don't believe my dry throat would have made a sound anyway. I just acted—and thank the Lord, my reflexes let me do something. I turned directly towards the ships with my nose down, and pulled up firing. I know now that if I had turned away from them they would have shot me down in their crossfire. As it was, I surprised them and went underneath them very fast and into the sun. Thus, when they looked around, I had the sun in my favor, and from that time on I was using it. But as I pulled up firing, I held the trigger down and "froze." I heard the cannon of the Zero—I felt the recoil of my six guns—I felt things hit "Old Exterminator"—and then I saw a cloud of black smoke in front of my nose. I shut my eyes involuntarily and dove again.

Something hit my ship with the same sound you get when you suddenly fly into heavy rain. I opened my eyes and everything was dark. I smelled the smoke and cordite and gasoline and thought I was on fire. Just then I realized I was still firing. I reached up, grabbed the handle, rolled the canopy open—and saw light. I rolled it shut again and realized that the blackness had been caused mostly by oil on my windshield. The speed of my dive had blown most of that off now, and though I couldn't see very well, I could make out the horizon.

With a long sigh of relief I levelled the speeding ship over the rice paddies, and as they say in the slang of fighter stations, "I took off like a scalded dog." I S-ed and skidded but tried not to lose speed. Looking back, I saw the smoke and oil that I had gone through, and down under the place where I had been I saw fire and a plume of smoke—one Jap that wouldn't fly again. I think I was halfway home before I fully realized that I had shot it down and hadn't run into it.

For twenty minutes I skimmed over the paddies, "jinking" to fool the enemy who might be pursuing, skidding to make him miss, and watching my boost read seventy inches of mercury. The engine heated up and the coolant light came on to warn me, before I eased the throttle back a little. I called Ajax Baumler on the radio and told him I was hit—had been intercepted, my engine was heating up and I didn't know what all was the matter with the ship, but I was on course for home and going like a bat out of hell. Ajax stood by to take my position if worse things should develop and I should have to land.

But the coolant light finally flickered and went off, the engine cooled off when I got a little of the boost off and stopped abusing it. And I breathed again, feeling that I'd been holding one breath for fifteen minutes. All was clear behind me, and I gradually climbed to ten thousand and went back home to Hengyang.

All the boys came out to see me. Of course Elias was missing and they'd been worried lest I was a goner too. There were cannon holes in my wings and tail; one had gone just across the back of the canopy. There were smaller holes in the fuselage from the cockpit back to the tail; there was oil from the spinner of the prop to the tail. Oil from your own ship can hardly get on the very tip of the nose of your ship, and this was proof that it was Jap oil.

As we looked the plane over, I got more and more settled down from my narrow escape. But then I realized that my ship, which I had now flown in combat from April until September 2nd, was badly damaged. "Old Exterminator" was shot to pieces.

We had tea in the alert shack and sent the other mission out to dive-bomb Nanchang and strafe the trains from Kukiang to the North towards Hankow. Also we got the Chinese net looking for Elias, and reported that I had shot down one Zero near Kukiang.

I was sitting there with a cup of very sorry Chinese tea, diligently making out my combat report, when somebody started a motorcycle about five feet from me. With the first explosion I thought of the cannon back there an hour or two before. I dropped my battered teacup, jumped clear over the table, and fell into the operations map trying to get out of the way. I tried to yell and rave at the poor Chinese messenger-boy who had started the motor, but I might as well have been talking to the moon. He saw my face, heard the fast, strange tongue, and just blandly smiled. When he held up his thumb, pointed to the sky, and said "Ding-hao," I got my poise back sufficiently to smile and call back to him—"Ding-hao."

27
Farewell to "Old Exterminator"

IN THE MEANTIME, down at Kweilin, Maj. Ed Rector, as CO of the Squadron, and Maj. Bruce Holloway as operations officer, were keeping the skies cleared of Japs and were escorting the little force of bombers under Colonel Haynes, who had now been made a Brigadier General. We were all happy over this promotion, not only because it was for a deserving officer but from the selfish standpoint that our China Air Task Force would get more bombers.

General Haynes led some missions on Canton, and after fair bombing results the fighters stayed behind and engaged the enemy Zeros. Lieut. Pat Daniels shot down his first Jap, and Charlie Sawyer got his third. In the next raid of the bombers General Haynes again led. Maj. Butch Morgan— who the newspapers used to say was the only Yankee on General Chennault's staff . . . "Wonder how he got there?"—was leaning over the lead bomb-sight and directing the bombing. This objective was to burn the docks of Haiphong on the coast of Indo-China.

The small bomber force of six B-25's went in with only three P-40's for escort. Maj. Ed Rector led the fighters, with Lieutenant Marks on one wing and Pat Daniels on the other. Just to make the bomb load against the Japs heavier, the fighters carried a five-hundred-pound bomb on each ship. With these they dive-bombed the docks after the bombers had blasted them and set them on fire. Here the attack was entirely successful; the fighter boys came back and said it was the best thing that they had ever seen. The bomb train had covered the Haiphong wharves from one end to the other, and when the ships went back to their forward field to refuel and return to base, the smoke was covering the town. Rector led his three fighters down in a strafing attack over the wharf fires and kept the fire-fighters from working.

We were brought back now from the Kweilin-Hengyang front to watch the situation in Burma and to harass the Jap to the South in Indo-China. Our situation was peculiar in

China—we were just about surrounded by the Japanese on all sides except to the North, towards Russia, and that was so far and over such mountains that it seemed not to matter. To our backs was Burma, filled with Japs. To the South was Indo-China and Thailand, and out to the front and North-east were Japanese. Where on earth could you find a worse situation?

But we got to fight all the time; we never had to sit on the defensive and worry. We liked it.

I had to wait at Hengyang a day longer than the others, for my ship was being repaired enough for me to fly it to the repair depot at Kunming. At Kunming the blow fell: the engine of "Old Exterminator" was bad and there were no more new or serviceable engines. The cannon from the Zero had damaged the wing so badly that pullouts would be dangerous. The fuselage was peppered with over two hundred holes from the last five months of combat.

But the old ship wasn't junked or salvaged, for we needed parts too badly in China. There were new planes on the way to us now in monthly increments, but we could take this plane and put several back in commission. The scheme that we devised helped my morale greatly, for to have junked the old ship that had been my fighter for five months would have been like seeing the horse that you've ridden for twenty years cast aside and destroyed. I could remember too well that day when I landed at Hengyang and looked at the damage the ship had suffered. There had been a lump in my throat and I had felt as though my sword had been taken away. "Old Exterminator" had taken me nearly five hundred hours into combat against the enemy. That's over a hundred thousand miles—and you just ask any pilot if that isn't a long way on trips where people shoot at you.

We took the guns out of the ship that General Chennault had given me in April and put them in my new P-40E. They were well broken in, and the Armament Officer, Captain Hoffman, who had been with the AVG and in my squadron in Panama seven years before, had worked them into perfection. I had had no jams or stoppages in over a month. The landing-gear we put on another ship; the instruments were scattered throughout the group; the armor plate was taken out to make a hot-cake griddle for the mess. All parts of the fighter were cannibalized, and in a month were spread out over eighteen P-40's in the organization. I remember especially that the automatic fuel-pump was put on a P-40B, which permitted the lighter ship to go higher than it had ever gone before, and on its second flight with the booster pump, the pilot, Lieut. T. R. Smith, shot down a Japanese observation plane over Kunming.

I never did go out and look at the old engine that had come out of my first fighter. After all, an engine is exchangeable anyway, and we get used to different ones. The shot-up shell of the fuselage, and the wing that had held me up over a hundred thousand miles of enemy country, I didn't want to see again. I just thought of my six fifty-calibre guns flying with me in my new fighter as the real soul of "Old Exterminator." And I thought of the hundreds of parts from Air Corps number 41-1456 that were helping to keep eighteen ships of our Group in the air to fight the Japs.

For the men of the Group, the cannibalized ship had been a help, but to me it had been a tradition to keep. In my mind, no matter how long I myself might be fighting in China, "Old Exterminator" would be on all those flights—some of it would be on every mission that we flew. And thus it would fly forever.

On September 25, Maj. Ed Rector led the assault of a flight down to raid Hanoi in Indo-China. I led the support, and we kept a thousand feet above the first echelon. Our mission was to escort ten bombers for the bombardment of Gia Lam airdrome. We went South and "topped-off" our gas load at a secret base, then routed our flight to the West of Laokay to keep from alerting the Jap warning net. Until we were close to Hanoi, we kept well West of the railroad that led to our objective.

Even with these precautions to keep from alerting the enemy, we found the Japanese I-45's in the air and over the field as we came in from the West. The twin-engine fighters absolutely ignored our fighters and made runs on the bombers, but they didn't get very far with their orders. Rector took the first four P-40's in on the leading Japs and hit them five hundred yards behind our bombers, who were already dropping their eggs. I saw two of Ed's flight gang-up on the first steeply climbing I-45, but before they could shoot it down Daniels went in fast to within a few yards of the Jap and shot him down in flames. As the ship exploded I thought Pat Daniels' plane was on fire too, they were so close. We all confirmed the first ship for the eager Daniels, who was from Van Nuys, California.

There were thirteen I-45's in the air over Gia Lam that

afternoon, and for the next few seconds, as they tried desperately to get to the bombers, our hands were full. We had ten fighters, and we felt that we outnumbered them many times —considering the way we usually had to fight.

The bombers were on the way home now, and we sighed with relief and tried to catch the Japs. Ed Rector took the next ship he got his sights on and blew it apart. Then he fought all the way to the ground with two others. Marks shot down one, and the others were about equally divided.

I caught a flight of three I-45's going hell-bent for the bombers from below and to the rear, and shot the last one in the formation down with a short burst. It was a point-blank range and occurred very fast. I first saw a thin trail of gray smoke that looked like the usual condensation cloud that forms behind the wings of fighter ships doing maneuvers at high altitude, when the atmospheric conditions are just right. And then flame poured from the right engine. It spread up over the cockpit and stretched thirty feet back in the slipstream. I moved up towards the second enemy fighter and didn't see the flamer go down.

With my first burst the next ship rolled over and dove, with one engine shot-up. By now I had caught up to the lead I-45, who was shooting at the bombers from exceedingly long range. I methodically aimed for his engines, putting a short burst into one and then into the other. The Jap must have felt the fire, for he went into a steep, climbing turn— which incidentally is very good if you have a ship that will outclimb your opponent. I thought this climbing turn might be a trick; so I watched closely for him to turn on me. But when he rolled over he dove not for me but for the clouds. I kept going after him and must have put two hundred shots into him before he got out of my sight in the cumulus cloud. Pieces had begun to come from his fuselage, and smoke was trailing behind. I believe his engines were hit and were failing, for the props seemed to be "windmilling." And yet I could only claim it as a "probable," for I didn't see it catch fire or crash.

We got all our bombers back, of course, and the pictures showed very good results for the bombing of Gia Lam field. We claimed nine of the thirteen enemy fighters definitely destroyed, and we hadn't even gotten a hole in one of our P-40's. In our opinion the new I-45 had turned out to be a flop for the Jap. Either it was not all they expected or the pilots didn't know how to use the fast-climbing ship. Sometimes I noticed that when I got on the tail of one, instead of *climbing* away from me—and he could easily have climbed away from a P-40—he tried to *dive* away from me, which is definitely a very poor thing to try with your opponent in a fast-diving Kittyhawk.

A short time after the Hanoi fight, we captured a French pilot, a Captain Penard, who had landed at Mengtze, just across the Indo-Chinese border. Though our questioning of him failed to yield much strategic information, we did get confirmation for the day's work of September 25th. He claimed to have observed the fight, and from his description his claim sounded probable. He said either nine or eleven enemy planes had been shot down, and as we of course knew, no American ships. Strangely enough, he told us of the way the Japanese surrounded the wrecks of their fighters and would not let the natives see them. He observed that they hastily painted out the rising-sun insignia of Japan and replaced it with the white star of the American Air Force. These trophies were then paraded through the country to impress the population with Japanese invincibility.

A poor way to have to impress conquered people, we thought. General Chennault said he'd furnish all the ships they wanted for that purpose. As far as we were concerned, the Japs could gather up all the Zeros and I-45's they wanted after we shot them down, and change the spots on them. We'd do all we could to help.

28

We've Got to Learn to Hate

JUST AS THE GENERAL had been expecting, heavy movement began in late September along the Burma Road, from Lashio North towards Lungling. The Japs were seen by our observation to be moving many trucks filled with troops. They were evidently going to renew the attempt to cross the Salween that the AVG had frustrated back in May.

Bruce Holloway and I caught these trucks the first day and burned twelve of them near Wanting. On the next afternoon, I got through the rain with a single fighter and caught four of them on a curve in the road at Chefang. From then on for six days, until the end of September, we harassed every movement on the wet and muddy road. Twelve of us burned ninety-six heavy trucks in six days. We used fragmentation bombs as well as the fifties. When we couldn't find their trucks, we'd hit the dark green troop barracks they were constructing from Lungling to Lashio.

One day Daniels dove on a truck column to find that the Japs had placed light tanks along with the truck convoy. When Daniels, who was an offensive-minded fighter anyway, saw the tanks he forgot about the trucks and concentrated on the more formidable vehicles. His Fifties tore two tanks rather badly, and his frag bombs knocked two more from the road, but he was wounded by the heavy fire from the tanks.

Lieutenant Welborn, his wing man, saw the tracers from the ground firing at his leader's ship and went to the aid of Pat Daniels. But the damage had been done. One bullet had come up through the side panel of Daniels' P-40 and had struck him in the shoulder. The wound was very bloody, and the shock had just about paralyzed the pilot's arm. Nevertheless, Cocky Daniels flew the ship back three hundred miles to Kunming and landed it there with his left hand.

On these same flights against the trucks, Bruce Holloway was shot down. All of us learned rapidly that this ground-strafing was tough business and not conducive to long life. Just about every ship on the strafing missions would be riddled with small holes from the constant ground-fire.

Maj. Bruce Holloway, the Group Executive, had been leading several fighters on the truck columns near Chefang. As he pulled from one diving attack he felt something strike his ship. At first he didn't notice it and continued to strafe from just about tree-top altitude. Then his coolant light popped on. Bruce turned immediately towards the friendly Chinese lines, which were nearly twenty miles away. He must have known immediately that the enemy bullet had punctured his prestone tank (the coolant of the American liquid-cooled engine). He had a very few minutes to stay in the air before the engine would catch fire or "freeze."

He must be getting closer to the river, he knew, for he was indicating over two hundred miles an hour, but in his anxiety it seemed to go farther away. With almost his last gasp he crossed the river into friendly Chinese country and crash-landed in one of the ever-present rice paddies.

Now begins Bruce's trip back from the interior of China to our base at Kunming. It's almost a saga, for Holloway was fêted, wined, and dined in the primitive fashion of the remote village people, who were tribesmen called "Miaows." Though Bruce was only fifty minutes by plane from Kunming, his mode of travel by sedan chair, donkey, and water buffalo required three weeks. From the moment he rode into headquarters on the last buffalo he had hired, he became known as the "Lochinvar of the Salween."

Later Lieutenant Welborn was shot down farther to the South. Welborn had gotten out of his burning plane two hundred miles South of Paoshan, and his trip out of the rough country was the longest of any man that was lost. I remember that when he reached the first village from which he could get word to us, he sent a message that at first sounds facetious, until you understand the conditions under which one travels in the interior of China; then you realize that he was conservative. His message read: "Landed safely such and such a sector. My motto is Kunming by Christmas."

It was then September, and Welborn beat his original estimate. He required fifty-four days to travel two hundred miles across the trails of southwestern Yunnan.

Our truck-strafing caused us to lose several planes and two pilots, but we cost the Japs lots of material. Towards the first of October, there were skeletons of enemy trucks and tanks from the Salween to Kutkai, near Lashio. The Jap may have moved a few at night, but not many after Morgan and Bayse got through bombing the bridges on the Burma Road. We caught a few Jap planes near Lashio and shot up several on the ground. I shot into a Zero there on October 5, and believe it went down, but only claimed it as a "probable."

The Japs kept coming towards Kunming from Indo-China nearly every day in early October, but I think they remembered that the last time they had been in the capital of Yunnan, they had lost all their ships to the AVG. Way back on Christmas Day, 1941.

Even with the hardships that a rugged country like China imposed, I was living a wonderful life there in Kunming. Those were days that I would never forget—not only for the adventure that I was sharing with the other fighters in the Group, but for the great privilege of living with my boss, General Chennault.

Gen. Caleb Haynes, Doctor Gentry, and I lived together with the General in a house the "Gissimo" had built for him. Situated near the field at Kunming, it was a modern home, or as modern as a bungalow could be in Yunnan. With a private room for each of us, with the Chinese houseboys the General had collected in his six years in China, we lived a wonderful life in a war-torn land.

There was "Wong Chauffeur" who drove the General's car. Wong had a little boy—of course called "Little Wong"—

who was suspicious of foreign devils and who used to cover his face with his hands when I spoke to him. The General told me that as far as he had been able to find out from a long time in China, we'd always be foreign to the Chinese. For, after all, the only word in China that could mean a person other than a Chinese was "foreign devil."

The General told me about an automobile trip he had made with Major Shu down the road from Chihkiang to Kweyang. This is bandit country, through the wilds of Kweyang province. Arriving at Kweyang, the capital, they had found an ancient walled city. The General, as a trusted servant of the Gissimo, had been taken to the Governor's house, and there dinner was served. All through the meal General Chennault noticed that strangers whom he did not meet would come in singly, sit down at the other end of the table, and after watching his every movement for a minute, would leave. Then another would come in and take the seat. After this had gone on during the entire meal, the General finally turned to Major Shu and asked what was going on—what all these staring people meant? Major Shu replied that here in Kweyang the people had never seen a foreign devil, and the Governor had given them permission to come in and look at one.

General Chennault's other houseboys were "Wang Cook," who had been on the US Gunboat *Panay*, and "Gunboat," who had served in the American Navy for three years.

The General used to take me hunting with him, and I came to understand that throughout these hunting trips he was giving me lessons in tactics, lessons he had learned the hard way against the Japanese. Without my knowing it, he would, in effect, criticize my method of former attacks and advise me about better ways to do the job. I used to listen to him for hours as he told of cases in which he had got his own ship shot up by going in too close, and then, after he learned how and knew that his longer range fifty-calibre guns would out-shoot the Jap, had accomplished the same destruction on the enemy without getting his own ship shot to pieces. These critiques taught me exactly what he meant to impart without his ever hurting my pride by telling me that I was wrong and could accomplish more by fighting in his way.

Coming home some nights from the exercise of our hunts together, I would think of my wife and little girl far away in Georgia, and get very homesick. Once I looked at the General and told him how I wished that I could press a button and to end the war, so that we could all go home. He thought for a second or two and then looked back, smiling.

"Aw now, Scotty," he said. "We don't want to do that. Why, if the war ended we'd all have to go back home and you know what that means—no cigarettes, no meat—why, you're better off right here." But the General's business was winning the war, and in spite of his kidding I knew he meant to finish the job.

We'd go home in the darkness, and Wang Cook would fix us a peppery dove-pie from the General's doves and some canned oysters out of the loot of Rangoon.

29
Calling Cards on Hongkong

COL. MERIAM C. COOPER was the Chief of Staff to the General. His business was war, too. Cooper had been one of the greatest heroes of the First World War, and was one of the greatest soldiers I have ever seen. I never discovered when it was he slept. At any time of night, he was apt to come into my room, when he visited us in Kunming from his usual headquarters in Chungking. Or when I'd go to see him, I could find him smoking his ever-present pipe at any hour. Cooper had served in the American Air Force in the last war, and when the war was over he had kept right on fighting. He had enlisted with the Poles in the Russian-Polish war, and had been second in command of the Kosciusko Squadron. After leading many dangerous strafing raids, he was awarded Poland's highest military decorations. Later he made a reputation as an explorer in Persia, Siam, and Africa. Following an active part in the formation of Pan-American Airways, he became one of the best known moving-picture producers in America.

Cooper was a soldier through and through, one of the most intelligent men that I could hope to meet, and the perfect Chief of Staff for General Chennault. Through his constant attention to our espionage in eastern China we learned of the Japanese Task Forces coming through Hongkong on their way to the Solomons and Saigon, and also of the large amount of shipping in Victoria harbor.

Now Cooper was working tirelessly to plan our greatest raid against the Japanese. I remember vividly how he toiled for six days and six nights at the General's house on the logistics for our proposed attack on the largest convoy that had come through Hongkong. Morning after morning, when I went in to breakfast, the floor around the table would be ankle-deep with "Walnut" tobacco from Cooper's pipe, but the plans would be those of a master. General Chennault and Colonel Cooper made, in fact, the perfect tactical team. Everything was ready for the bombing raid by the middle of October, and we merely waited for word from the East that the harbor between Kowloon and Hongkong was filled with Japs.

General Haynes had come to China to lead General Chennault's bombers when he left the leadership of the Ferry Command. He had hurt the Jap plenty with his precision bombing, and had built up a great bombing force, mainly through the inspiration of his personal leadership on the most dangerous missions.

Radio Tokyo had recently been "panning" Haynes, referring to him as "the old broken-down transport pilot." In a way, this was music to our ears, for it meant that the Japanese were being hurt by his bombings or they would not have resorted to such propaganda. But it made General Haynes so mad that he could have torn the Jap to pieces with his bare hands. After all, he had been a pursuit pilot for years, and for the last ten years he had been dean of American four-engine bombers. The records he had set with the B-15 had made history and were inspirations to the Air Corps. It had been only recently, when he had been taken from his thirteen four-engine bombers on the way to blast Tokyo, that he had been assigned to transports. The Japs must have known just how to get under his skin, but in the end I think the knowledge worked against them.

Now he was getting back at them by having thousands of little leaflets printed in several languages, especially in Japanese. They read:

COMPLIMENTS OF THE OLD BROKEN-DOWN
TRANSPORT PILOT

He used to drop some of these on every bombing mission he led. He'd go out and tie some to each bomb; put them in the bomb bay so that they fell out when the doors were opened; even throw them out over the Japanese-occupied cities that he blasted. I knew now that he was getting a new supply ready for Hongkong.

Towards the end of October came the word we had so long

been waiting for. Victoria harbor was filled with Japanese shipping. In deepest secret we got ready to go.

Our ships would leave from Kunming, but we would of course use the intermediate bases in the Kweilin-Hengyang section, 500 miles to the East. Hongkong, you will recall, is about 325 miles Southeast of Kweilin. It is protected by surrounding enemy fighter fields at Canton and Kowloon. Our objectives would be the shipping in the harbor, the shipping at the docks in Kowloon, and the ships at the drydocks in Hongkong.

Early on the morning of October 25 our twelve bombers took off from Yunnan for Kweilin, and shortly afterwards Hill, Alison, Holloway and I led the fighters off. We were all to infiltrate into Kweilin, a few ships at a time, so as not to alert the coast of eastern China.

For two weeks I had worried about this attack. I thought it would come any day, and because of the tension I couldn't sleep. Each night when I shut my eyes I'd wonder if I would do the right thing when the time came. I'd picture myself flying in the lead, and see planes on my wing going down in flames. I'd roll my head down in bed and with my eyes tightly closed see formations of Zeros passing in endless review, climbing steeply, rolling over in arrogance, with grinning Japanese faces. I'd get up every morning at three o'clock hoping that the word had come, yet also fearing that it had. Today might be the day that I made the mistake that would lose my Group.

When I learned that word hadn't come, I'd spend another sleepless night. I got the doctor to give me something to make me sleep and I had a headache the next day. I knew "my wind was up," as the British say—*but why didn't we go on and get the attack over with!*

But now I was on the way. I could see the shark-mouths of the P-40's all around, and the whole thing was easy—just what I had wanted all the time. We sat down at Kweilin at one-minute intervals at eight o'clock. The bombers were soon in, and the Chinese were busy servicing the field full of ships. They were the happiest people I had ever seen. They'd point towards Japan and point down with their thumbs and say, "Bu-hao."

While they serviced the ships, we hurried to the alert cave and were "briefed" by the General. We had to work fast, for we were so close to Japanese bases that we could have been caught on the ground with our Air Force if we hadn't been careful. In fifty minutes we were away, the fighters first, and then the bombers. Making our assembly over the designated point, we were off on our greatest mission to date.

All of us were proud to be going. But as I looked at those seven P-40's escorting ten bombers, I could not help feeling apologetic for that greatest country in the world that we were representing. Oh, God, if the day could soon come when we could go against this enemy with a thousand bombers, even a hundred bombers!

Maybe the small fighter force that we had made us lucky ones who were privileged to go resolve all the more that we would make up in quality what we lacked in quantity. Personally I felt like a veteran football player who has been on the bench and has now been called into the big game. Nearly a year before, when Hongkong had fallen to the Japanese attacks from the Asiatic mainland of Kowloon, I had sworn that I would see the first bombs hit the Crown Colony. I had no idea then that I would lead the fighters, that I would shoot down Japanese fighters in the raid, that we would be intercepted by a superior force of the enemy, but that in less than three minutes after the interception there would be only ships of the U. S. Army Air Force over Victoria harbor.

"Now I had the familiar "wind up" feeling that precedes combat. The palms of my hands perspired freely. As I wiped them on the legs of my trousers I saw that the sweat was like mud; it had mixed with the red dust of Kweilin Field through which we had taken off.

Our altitude kept increasing to 20,000 feet, while down below at seventeen thousand were the medium bombers in javelin formation: two Vee's of three, and the last element a diamond of four. We passed one of the river junction checkpoints that enabled me to compute our ground speed. In fifty minutes I could see the glint of the sun on the Pacific Ocean. As I saw the bomber formation again, I felt proud of the crews of those perfectly spaced ships. This really was like a football game: the bombers were carrying the ball while we in the pea-shooters ran the interference.

I imagined General Haynes, down there in the lead bomber, grinning as he thought of dropping a few hundred more of his leaflet souvenirs to the Japs, "Compliments of the old broken-down transport pilot"—along with at least sixty 500-pound bombs. Big "Butch" Morgan, the best bombardier in the Air Force, had probably wormed his huge bulk through the tunnel into the nose of Haynes's bomber and was even now intensely interested in his pet bomb-sight.

Now I could even smell the freshness of the Pacific. The

sky had never been so blue. The beauty of the day and the beauty of those weapons flying so smoothly under us made me forget the scratching of the oxygen mask on my sunburned neck. It was a joy to look back and see the six shark-mouths on the other P-40's grinning at me. Some day, I thought, Jap mothers were going to frighten their children by referring to them and reminding the brats of Nippon that their fathers had more than likely had that view of an American P-40 for a last memory.

As we got closer to the target, we split our formation of fighters automatically. Tex Hill, Hampshire, and Sher stayed with me; Marks took the other three on the opposite flank of the bombers. The country below had become lower in elevation but was green and still hilly. Over the radio, as we reached the point North of Macao, came the jabbering of Japanese voices on our frequency, and we knew from its ominous sound that they were warning of our attack.

I tensed a little and looked about for enemy planes. Far to my left I could see the three rivers meeting at Canton, could see two fields from which I knew Zeros were taking off to intercept us. We had by-passed Canton purposely by thirty miles. I saw the bombers changing course: we were around Canton now, and were going to steer straight for the North of Kowloon peninsula. The blue Pacific looked friendly, reminding me of the southern California coast. The old, familiar fog banks that should have been covering San Clemente and Catalina were shrouding instead the Ladrones Islands, with only their hilltops visible, sticking out from the fog on the China Sea.

We were turning over Macao, where the Clippers used to land. To the South I could see another Jap field, Sanchau Island. Now to the right was Hongkong Island, shaped like a kidney and mountainous, just about nine miles long and three or four miles across. I could make out the indentations of the romantic-sounding bays whose names I knew—Sandy, Telegraph, Kellet, and Repulse. There were points of land jutting towards the mainland—Quarry Point, with its Naval Drydock, and Shek Tong Tsui, the point over which we would fight our aerial battle. Reaching towards the island like a finger was Kowloon peninsula, separated from it by the blue waters of Victoria harbor. Near the end of the spit of land closest to Hongkong, I saw the large modern Peninsular Hotel. All of us knew that Japanese Generals and staff officers slept there.

We came across the Great West Channel, passed North of

Stonecutters Island, and came to our turning point, seven miles North of Kowloon. The bombers were turning South now for the bombing run. This was the crucial moment.

I crossed around and over General Haynes and his formation, watching vigilantly. Far below I saw dust on Kai Tak airdrome, and knew that enemy ships were taking off to attack us. My throat felt dry and I had trouble swallowing; I turned my gun switch off and on nervously.

Now I saw the bomb-bay doors opening, and I couldn't keep the tears of excitement from burning my eyes. Anti-aircraft was beginning to dot the sky with black and white puffs. As I dove almost to the level of the bombers, I could feel the ack-ack rock my fighter ship. I kept S-ing to watch for the enemy fighters that must be coming. The white stars on the upper wings of the bombers below were like an American flag waving, and it gave me the same feeling that I get when I see home after a long absence. As loud as I could against the roar of the engine, I shouted: "Come up, you devils!"

I saw the yellow bombs begin to fall in long strings, imposed on the dark green of the world below. They got smaller and smaller as the noses pointed slowly down. Remembering my movie camera, I tried to take pictures of the explosions. The bombs seemed to take years to fall, and I began to think they were all duds. The ack-ack burst closer as the Japs got the range while we went straight in. I know I was never more excited in all my life. I yelled, "Okay, Hirohito—we have lots more where those came from!" I kept looking behind and under us for the bombs to burst.

And then I saw the first white explosion—right on the docks of Kowloon. After that they came so fast you couldn't count them. I let my camera run as the explosions turned from white to black—there were oil-fires now. I could see the flash of the anti-aircraft guns from the North shore of Hongkong Island, as we continued across Victoria harbor. I risked another look at the target; it was covered with smoke from one end to the other. Then I got my eyes back to searching for enemy interceptors—we had to be extra careful now.

Why didn't the bombers turn for home? They had dropped the bombs, but they were still going on endlessly towards that point of Shek Tong Tsui. All of us were keyed up. But then the long javelin of B-25's began to turn to the right. Mission accomplished—now they had the down-hill run to base, and I began to get that old feeling of relief. Then, somehow, I felt cheated. Where were the enemy fighters? I raised my camera, sighted again, and took the formation as it swung over the burning docks.

Then, as I glanced about, I saw them, silhouette after silhouette, climbing terribly steeply towards the bombers. I know now that they had got there from Kai Tak below in four minutes; they had made the sixteen thousand feet in that short time. I felt my camera drop to my lap, hit my knee, then drop to the metal floor of the fighter. I was fumbling now for the "mike" button on the throttle; then I was calling: "Bandits ahead—Zeroooos! At eleven o'clock." Fumbling again for the throttle quadrant, shoving everything as far forward as I could, I marvelled at the steepness of the climb the enemy ships were maintaining. I called: "Zeros at twelve o'clock," to designate their direction clock-fashion from us. I heard Tex Hill reply: "Yes, I see 'em." I could hear the jabber of the Japs still trying to block our frequency.

I was diving now, aiming for the lead Zero, turning my gunsight on and off, a little nervously checking again and again to see that the gun-switch was at "on." I jerked the belly-tank release and felt the underslung fifty-gallon bamboo tank drop off. We rolled to our backs to gain speed for the attack and went straight for the Zeros. I kept the first Zero right in the lighted sight and began to fire from over a thousand yards, for he was too close to the bombers. Orange tracers were coming from the B-25's too, as the turret gunners went to work.

Five hundred yards before I got to the Zero, I saw another P-40 bearing the number 151 speed in and take it. That was Tex Hill. He followed the Zero as it tried to turn sharply into the bombers and shot it down. Tex spun from his tight turn as the Jap burst into flames. I took the next Zero—they seemed to be all over the sky now. I went so close that I could see the pilot's head through the glass canopy and the little tail-wheel that was not retracted, and I knew it was a Navy Zero—the little wheel was built for the arresting-gear of a carrier. My tracers entered the cockpit and smoke poured back, hiding the canopy, and I went by.

As I turned to take another ship below me, I saw four airplanes falling in flames towards the waters of Victoria harbor. I half rolled again and skidded in my dive to shake any Zero that might be on my tail. I saw another P-40 shooting at a Jap, but there was a Zero right on his tail. I dove for this one. He grew in my sights, and as my tracers crossed in front of him he turned into me. I shot him down as his ship seemed to stand still in the vertical bank. The ship was three or four hundred yards from me, and it fell towards the water for a time that seemed ages. An explosion came, and there was only black smoke; then I could see the ship again, falling, turning in a slow spin, down—down—down.

I shot at everything I saw. Sometimes it was just a short burst as the Jap went in for our bombers. Sometimes I fired at one that was turning, and as I'd keep reefing back on my stick, my ship would spin, and I'd recover far below. I shot down another ship that didn't see me. I got it with one short burst from directly astern, a no-deflection shot. In this attack I could see the Japanese ship vibrate as my burst of six fifty-calibre guns hit it. First it just shook, then one wing went up. I saw the canopy shot completely off; then I went across it. Turning back in a dive to keep my speed, I watched the enemy ship, as it dove straight down, stream flames for a distance the length of the airplane behind.

As I looked around now the bombers were gone, but climbing up from the South I saw four twin-engine ships that I thought were I-45's; later we decided they were Japanese Messerschmitts. I had plenty of altitude on the leader, and started shooting at him from long range, concentrating on his right engine. He turned to dive, and I followed him straight for the water. I remember grinning, for he had made the usual mistake of diving instead of climbing. But as I drew up on the twin-engine ship, I began to believe that I had hit him from the long range. His ship was losing altitude rapidly in a power glide, but he was making no effort to turn. I came up to within fifty yards and fired into him until he burned. I saw the ship hit the water and continue to burn. We had been going towards the fog bank in the direction of the Philippines, and I wondered if the Jap had been running for Manila.

I shot at two of the other twin-engine ships from long range but couldn't climb up to them. Then I passed over Hong-kong Island, flying at a thousand feet; as I was too low but didn't want to waste any time climbing. And I saw something that gripped my heart—a fenced-in enclosure which I knew was Fort Stanley, the British and American prison camp. There was a large group standing in the camp and waving at my ship. My saddest feeling of the war came over me then. Here were soldiers who had been prisoners of the Japanese for nearly a year. Month after month they had waited for the sight of Allied airplanes attacking Hongkong—and at last it had come. Even in their suffering they were waving a cheer to the few United States planes that had finally come, and I swore to myself I'd come back again and again.

Then I saw above me the criss-crossing vapor paths of an area where fighter ships have sped through an air attack. They almost covered the sky in a cloud. Here and there were darker lines that could have been smoke paths where ships had burned and gone down to destruction.

I was rudely jerked back to attention by a slow voice that yet was sharp: "If that's a P-40 in front of me, waggle your wings." I rocked my wings before I looked. Then I saw the other ship, a P-40 nearly a mile away. I think from the voice it was Tex Hill. I went over towards him and together we dove towards home.

The presence of the other P-40 made me feel very arrogant and egotistical, for I had shot down four enemy ships and had damaged others. So I looped above Victoria harbor and dove for the Peninsular Hotel. My tracers ripped into the shining plateglass of the pent-houses on its top, and I saw the broken windows cascade like snow to the streets, many floors below. I laughed, for I knew that behind those windows were Japanese high officers, enjoying that modern hotel. When I got closer I could see uniformed figures going down the fire-escapes, and I shot at them. In the smoke of Kowloon I could smell oil and rubber. I turned for one more run on the packed fire-escapes filled with Jap soldiers, but my next burst ended very suddenly. I was out of ammunition. Then, right into the smoke and through it right down to the tree-top levels, I headed Northwest to get out of Japanese territory sooner, and went as fast as I could for Kweilin.

I was the last ship in, and the General was anxiously waiting for me, scanning the sky for ships to come in. He knew I had shot down an enemy, for I had come in with my low-altitude roll of victory. But when I jumped from my cramped seat and said, "General, I got four definitely," he shook my hand and looked very happy. "That makes nineteen then," he said, "for the fighters and the bombers."

We had lost a fighter and a bomber. The bomber had become a straggler when one engine was hit by anti-aircraft; then it was shot to pieces by one of the twin-engined Jap fighters. The pilot had managed even then to get it down, but he had remained in the ship to destroy the bomb-sight, and had been shot through the foot by a Jap cannon. Two of the bomber crew had bailed out and were captured. The other two carried the injured pilot until he had begged them to leave him alone and escape. They had bandaged his foot tightly, but had refused to go without him.

As they moved on through the enemy lines that night, they stopped to rest, and the wounded pilot crawled away from them to insure their getting away to the guerrilla lines. They escaped, and later we received a letter signed by the other two crewmen which said that the pilot had been captured and was then in a Japanese hospital. The letter was a Japanese propaganda leaflet that the Japs had dropped near Kweilin, but being properly signed, it gave us hope for the remainder of the crew, and for the heroic pilot, Lieutenant Allers.

That night Morgan led a night raid to bomb Canton, and had a successful attack. Later the same night, Ed Bayse led six bombers to destroy the power station on Hongkong Island. In his return to Kweilin, five of his ships landed but the other continued to circle—informing the radioman that he had no air speed and thus was having difficulty bringing the fast bomber in to land.

Bayse, who had worked all the day and most of the night over enemy lines, started his ship and went aloft, got the other ship on his wing in formation, and told the pilot to keep the position. And then this experienced bomber pilot led the younger pilot in to a safe landing. It was teamwork of the sort that had begun to appear among the bomber crews, and more important still, as the co-ordinated attack had shown, between the fighters and bombers. This was what Colonel Cooper had been working for during the past several months.

Cooper had done another fine job, one that we learned of only after we returned to Kunming from the attack. In India the field in Assam had been raided heavily by the Japanese at the same hour as our attack on Kowloon, and simultaneously the Japanese had tried to strike at Kunming with a large force. Colonel Cooper had been left behind in the hospital with a sinus infection. He was chafing at the bit, and we sympathized with him—for after having planned the greatest raid of the war in China, he had been forced out of accompanying the mission. But it has always been our contention out there that "everything happens for the best." And it proved out again. When the enemy planes approached Kunming, Cooper left the hospital and took charge of the defense of the home base. He sent Schiel's Squadron towards the South at exactly the right time. They not only intercepted the enemy and foiled the attack but shot down eight of the enemy. That made the score for the Group twenty-seven enemy planes on October 25th, and three highly successful bombing raids.

We were ordered home the next day, although we now had the enemy at our mercy without fighter protection against future raids towards Hongkong. But heavy attacks had come to India, and we were needed to protect the terminus of the ferry route to China.

We managed, however, to leave a small force of P-40's under Holloway and Alison, with mission to dive-bomb shipping in Victoria harbor within the next few days. They took eight planes down and dove through the overcast towards some big enemy freighters that were on the way South towards the Solomons. Their bombs damaged two 8-000-ton freighters and sank a 12,000-ton vessel. Captain O'Connell made this last direct hit by almost taking his bomb down the smokestack of the enemy vessel, and in doing so he was shot down. He took the bomb very low, and in recovering from the dive he was attacked by a single enemy, who got one of the best pilots in the Squadron. Clinger and Alison saw the enemy ship, but from their distance they could do nothing in time to save O'Connell. While Alison was getting the lone enemy ship, Clinger dove in anger along the docks of Kowloon, strafing three anti-aircraft positions in the face of very heavy ground-fire.

30

So Sorry, Please, So Sorry

THE MOST VIVID memories of our air war in China come from the little things. Like the memory of General Chennault, sitting there at the mouth of the cave in Kweilin through the long hours while we were away on the attack missions. Sitting there smoking his pipe and, like a football coach, planning the next week's work. Joe, the General's little black dachshund, would be burrowing into the rocks, looking for the inevitable rats. When with the passing minutes the P-40's or the bombers were due to return, the General would begin to watch the eastern sky. There he would sit without a word until the last ship was accounted for. Sometimes I thought: The General lives through every second of the combat with us. With his keen knowledge of tactics and of the Jap too, he sees exactly what we are doing.

Another memory that always brings a smile is Lieutenant Couch's face when he was explaining what happened the first time he got a Jap Zero in his sights. The enemy ship was a lone "sitter," probably some inexperienced Japanese pilot who wasn't looking around and didn't know the P-40 was behind him. Couch said he kept moving up closer and closer until he knew the Jap was going to be dead the instant he pressed his trigger. Then he pressed—and nothing happened. He squeezed the trigger until he thought he'd press the top off the stick; he found that he shut his eyes, flinched, and bit his lip, but still the guns didn't fire.

The American pilot from the Carolinas swore and throttled back, dropping to the rear while the Jap kept flying innocently on. After Couch had recharged his guns he began to stalk the Zero again, going closer and closer until he could see the enemy pilot at the controls. He set his sights right on the cockpit and pressed the trigger once more. And again nothing happened.

Couch came home disgusted, and I think he worked on his guns all night.

One memory brings back a joke on myself. I had been on a long flight towards Hankow, and from the time of take-off, all the way to the enemy base, all during combat, and then back home, I had been forced to pump my landing-gear up manually every ten miles. At eighteen thousand feet, in the rarefied air and with an oxygen mask on, this becomes monotonous work, but in combat it's even a dangerous kind of work. I had pumped and pumped, and just as I'd get the wheels back up, the defective hydraulic valve would release the pressure and I'd feel that the wheels were slowly dropping again. Now, after nearly seven hundred miles of it, over some three hours and a half, I pumped them up once more and they seemed to hold. I asked my wing man to fly up close and investigate.

Bruce Holloway told me later that they had all been listening for reports of the fight, via the Command Radio back in Kunming—when over the ether they heard a very Southern drawl disgustedly calling, "Dubois, fly up close to me and see if that blasted wheel is down again."

We tried to hold the chatter over the radios to a minimum, but there were times when the men released their emotions into the microphone, and we thought it better not to try to cut it out altogether. We had codes for every purpose, but we found that when you really needed something, it was just as good to ask for it in the clear or in veiled American slang. Sometimes the retorts that came as a natural response to actions were better than any that could have been planned and written by the masters.

Up between Hengyang and Lingling we had broken the main Jap force with several attacks and there were only stragglers around the sky. We had been searching them out for fifteen minutes when I saw and heard a remark that was nothing short of classic. From 21,000 feet I observed a lone Zero. But there was a P-40 trailing him, and so I held my altitude and watched. The P-40 closed the gap more and more, following the acrobatics of the Jap, and then drew up for the kill. As the tracers from the six guns went into the Zero I heard the voice of Captain Goss say, "That's for you, God rest your soul." Over the radio you could also hear the staccato roll of the six Fifties. The Zero slowly rolled over to destruction.

Sometimes the hated Japs had the last word. In regions where the air-warning net was working poorly or not at all, our first knowledge of the approach of the enemy would be the sight of Japanese bombers overhead. As the bombs blasted the runways and the Jap radial engines were taking their ships at high altitude back towards their bases, we would hear over the radio on our exact frequency, in perfect English: "So sorry, please, so sorry."

We would just shake our fists and wait for better days.

When I first brought "Old Exterminator" to China, I had painted the number 10 on the fuselage. Later on we used the last three numerals of the Air Corps numbers for call letters, or were assigned some name like "ash," "oak," or "pine." But the first time I came back from Chungking, late one afternoon, I approached Kunming down the usual corridor, expecting that to identify me automatically, and from far out I called by radio: "One-Zero, coming in from the North." Of course I was using the numerals of the number "ten" to identify me to the radioman. Instead, as I came over the field I saw anti-aircraft men of the Chinese Army running for their guns, and I saw six P-40's taking off to shoot the invader down. Meaning me. You've probably guessed it by now—the radioman gathered that some one had just warned him that one enemy Zero was about to strafe the field. Needless to say, I took myself to safer places for a few minutes until I could properly identify my ship. Then I landed and changed the fuselage number to lucky "seven"—but definitely not seventy.

There just wasn't much relaxation in China with Scotch at one hundred dollars gold a bottle—when you could find it. In fact, we didn't get to drink anything except boiled water and that really terrible rice wine. This we had to learn to down with the Chinese and in their manner, which was with the inevitable salute, "Gambey," or "bottoms up." Then they'd come and proudly show you the bottoms of their glasses, and you'd have to follow suit with a weak little gambey.

Then there was the incessant ringing of the telephones in the warning-net plotting-room that got on all our nerves. After months I found out that without exception every pilot tried not to let others know of his nervousness. But it became unmistakable, for the tension that built up around the card-tables in the alert shacks was not the most effectively disguised in the world.

Pilots waiting for the order to go into the air. Sitting at the crude table, waiting for the chow wagon or for an alert. Listening with keen ears for the jingle of the telephone. Playing gin rummy or poker, but hearing everything that was going on. A player would be dealing the deck, and in the middle of the routine of dropping a card here, and one there, the phone would ring. The card would stop in the air, poised over the table while we all heard the Chinese interpreters pick up the magneto phone and utter the familiar "Wey-wey," as they say "hello." The card would remain there over the table, undealt throughout the telephone conversation—until the player realized what he was doing. Then he'd go hesitatingly on.

Perhaps the call was one of the hundreds that meant nothing; only the Chinese really knew, and we could only wait and find out. Then again, the receiver of the telephone might drop back into place and the interpreter would say something to another Chinese. This second one would go to the plotting-board, look at the marked co-ordinates, and quietly put a little red flag down over a certain city towards Japanese territory. Even then, with one warning only, the game could go on for a long time in confidence.

But as the phone kept ringing and the proximity of an attack became more certain, the game would get slower. More and more words would be left hanging in the air, more sentences would never end, nervous laughs would become more frequent. You'd realize finally that you were listening to that damned telephone and to nothing else, and wishing subconsciously that you could pull it off the wall. But there would always be more to come, with Chinese saying "Wey, wey—wey—wey." More little flags would form a line on the map, and more Chinese would walk soundlessly across the room; no jabbering from them—it was their business, and they knew when the flags got to a certain point, or quit advancing and turned back, that something would happen.

Maybe at this stage some one in the game would get up to investigate, and would come back and say, "Eighteen unknown in L-5," or "Heavy engine noise to the East." It might be the something that let the tension off a bit, such as, "One Enemy plane over in S-15." Then somebody else would grin hopefully and say, "That's old reliable—he reports every day."

Perhaps the Squadron commander or the officer who was on the alert that day would move out of the game and start looking the map and the flags over, sizing up the situation. As the picture formed and it became apparent that this was a real attack he'd just go over and tell the card-game about it. Or maybe two or three men would begin to get helmets out. The game would silently break up, with cards and CN left where they were. Helmets and gloves would be put on. Men who were pretending to be sleeping in the bags on the floor would be awakened.

And the tension dropped off like a cloak. It wasn't the actual combat these fighter pilots feared, for we all wanted combat more than anything else; it was the damnable uncertainty—the ringing of a telephone, an ominous sound that most of the time meant nothing.

When men went out of the door to get into their ships and take off there was no handing to friends on the ground of last letters to take care of, no entrusting of rings and watches to room-mates. For fighter pilots don't think of not coming back. They are invincible, or think they are, and they have to be that way. Down in our hearts we may figure that some accident will get us some day, when we are old and gray, when our beards get in the way of the controls, or we get to where we don't see well or react fast—but we know that no enemy fighter is good enough to shoot us down. If that happens it's just an accident.

These thoughts are the "chips" that we carry on our shoulders, and they have to be there—arrogant, egotistical chips mellowed by flying technique and experience and fortified by the motto, "Attack!" Never be on the defensive. Shoot the enemy down before he can shoot you down. You are better than he is, but don't give him a chance. He may get in a lucky shot but you're invincible. Move towards any dot in the sky that remotely resembles an airplane. Move to attack, with switches on and the sight ready. If it's not a ship or if it's a friendly one you'll be ready anyway, and your arrogant luck will last a lot longer.

The worry comes before you get to take off for combat—wondering whether or not you'll do the right thing out of habit. After you're in the air it's all the fun of flying and doing the greatest job in the world. You are up there, pitying all earthbound creatures who are not privileged to breathe this purer air on high. Your training makes you do the combat work that is ahead without thinking about the movements.

Months and years of training . . . hours of waiting on the ground . . . high-powered engines pulling you up and up to the attack—and then in a few fleeting seconds the combat is over, your ship is all that's in the sky, and you're on the way home again to base, whistling and thinking how easy it was and what a great and glorious life it really is. You're wondering if you can pick those cards up and finish the game and take your CN back from Ajax or Johnny or Mack. You might be thinking how good that sleeping bag is going to feel, or wondering whether the transports that can land on the field, now that the air raid alert is over, have brought you any mail. . . . "Dog-gone, I wonder if that woman is writing me?"

Maybe they've even made some mistake back over there in the States and have sent some new planes out here, and we're going to get the best in the world, planes that go a hundred miles an hour faster and climb 4500 feet in a minute to fifty thousand feet. But there's your crew-chief now, waving you in—and he's looking at the patches you've shot from the blast tubes of your guns and knows you've fired at the enemy. Or maybe your "victory roll" warned him anyway. . . . Who knows?

31

Keeping the Japs Guessing

DAY AFTER DAY, through the early part of November, we actually prayed that the weather East would clear, so that we could stop our small, piddling attacks on Burma and go back to Hongkong. I knew that General Chennault and Colonel Cooper were planning a big one for the next time, for now we had the largest force of fighters we had ever seen in China. New P-40's had been arriving in small numbers, but steadily. The Group was actually being built up to strength at last.

With the first breaks in the heavy winter clouds, Bert Carleton was sent with his transport and our ground personnel to Kweilin. Aviation fuel and bombs were placed ready for instant use, and I could feel the tension in the air again. From the daily reports on the air-warning net it could be seen that the Japanese had maintained a constant aerial patrol over Hongkong and vicinity since our last attack. With the first break in the clouds we sent observation planes over with a top-cover of several fighters, but the Jap would not come up to fight the shark-mouthed planes. His instructions appear to have been: Wait for the American bombers.

On November 21, the ground crews got to Kweilin. Instead of keeping them in the hostel that first night to insure that information would not leak out to the enemy, we sent them to town, first casually remarking that we were here now for the second attack on Hongkong. News traveled fast, as the General expected it would, via those of the Koreans who were in Japanese pay. General Chennault knew that within four hours the enemy would be waiting for us to strike Victoria harbor again, for his aerial patrol over the city had doubled. Our warning net showed that.

Early next morning our twelve bombers slipped into Kweilin with Colonel* Butch Morgan in the lead ship. The strengthened fighter force of between thirty and forty planes infiltrated for reservice—some went to Kweilin, others scattered to the surrounding emergency fields for better protection of the bombers. As soon as I landed I ran up to the cave and the General took me in and showed me the plotting-board. The little red flags indicated increased vigilance at Hongkong. Then I got my orders: "Strike Hongay." In an hour the bombers were off to bomb the coal mines and docks of that Indo-Chinese port North of Haiphong. Morgan sank a 12,000-ton ship that was reported to have been an aircraft carrier. The fighter escort strafed ferry boats, small surface craft, and looked for Jap fighters trying to intercept. But none came.

That night the enemy sent up a flight of three bombers to each of our fields, looking for our forces. But we were so scattered that their luck was bad. Night fighters from all stations took off, but those under Maj. Harry Pike at Kweilin made perfect contact. The entire Japanese formation of three

*Morgan had been promoted since the last attack.

bombers was shot down over the field. Pike, Lombard, and Griffin each added an enemy ship to their scores, but Lombard was shot down in flames when the Jap gunners blew up his belly tank. Lombard had made the tactical error of pulling up over the bombers after delivering fire that shot one down. We had given him up for lost when he walked in carrying his chute—and begging for another ship.

At dawn the next day, November 23, I led the group to escort Morgan to Sanchau Island with twelve bombers. We had noted that the Japs were strengthening the air patrol over Hongkong even more. The General had smiled and said, "We're making them waste a terrible amount of gasoline."

We saw Morgan's bombs take out two of the three hangars on the island field, and we went down to strafe and watch for interceptors taking off. Some of the flight got three, but my plane was hit by the ack-ack, and when the oil pressure began immediately to fail, I started for the mainland and home. With the oil pressure slowly going from seventy to fifty and finally to nothing, I sweated out my return to Kweilin and just made it by mentally lifting the ship onto the strip between the jagged stalagmites that seemed to guard our field.

That afternoon I led sixteen fighters to escort our twelve bombers to Canton. Capt. Brick Holstrom, who had participated in the raid on Tokyo the preceding April, led the bombers. As the fighters kept the new tactical "squirrel cage" about his formation he deliberately circled to the South of Tien Ho airdrome and covered the target area perfectly with his long string of bombs. The anti-aircraft was heavy and increased as we went on North over White Cloud field. I looked back at the results of Tien Ho and felt a surge of pride at that perfect bombing from fourteen thousand feet. This was teamwork, I knew now, with bombers and fighters properly proportioned. All of us were mad because the Japs wouldn't come up. The bomber crews had reported them taking off from both fields and keeping low, but heading in all directions. The accurate bombing must have destroyed many of them on the ground, for we had made a feint of continuing on South to Hongkong. I sent one ship home with each bomber. The rest of us hung back and tried to tempt the enemy Zeros to come up; but they had evidently received their orders.

Next morning Lieut. Pat Daniels got up begging the General to let him lead a dive-bombing attack on an aircraft assembly plant in Canton. His plan was good, and the mission was made ready. All of us went down to the alert shack and watched the ground crew loading the little yellow fragmentation bombs under the wings of six P-40E's. A short time later they were off, with Daniels waiting to blow up the factory, and all set with his movie camera to take pictures automatically as he dove the bombs into the target.

Three hours later only five of the six returned. Pat Daniels was missing in action. His wing man had seen his leader lose part of his wing in an explosion on the way in with the bombs. Anti-aircraft could have done it, but most of us agreed from the description that Daniels' bombs might have hit his own propeller. At the tremendous speed that a fast fighter-ship builds up in a long and nearly vertical dive, pressures are also built up from the increased speed. This torque necessitates so much compensating pressure on the rudder that one must actually stand on the rudder control. While doing this, Pat might have relaxed pressure just as he reached down to pull the bomb release; this would have allowed the speeding plane to "yaw" or skid, and the bombs could have struck the arc of the prop.

The only note of encouragement was that a chute had been seen when the fighters left the target. Lieut. Patrick Daniels was one of our best and most aggressive pilots, and we missed him immediately—and hoped for the best.

That same night, Johnny Alison led eight ships, in a fighter sweep and dive-bombing attack on the docks at Hankow, over four hundred miles to the North. In the river harbor, with the sky criss-crossed by tracers from the ground, Johnny dropped his bombs on the hangars and on a large freighter. Then for ten minutes he strafed the enemy vessel and badly disabled it. Captain Hampshire dove and shot the search-lights out until he was out of ammunition. The night attack so deep into enemy territory was a daring one and did much to confuse the Japs further. Johnny's ships were rather badly shot up from the ground-fire, and he was lucky to get them all back to base safely. But it was such missions as these which built up the circumstances that would assure the success of the big attack the General was planning.

Next day, with eighteen fighters, we escorted the bombers to raid Sienning, an occupied town near Hankow. We kept the circling movement all around our B-25's and tried to give them an added feeling of security by our presence. Through heavy anti-aircraft fire, Morgan led the attack in and didn't waste a bomb. We left the warehouses in flames, and there was much less ack-ack coming up towards us than when we first approached.

Arriving back at our advanced base, we refueled and bombed up again. Then we made the second raid of the day towards Hankow, over the town of Yoyang. Once again Morgan blasted the target, with black bursts of anti-aircraft fire bouncing around the formation. But there was no interception, and now we were feeling blue. We couldn't destroy the Jap Air Force if they were going to try to save their airplanes.

We spent the next day, Thanksgiving, working on the airplanes and resting. We had flown seven missions in four days, and both men and machines were tired and in need of repair. We had a special dinner that night, but remained extra vigilant against a surprise by the Jap.

On that Thanksgiving evening, as we were grouped around the General, he brought out a bottle of Scotch some one had given him. We figured that some important announcement was about to be made, and out there in the hostel area everything was quiet. The amber liquid was divided among some forty men, and each of us got a few drops in a Chinese teacup —but it was enough for the ceremony.

The General grinned at us and said, "We've got the Japs worried now, we've hit everywhere except what he thought we'd attack. *Tomorrow is the Day*." We could hardly keep from cheering. But we held up our "brimming cups" and just said, "To you, General." The drops never tasted better.

That night, after the announcement, we closed the post and kept all men from going into town. This would cause talk in the right places. Colonel Cooper went into Kweilin and discreetly passed out the news that we were ready for the main attack. Somehow he arranged for just the right information to begin its round-about journey to the Japanese.

The seed had now been sown.

32

Our Biggest Bombing

ON NOVEMBER 27 the largest force of bombers we had ever used in China, escorted by the largest force of fighters, rolled down the runway at Kweilin. There were fourteen bombers, with twenty-two P-40's for escort. We had also left a strong force on the ground at Kweilin, just in case the Jap tried something while we were away. I led the headquarters section of the fighter escort and made up the reserve. My position in the escort would be three thousand feet above the bombers. Down below me a thousand feet was Johnny Alison with his flight of eight, on the right flank of Morgan's bombers. Colonel Bruce Holloway had the flight on the left flank, another thousand feet lower. Colonel Cooper was riding in the lead bomber as intelligence officer, and that day was going to demonstrate the teamwork that he had striven for, between the fighters and the bombers.

Cooper had been so anxious to accompany our raids that he seemed keenly disappointed whenever other duties interfered. He was threatening today to take over one of the turrets in the lead bomber and shoot down the first Jap. I joked with Coop on the way to our fighters that morning, and told him that we in the fighters were so glad to have him along that we were going to let one Jap through, just so he could shoot it down and get the pilot's ears for his little boy. We laughed as we separated.

The large formation—large for us in China—assembled over the airdrome and took a course North in the direction of Hankow. We wanted reports from other spies in Kweilin to get started, for this mission was planned mainly to get the Jap Air Force into the air where we could get at it. We usually evaded towns as we began our attacks, but today we went low over Kweilin, and then to the North. When we were beyond the prying and ready ears of any spies, we turned to a direct heading for Hongkong.

Now we climbed above high overcast to twenty-thousand feet, and settled down for the three hundred miles ahead. In fifty-five minutes the clouds began to break and scatter, and we approached enemy territory with a cloudless sky and perfect visibility. Over to the right now I caught the glint of the sun on the junction of the three rivers that meet near Canton in a figure like a trident. Far ahead I saw the hills of Hongkong Island and the ever-present fog banks out in the Pacific.

We crossed the East River that led down to Canton, and the bombers turned ninety degrees to the right, away from Hongkong—and we swept towards Canton. For again we were going where the enemy were not expecting us. The General was about to outguess the Japanese as always.

I could imagine the small aerial screen over Hongkong watching and waiting, while on the ground at Kai Tak in Kowloon, on Sanchau Island, at Tien Ho and White Cloud in Canton, the enemy Zeros were waiting to take off after we had passed Canton, to come and get us over Hongkong or to intercept us on the way home. We bored in towards our targets— shipping on the East River at Canton and at Whangpoo Docks. We had special reports that two freighters were unloading new Zeros and spare airplane engines at Canton that morning.

Just South of Tien Ho airdrome, we split the bomber formation, and one of the fighter echelons went with each of the three bomber flights, each with an assigned target. My flight stayed with the lead bomber formation, and I saw our target, an 8,000-ton freighter surrounded by many lighters, there in the river. The smoke from the single stack was lazily going straight up. Morgan's bombardier was bending tensely over his bomb-sight now, keeping the cross-hairs on the target. I knew the A.F.C.E. was flying the lead bomber as we went on the straight bombing run towards our target.

I saw the string of bombs bracket the freighter perfectly, and later photos showed four direct hits from the first flight. The lighters around the doomed vessel were blown high and in all directions. Down to our left, Holloway, escorting the other flight whose target was a freighter, saw the vessel hit, then saw the smoke. Alison had his fighter force with the third flight; they had already bombed the docks and were fighting Zeros from getting to the bombers. I heard the bomber commanders call that bombs were away, and give orders to close the bomb-bay doors. As we wheeled over our targets, turned from West to North, and started home, I heard Morgan call "California," which was my signal that he was on the way home with the big ships.

Then, under the lead flight of bombers, I saw the enemy fighters coming up and I knew we had them. All the enemy planes were below us, climbing steeply for the bellies of the bombers. They had waited on the ground too long, had waited for us to pass Canton and go on to Hongkong. Now we had every advantage. General Chennault had foxed them again, and I had an idea that we were in for a profitable day.

I called directions to the Group as the bombers closed up and I started down. Alison was even now shooting down Zeros around the last formation of bombers. Holloway called to one of his elements to take the climbing Jap ships and return to formation. We were fighting this battle like a business, and we were going to keep together until every bomber was safely on the way home to lunch at Kweilin.

About four thousand feet under the leading three bombers I could see the first of the steeply climbing Japs. As I dove closer I could even see the white smoke rings that formed in front of his wings, and I knew from experience that he was firing his cannon at the bottom of the bombers as he climbed. The Jap carries in his wings smaller guns that have tracers; he gets these on his target, then shoots his cannon. As I took this first enemy ship, I had one moment of panic: it seemed very close to Morgan's lead ship—maybe I couldn't get to it in time. Then my dive took me right up above the Zero, between him and the bomber. I held my fire until the last two hundred yards, and shot the Zero down with a two-second burst. It exploded within a hundred yards of the ship in which Colonel Cooper was—he confirmed it for me later. But as I pulled up and looked for the next enemy ship, I recalled that I had almost made my joking threat too good. For the Jap had got too close to the bomber in which the Chief of Staff was riding.

My wing man stayed with me and we fired on the second Zero together. I could see his tracers coming from my right. I closed in with a full-deflection shot and held a burst ahead of the next enemy ship. He climbed on up towards the bombers and flew right through my tracers. His ship turned in a slow, almost too deliberate half-loop, stalled out, then dove straight down. At first I thought that I had fired too far in front of him and he'd turned to evade the fire; then, as I watched the speeding ship go straight into the hills between Tien Ho field and White Cloud, I knew I had shot the pilot. The ship did not burn until it crashed.

I fired at six Japanese fighters so fast that I didn't see what happened to any of them. You get a snap shot and then the Zero is gone, rolling over, or you're turning for another one, or you're getting your nose down to make sure that you never lose your speed and too much altitude when you're fighting those highly maneuverable ships.

One other I saw trailing smoke as he rolled over, but I didn't get to see him catch fire or crash. The bombers had outrun our dog-fight and were going down-hill fast for Kweilin. I heard Morgan call that chow was on, and I knew he considered his bombers safe. I called and told Captain Goss to escort the bombers to base.

The others of us broke away looking for straggling Japs. I took my flight over towards White Cloud airdrome, where ack-ack was so heavy that it was just about making the sky black. I guess I must have thought of Lieutenant Daniels—for I dove. I hadn't heard a single P-40 call for help; so I was fairly confident that we had won the battle. My wing man must have got lost in my dive, for I went down towards the anti-aircraft pretty fast.

From the altitude at which I had started my dive I couldn't

see what was on White Cloud field, but as I pulled half out of the four-hundred-mile-an-hour dive over the hills South of the airdrome, I saw an airplane. It was a big ship, which I soon saw had three engines. The door was open, and I think men were hurrying to get in or out. Two cars were driving away from the ship. Even at my speed I tried a burst at the tri-motored Junkers 52, but I saw the tracers go short, and when I got closer I could see the dust far to the left of the target. My speed was so great that I couldn't hold enough pressure on the rudder steadily for accurate shooting. But I must have gotten a few tracers in, for as I swept low over the ship it seemed that dust was churned up all about.

Turning low, I came back for a better shot. The ack-ack was so thick that I nearly forgot and turned back. After all, that which I could see had already exploded, and if I wasn't hit yet I was as well off one place as another. My burst caught the engines of the transport, which I could see now were running. Uniformed passengers were jumping out of the door. I turned steeply and fired on the door, then into the fuselage. The ship was smoking, and the engines had either been shot up or had been cut off, for they had stopped.

My engine missed several times, as it had done from some poor gasoline earlier in the flight, and I decided to let well enough alone and get away from White Cloud. Keeping just about down in the rice, I went straight North to the river. With the engine missing every now and then, I spent a miserable few minutes that seemed like a year until I got out of Jap territory. "Why is it," I asked myself, "I always do some fool thing and wind up in these attacks coming home solo?" I always hated to think of an engine failing and of myself captured near a Jap field that I'd just strafed. Especially where I'd just shot up a transport-load of "brass hats."

In thirty miles I crossed the Wen-Kiang and was in friendly territory. I heard Holloway call that he'd slipped up on a twin-engine Jap I-45 that had been trailing the bombers home and had shot it down. I laughed, for Bruce was always getting to slip up on some luckless Jap and blow him up. Several weeks before, we'd kidded him about two Jap biplanes he'd shot down in Indo-China. Everybody said they were going to let him paint half a flag on the side of his ship to represent the victory—and besides he was going to have Vichy France mad at him for shooting down those Frenchmen, and he'd be sure to get a letter from Washington to answer by endorsement. Later it came out that the ships were flown by Japs, and that they were being trained in these ships in Indo-China. It was just kidding, anyway, for Bruce Holloway was one of the most eager pilots in all the world and was running up a good score.

I landed at Kweilin, and while I counted the holes in my plane I watched for the last of the fighters to come in—half trying to count the twenty-seven holes from the ground-fire around White Cloud and half trying to sweat all the twenty-two fighters back. All the bombers were in and were being serviced and bombed up again. Eighteen fighters finally came in, and we worried until we got word that the other four were at another field and would be back later in the afternoon.

We made our reports to the General and we knew he was pleased. Out of 45 Zeros that had come up for us over Canton we had shot down 29 that were confirmed. Alison had stayed back there for twenty-five minutes and definitely had seen that the two freighters loaded with Zeros and engines had been sunk. The nature of the cargo was eventually confirmed. Three weeks later we dive-bombed the salvage parties that were diligently trying to raise the sunken freighters. Evidently there had been something very valuable to the Japanese on the two big vessels.

That afternoon we bombed Hongay for the second time, making nine raids in six days. Now we were worn out, gasoline was getting low, and the enemy were making heavier movements in western Yunnan.

We went on back to Kunming. Sometimes I wonder if the Jap ever did find out where General Chennault was going. Years after maybe they'd still be flying that patrol over Hongkong, waiting for the attack that we were supposed to make.

33
The "Chip" of Invincibility

As WE CARRIED out the long missions into Burma in the days that followed, I thought about how the spirit of our air warfare had changed from what I had heard about and read of the last World War in the air. There had been an element of knighthood depicted in that first struggle in the skies. Now I thought I knew why.

Back there the pilots had been carefully hand-picked. They were the adventurous, devil-may-care hot-bloods, like those boys who had been the Confederate cavalry in the War Between the States. More than likely when they fired at another pilot and then saw that their victim's guns were "jammed," they may have "saluted" and dived away, unwilling to destroy the helpless enemy. But this was a different type of war, against a race of fanatics, who had been repressed for so long in their warped minds that they were barbaric madmen.

From what I had already seen, I knew that the Japanese soldier and the Japanese war machine were not out merely to beat us in war—they were out to EXTERMINATE US, even to the extent of killing our pilots whom they captured as prisoners. And we knew that this had been done even in April of 1942. We learned of it again after the Hongkong raid. They would never give up—they had gone all-out in a war to the bitter end. There was no romance about it. We knew that if we were shot down and were not killed in the crash, or if we were captured, we would most certainly be tortured and executed. That's why all of us never considered the element of capture. Get out of the crash-landing shooting, we always said.

Another theory was that the realization that you had strafed enemy ground troops, shot down Japanese pilots, strafed troops getting out of an enemy transport, or even killed Japanese satellites, would come back to you at night, and you'd wake up in horror at having "blood on your hands." To that I say "Nuts." I never knew a pilot who thought about it. All the pilots I ever saw were so happy over even their first enemy kill that I began right off to know that we were not the soft race we had been charged with being early in the war. Personally, every time I cut Japanese columns to pieces in Burma, strafed Japs swimming from boats we were sinking, or blew a Jap pilot right out of the sky, I just laughed in my heart and knew that I had stepped a day closer to victory.

Later, when the newness of combat had worn off, I used to watch a Japanese pilot come towards me on a head-on run, picking me out, I guess, because I was leading the Group. I'd get my sights on him and yell, perhaps a bit hysterically: "You poor sucker, with my six Fifties that out-range your short-range little cannons that jam lots of times, I'm going to blow you apart before you get close enough to hit me!" Overconfidence, perhaps, for I didn't get every one who came at me, and I took lots of hits in my own ship—even had to dive away sometimes when two came on me at once. But I'm still here, and from thirteen to twenty-two Jap pilots who fought against me are dead.

That's the "chip" of invincibility that I carried on my shoulder into combat. That's the combat spirit that a fighter pilot must have who fights alone in a little ship where he's the loneliest person in the world—sometimes. But do you know what makes the pilot understand that he's got to be better than the Japanese, makes him know what we are fighting for, gives him faith that in the end, when we're all properly trained and equipped, we'll be the best Air Force in all the world? It's the understanding that comes when you've seen the rest of the world, when you've glimpsed the filth and corruption of all the hell-holes that Americans are fighting in today, when you've had the blood and brains of your brother officers or of your soldiers splashed in your face by an enemy bomb. Then you know—for it's seared on your soul—that we have the best country in the Universe, whether it's run by the Democrats or the Republicans or the new party that springs up tomorrow.

You know that you have everything to live for, and that the Jap has everything to die for. That's his only hope of reaching the heaven that we already have.

Yes, they are suicide pilots; at times they will try to ram your plane, or will dive their ships into our carriers. I've seen a Japanese dive low over Hengyang and circle while they shot at him with everything on the field and we shot at him with every ship above the field. But he flew his ship in a slow circle, as if he were blinded and couldn't see, or were only partly conscious. Then, with a half roll at barely three hundred feet, he dove his plane into the only building on the field—our thatched-roof alert shack, which burned with the Jap in his ship. When the wreckage had cooled enough we finally pulled his charred body out—and by his side was his Samurai sword, and through his body the doctor found one lone bullet-hole, severing his spinal cord near the small of the back. He had been able to move his hands but not his feet. But with his last consciousness he had picked out one more object on our field to destroy for the gods of the Shinto Shrine.

But they have fear too. Don't think they're supermen, for I assure you they're not. They're little, warped-brained savages, with an inbred persecution complex—but they have fear, like any one else. Their fear is worse, for there's that phobia of having nothing to live for—the inferiority-complex they try to overcome.

I once saw that fear on the face of a Japanese pilot when he knew he was going to die, and it did me lots of good. I told of it many times to youngsters in my Group and it always made them feel better to know that the Japs were afraid when they met them—probably more afraid than we were. Oh, the Jap is a wonderful pilot when he meets no or little opposition. They come in over undefended Chinese cities and loop and roll and zoom, shooting at the helpless pedestrians while arrogantly flying inverted on their backs. But when they meet good American fighters, with pilots who know how to fight them, they are the most anxious people I've ever met to leave our territory and go "hell for leather" towards Japan.

One day I flew up very close to a lone Jap pilot during a fight near Kweilin. I placed my sights right where his wing joined the fuselage of the 1-97-2 and steadily squeezed a burst from two hundred yards, holding the trigger down while I moved into closer range. Then I swerved out from behind the enemy ship, expecting it to stream fire and perhaps explode. I had seen pieces come off, and I had seen the canopy glass turn to a fine, shining powder that sparkled in the slipstream as the ship nosed almost straight up. But when it didn't burn, I skidded back across its tail, first with a look to my rear quarter lest I be surprised.

I saw into the cockpit. The canopy had been shot away and I could see the Jap's face—and on it was a look of terror such as I had never seen before. The realization went through me with such force that as I nosed down to fire again I nearly cut the tail from the Jap fighter with my prop. Then I savagely held a long burst from less than fifty yards while I shot the ship to pieces. Even after the enemy plane had fallen and I had flown through the debris, I found that I was continuing to fire at the empty heavens, for I had learned to hate also.

No, the Jap is far from a superman. But we must never again belittle the fanaticism of the Japanese. They are as dangerous as mad dogs. They think they will win—and they can if we continue to under-estimate them.

Strange things happen in the air, strange as the fiction of the ages. Six of us shot into a ship that detached itself from one of the circling Japanese "circuses" we encountered one day East of Hengyang. When you meet the Jap in his larger-numbered formation, he at once goes into the circling technique that Baron von Richthofen made famous in the last war. This "circus" gradually moves in on or away from their objective as a defensive maneuver, for in it the ship beyond protects the tail of the one in front. Our tactics were to dive through the "squirrel cage" and get snap shots at as many ships as we could, but keep our speed to prevent their getting on our tails.

It was in one of these attacks that this lone Jap Zero left the protection of his other ships and began to do aerobatics—sloppy loops, wingovers, stalls, and then another loop. Thinking it was a trick, we were wary; but after two of our pilots had made passes on it, two more of us went down towards it.

As I kept getting closer and closer to the enemy plane I could see that the pilot was evidently hurt, but when I crossed the top of the strange-acting plane I saw that he was leaning forward over the stick control, obviously dead.

As the speed of the dive would build up pressures on the tail surfaces, the nose would rise, for a Jap ship is rigged that way. As the ship climbed more steeply, the pilot's upper body swung to the back of the seat in the normal position and the plane made a sloppy loop.

For several minutes we watched the pilotless Zero in fascination. From 16,000 feet a ship that is shot down can dive into the ground in a few seconds—it can even spin in from an explosion in a little longer than that; but we watched this plane for twice the time that it would normally have taken. It worked closer and closer to the ground over the same area, as it lost altitude gradually in the maneuvers. Then, after the longest wait that I can remember having gone through in the air, in one of its dives from a loop it struck the hills below and burned. We could have burned it with a long burst many times during the minutes of our watching, but I imagine we were all spellbound at the spectacle.

No one spoke for several minutes as we turned back to Hengyang. Then some call over the radio broke the spell, and we just marked the Jap off as another confirmed Zero—another "good" Jap.

Over in Yunnan we fought the Japs a few times in Burma and had the sadness of another military funeral. Those moments in the Buddhist burial grounds were the hardest in China. As the Chaplain read the prayer and the flag-draped casket was lowered into the red earth of Yunnan, a small formation, with slow-turning engines that gave forth a muffled sound, would fly over the grave. There would be one vacant niche in the evenly spaced fighters, in honor of the brother airman who would fly no more.

After eight months in combat I was sent with five other pilots to ferry six new P-40K's over from the air base at Karachi. During our wait for the planes to be ready for combat, we were permitted to go to Bombay for the detached service. There, in the splendor of the Hotel Taj Mahal, we had a glorious time. In fact, it became very hard to realize that a war was going on over in Burma and China, as we looked at the night clubs from Malabar Hill and from inside them too, at the horse-races for the Aga Khan's Purse—and at all the things that we had forgotten to remember.

The return across India was a happy one, for we were ferrying new and higher-powered ships back to the war, and all of us were eager to try them out in combat. From Assam we took the old familiar trail that I used to fly with the transports, and it felt especially good to look around and see those friendly looking P-40's along with me over the Burma Road where I had, in earlier months, been compelled to fly alone. The sharkmouths had not yet been painted on, but the silhouettes of the new fighters looked friendly nevertheless.

A fast trip over the five hundred miles from Assam is like this:

We're off from our base and heading 118 degrees across the twelve-thousand-foot Naga Hills to the first check-point, where the upper fork of the Chindwin forms the likeness of a shamrock. Up to our left now, from the altitude of eighteen thousand that we've attained so effortlessly with the new ships, can be seen the higher snow-capped peaks of Tibet and Chinese Turkestan. Down below us the valley of the Irrawaddy is low and green, but forbidding nonetheless. Ahead, as we cross the "Y" in the little known "triangle of the Irrawaddy," we see the real hills of the "hump" begin to rise. Snow-capped peaks everywhere. Our map reads that our highest peak is going to be 15,800 feet; yet we well know from experience that we've tried it many times and we need to be very sure that we are at 18,000 to clear the mountains from the Irrawaddy to Tali Lake.

Below us are the villages of the Miaows. We climb to 25,000 feet to test the "suped-up" ships, and a smile comes to our faces under the oxygen masks—for this is going to surprise the Jap. We're going over the Mekong now, and from the time that has elapsed we've certainly picked up a tail wind—must be making over three hundred. The gorge of the Mekong runs like a gash in the sinister country of Burma to the South, and we know it goes on and on towards Saigon and the sea.

It's barely twenty miles to the Salween, and we make it so quickly that we begin to doubt that the other river had been the Mekong. Our ground speed is well over three hundred as we see Lake Tali and start the down-hill run to Kunming. Now we catch the first glimpse of the Burma Road, North of Yunnanyi, and soon we see the small lake that is near our field at that town. The mountains to the North are very high, and we know they get higher and higher and stretch almost without break to the East and the Pacific. We see the hairpin turns of the Burma

Road near Tsuyung, and know that we're nearly home from the Taj Mahal and India.

We dive over the field of our headquarters just one hour and twenty-five minutes from the time we took off from Assam, five hundred miles away. I can tell by the smiles on the faces of the other men in the flight that we're all thinking the same thing: We have bad medicine for the Jap packed into the increased horsepower of these new "Kays"—our Warhawks. They are the latest of the P-40 series, and coming to us this time of year we look upon them as Christmas presents from the States.

The P-40 was in production when the war began. Then the decks were definitely stacked against us, and everything was in favor of the enemy. During the past year of our war these ships produced as no other fighter plane did, for they were serving on every front. Any pilot who actually fought the Axis enemies in the P-40 Tomahawks, Kittyhawks, or Warhawks will tell you they are tough and dependable. They will dive with the best of projectiles—including a bomb. All of us hope that the best fighter plane has not been produced, but we know that America will develop it.

In the meantime, through those lean months when America had to fight on many fronts with so little, the glorious P-40 series paid off when the chips were down in a ratio of between twelve and fifteen to one—twelve to fifteen enemy ships for every one of ours lost.

Some day, when the war is over and our sturdy American engines driving great American ships have won victory with air power, I hope and pray—with all fighter pilots who have faced our enemies in aerial combat, from the hot sands of Libya to the cold tundra of the Aleutians, from the jungle heat of Guadalcanal to those torrential rains of the Burmese Monsoons—that some understanding group of citizens will go to Kitty Hawk, North Carolina. There, beside the statue that commemorates the first flight of the Wright Brothers, I hope that they will build a monument to the Curtiss P-40 with its Allison Engine.

34

Goose for Christmas

AND NOW, with a few minor battles in the air, we saw Christmas in China draw near, and I couldn't help wishing for fast action somewhere. After all, there's only one place a person wants to be at Christmas time, and that place for all of us was far away.

I took off from Kunming one day just before Christmas to inspect the warning net in western Yunnan. It didn't take long to find out that it was very inefficient near the Burma border, where a steady influx of fifth-columnists and Japanese money was filtering across the Salween. Even then I knew that instead of getting the Chinese officers who were in charge of the net to investigate, it would be much better to have a few engagements with the Jap over the failing net-area. There was no tonic like a few burning Jap planes over the country to improve the functioning of the air-raid warning net. It looked as if we'd get the chance very soon, too, for the field in western Yunnan had been selected by the newly formed Air Transport Command, which was superseding the Ferry Command, as the Eastern terminus of the route to China.

For the purpose of security in future operations, I will not name our base in western Yunnan. But there was a big turquoise-blue lake less than ten miles away which the General and I called Yeching. To us that meant "good hunting," for ducks and geese abounded. The landmark for our base was just one of the many lakes in Yunnan.

Next morning I went out on Lake Yeching, and from the bow of a native sampan I soon shot eighteen of the biggest geese I had ever seen. Even if we were remote from the loved ones at home, we'd have meat for Christmas dinner that was filled with the vitamins we needed.

I had hurried back to the field before taking off for Kunming with my report on the efficiency of the warning net, and was taking pictures of some little mongol-appearing Miaows who were holding my geese aloft—when we had an air raid alert. There was heavy engine-noise from the reporting stations over towards Burma. We tossed the eighteen geese into the baggage compartment, winding their necks around among the conduits of the radio so that the cargo wouldn't shift, and I took off for Kunming. Then as I heard more reports from the Southwest, I turned South, joined the other fighters on patrol, and looked for the enemy. In about forty-five minutes we spread out to cover more territory, and I caught sight of two enemy planes—Zeros I thought, at first sight. I called to the others and attacked. Even as I approached the Japs I knew they were too slow and too large for Zeros. Then I saw that they were single-engine reconnaissance-bombers. I caught the rear one and gave it a short burst, keeping my eye on the other. The first one went down with most of one wing gone. The next I chased down every valley on the Mekong, getting in several good shots, but I never did see him go down or crash. From the evidence of the thin trail of smoke that I last saw coming from it as I dove and circled to look around again, I claimed it as a "probable." The first one I had confirmed as a "certain." The others in our patrol engaged four other planes and probably shot down two of them. The General had been correct as usual—the Japs were keeping the end of the ferry route under close surveillance.

When I told the General about my victory, which had been my twelfth confirmed enemy ship, and told him about the geese in the baggage compartment, he said he didn't know whether to congratulate me for the meat or for the Japs—at that time of the year Christmas dinner was more important. As for myself, I told him, I hadn't worried so much about the Japs' shooting me down as I had about their getting a lucky burst through my fuselage and ruining all that good meat with their explosive bullets. Besides, in the maneuvers of combat, if the necks of all those geese had jammed the controls and had made me spin in, the Chinese who found me would have talked a long time about the pilot whom they'd found dead with feathers all over him.

Christmas night, while we were enjoying the geese, George Hazelett came in with his Squadron to report that the Japs had bombed our base near Lake Yeching with eighteen ships on that afternoon of Christmas Day, and the first warning the field had was the sight of the enemy bombers in the clear blue Yunnan sky. Luckily the bombing had missed the field and no ships were damaged, but many Chinese in the village had been killed. Definitely the warning net in western Yunnan made the operation of the Transport Command at Yeching hazardous. I could tell by the General's face that he had some plans he would tell me about in private.

The General had been sick with a cold over Christmas and had a fever that night, when he told me what he had to do at Yeching. At dawn the next morning—December 26th in China, but actually Christmas Day in America—I took off with full instructions. When I left, the Doctor told me General Chennault was running a temperature of 103. All of us were worried about him, and knew that the defeats on Christmas Day hadn't helped his spirits.

As I flew West towards Yeching, 145 miles away, in the half light I saw the coolies carrying drums of gasoline on wheelbarrows up the Burma Road. Some of these I knew would go on through Kunming to Chungking, 390 miles away by air. Trundling these crude wooden-wheeled vehicles of the ages gone-by, these patient workers would require seventy days of constant effort, at their dogged trot, to reach the capital at Chungking. The two-wheeled Peking carts with three drums would take a shorter time—44 days. I saw coolie boys plowing in the rice paddies halfway up the sides of the mountains— paddies built like steps from the top of the hill to the valley, so that the irrigation water could be used over and over. I laughed as I saw the ancient means of cultivation—the boy, standing with his feet on the wooden scraper, was using his own weight to make it scratch the mud, but was holding on to the water buffalo, with his hand gripping the tail of the ponderous animal.

Again I found myself pitying these earthbound creatures. I said to myself: "When you reach the end of that paddy, I'll be many miles from here." I suppose I get arrogant like that because I'm sitting up there with six good American fifty-calibre guns in front of me charged and ready, and off on a mission bound to be exciting. It didn't matter now that some other day I might be letting down somewhere around there in bad weather, with night coming on or with my fuel running low; I might see that same coolie boy and might reflect how lucky he was to know his whereabouts and not be on the point of cracking up a good airplane that couldn't be replaced. For a moment might come when I would give anything just to be able to ask in sign language: "Where is the Burma Road?" or "Is Yunnanfu this way?"

35
How to Cure a General

LANDING at the threatened airdrome, I put the General's plan into immediate effect.

I commandeered the necessary transportation on Yeching field and placed it ready for the instant movement of pilots to their dispersed fighters, which were scattered to all parts of the airdrome. The P-40's were pointed in the direction of a run for immediate take-off. All this was to save even the barest minimum of lost time, for when the alert came we would have to move fast and furious. Every one of the thirty pilots was kept on alert, and constant patrols were begun at dawn. We sent two ships above the field at seven o'clock and doubled the number at nine. At eleven o'clock we doubled again and continually had eight high in the sky.

The Jap had attacked the day before at 2:35 in the afternoon, or 14:35. The General had told me many times of the propensity of the Japanese for the exact duplication of former military operations. We were going to get gradually more vigilant and stronger above the field for the expected blow. At the same time we were going as far as was commensurate with safety to conserve the invaluable aviation gasoline. Most of the fighters kept right over the field or slightly away in the direction of the expected attack from Burmese bases. Four fighters began to patrol from Yeching to the Mekong, on course to Lashio and seventy miles from where we were waiting.

At two o'clock I sent all planes into the sky except mine. I sat in that on the ground, listening for Harry Pike's expected report from his patrol to the Mekong River. I was within shouting distance of the ground radio operator, who would tell me of any developments on the weak-functioning warning net. The Jap would come today, I knew, between two and four—that's 14:00 to 16:00 hours.

At 14:54 I saw the radio operator wildly running for my ship. He yelled, "Report from W-7 says heavy engine noise coming this way—the report is right recent." I was already energizing my starter when Harry Pike called excitedly: "Here they come—fighters and bombers—I'm just East of the river." I knew then that the Japs were close to fifty miles away; we had all we could do to get set and be waiting for them.

When Pike called in, as I got the engine started, I heard that the Japs were at seventeen thousand, and I called to him to take the fighters, for I hoped by that move to make the bombers come in unescorted. From Yeching at its level of 6500 feet I was climbing with full gun, climbing for all the altitude I could grab. I watched the temperature but drew all the boost I could without detonating too badly. At exactly three o'clock I reached twenty thousand feet and picked up most of my Group, which today was made up of Hazelett's Squadron.

Just six minutes from the time I had given the ship the gun, I saw flashes reflected by Japanese windshields in the sun. They weren't far away, but I grinned—for they were below us. I heard from the chatter on our frequency that there was a fight going on towards where Pike had seen the formation cross the river. As the enemy ships materialized on the horizon, I knew that Pike had done his job well, for there was only one fighter with the bombers as escort—one fighter with nine heavy bombers. I think I knew then that we were going to make it tough for the Japs.

I called for the attack, in order to get the enemy before he could bomb the field. As I dove for the attack that I had always longed for, I saw one P-40 take the lone Zero head-on and shoot it down, and I knew from the way the shark-nosed ship pulled up in his chandelle of glory that Dallas Clinger had become an ace with his fifth enemy ship.

We made the attack from three directions simultaneously. Lieutenant Couch led his ships on a stern attack that I did not see, for I was diving on the course of the bombers from the flank where the low sun was. I was going in for a full-deflection shot from out of that sun, for I had planned this method of how I wanted to attack a bomber formation long ago. On my wings were six fighters in two ship elements. In Couch's flight were four fighters, and Hazelett had four coming from above the Japs on the other flank.

I had to dive from 20,000 feet to 17,000 feet to get on the level with the enemy formation, and when I got there I had plenty of excess speed over the Japs. I passed them rapidly from out of their range, but could see their tracers curving short of my flight. When I had over-run them a thousand yards, I turned right into the bombers and we went after the three Vee's of Mitsubishi bombers. By being on the same level with them I'm sure we caused part of the enemy formation to blanket out some of their own ships from firing at us. I opened fire from six hundred yards and led the enemy leader by at least a hundred yards; it must have been just right, for the tracers seemed to go into the top of the wing. I just held the trigger down and kept going into the sides of the Japs—they blossomed out of the sky at me, growing larger and larger, "mushrooming" in my windshield. As the bombers passed by, my bullets were raking them with full-deflection shots, and as fast as my formation turned the other five men were doing the same. I saw the lead bomber climb a little, then settle back towards the formation with one wing down.

As I saw the second Jap in front of me—the left wing man of the leader—I realized I'd have to dive under the enemy very soon or I'd run into them. Things hit my ship now, and with noise like a wing coming off, the side glass of my windshield was shot out. I was three hundred to two hundred yards from the second bomber when I got my long burst into it. There was a flash ahead, and I dove as fast as I could shove the nose down. As I went under the smoke and orange flame, I thought that the Jap I was shooting at had caught fire, but as I pulled around, back to the direction the formation had been going, and climbed, I saw what had happened.

There was only smoke above, and the formation had broken, for I knew the bomber had exploded—the bombs had been detonated by the fifty-calibre fire. Behind, over the trail the Japs had come, were four plumes of smoke where their bombers were going down. Below there were bomb bursts all over the paddy fields where bombs had been jettisoned in the unanticipated interception. I pulled up behind one of the lone bombers that I could see and began to shoot at it methodically from long range. Over on the left were three more, and I saw P-40's making passes at them. Over the radio I could hear happy American English, with unauthorized swear words aimed at the Jap that the individual pilot was shooting at, and by the tone of the pilots I knew that we were winning this battle and that the General was also going to be very happy.

From 800 yards I'd squeeze out a short burst at one engine, then skid over and aim carefully at the other engine and throw out another short burst. The Jap ship was diving with all the speed he could get, but the P-40 kept moving up. I think all their ammunition was gone, for I saw no tracers. In my second burst on the right engine I saw some gray smoke—thin, like gasoline overflowing a tank and blowing back into the slipstream. The next time I came over behind that engine from closer range I saw two red dots near the engine, two dots that became fire. The flame ran to the engine and to the fuselage, but by that time I was over shooting at the other engine again. I last saw the bomber diving, with flames that were orange against the green of the mountains below.

There were no more bombers to be seen, but I saw seven P-40's. Clinger came over and got on my wing; as I recognized his ship I slid my hatch-cover back and waved at him. Even before we landed I thought that we had gotten all the bombers. As we circled the field, with me trying to dodge the cold air that was knifing through the hole in my windshield and bringing a particle of glass against my face every now and then, I realized why we still had to wear goggles in fighter ships in combat. Below on the Yunnan hills, I saw eight forest-fires that could have been started only by burning airplane wrecks, for they had not been there when I took off.

I kept some of the planes up for top-cover while we landed those that were shot up or low on fuel. Later, when I had the combat reports made out before the pilots could talk the battle over between them, the "certains" out of the nineteen that had come in—nine fighters and nine bombers and one observation plane—were fifteen. But from the patrol that had been at the Mekong and from the "probables," we knew that we had not let one Jap escape from the December 26th attempted bombing of Yeching. I felt so good I wanted to radio the General, but I waited until we checked up on those who were missing, so that I could go and tell him in person.

Our victory had not been without loss. Lieutenant Couch, who had led the rear attack on the bombers, had failed to return. His wing man had seen him pulling up over the tail of the bomber formation after shooting down one of the Japs; but they had concentrated their fire on him and had shot him down in flames. No one knew whether or not the Carolina pilot had gotten out. In the speed with which that attack had moved you didn't have time to see parachutes opening.

Another pilot, Lieutenant Mooney, had been seen to shoot one bomber down, and then, in another head-on attack, had either collided with another of the enemy or had exploded it so close to his own ship that the observing pilot had not been able to see Mooney's P-40 again.

Sending out the usual search parties, I took off into a setting sun for Kunming. My heart was heavy with the loss of two fine pilots, but there was still hope that they had gotten out. And at the same time my spirits were singing with victory.

I landed at headquarters in the dark and went to the General's house. Over the rough road that led there, my mind was on the speedy happenings since I had driven out to the ship that morning. Then I drove past the guard at the gate, who smiled and yelled, "AVG—ding-hao." I called a cheerful greeting to him, for everything was good now. There was a full moon rising in the sky—a "bombing moon," the Chinese call it —and the cedar trees around the house that the Gissimo had built for the General were casting long shadows in its light.

I tossed my flying gear on the bed in my room and hurried to the General. I saw "Gunboat" the houseboy coming out of the General's corner room. He said softly, "General still feel pretty bad." I went in.

General Chennault was in bed, propped up by pillows. He glanced up from a map and looked at me. "Well, Scotty," he said, "I hear there was a fight over Yeching this afternoon and I see blood on your face, so I know you made contact. What happened?"

Trying to look real stern, I told the General that nineteen Japs had come in, just as he said they would, at the same time as the day before—only this time we were higher than they and were waiting for them. "General," I said, with a tremor of pride in my voice, "we shot 'em all down."

The General was looking more like a well man every moment. He asked about our losses and I told him about the two missing pilots. He thought a minute, then started to get up.

"Scotty, if you'll look over behind you in that pretty box, you'll find a bottle of Haig & Haig, pinch bottle, that the Soong sisters sent us for Christmas. We're going to open that and celebrate."

We were celebrating when Doctor Tom Gentry came back and began to ask the General why he wasn't in bed with his fever. The General looked so happy, I guess, that Doctor took his temperature again. Then he gave me a funny look. "Normal," he said. "Sometimes I think if you all shot down a few Japs every day, the General would even get to where he could hear as well as he could when he was a boy in Louisiana."

The General filled his glass again and handed me the bottle. Then he raised the glass at me and said, "How!" We drank to the victory of the afternoon.

36
No Use Fooling Ourselves

EARLY NEXT DAY I went over again with Holloway, just in case the Jap came again. We learned that the victory had not been without cost. Lieutenant Mooney had been found dead, close to the wrecks of two burned airplanes—a Mitsubishi Japanese bomber and his P-40. We now knew from the different stories of pilot witnesses that he had gone down on the tail of one Japanese bomber against the withering fire of several planes. He had shot one down, but had evidently been hit badly himself, for his plane was smoking. Mooney's speed had carried him on past the enemy formation, and he had come back for a head-on run against a single plane after the formation had been broken. They had either flown together because of Mooney's determination to keep coming until he shot the Jap down, or Mooney had been badly hit. The opinion of two of the witnesses was that he had flown his fighter into the Jap. Perhaps when the chips were down, others besides the Japanese could take just one more enemy with them when the end was near.

We rolled Lieutenant Mooney in his chute and placed him aboard the transport for Kunming. There would be another funeral in the graveyard of the 23rd Group, with a formation, and the Chinese bugler blowing taps.

Couch had had better luck and was in the hospital. I went up to see him as soon as we assigned the "aerial umbrella" of P-40's that were going to patrol the skies for a recurrence of the Jap raids. Lieutenant Couch was badly burned but was resting easy. He told me that the bomber he had fired on had begun to smoke and he'd taken his plane in very close to make certain that the Jap burned. This had been a mistake, he knew, for the guns of three or more of the enemy had converged on his fighter, and when he dove out he was on fire; the flames streaming out of his engine covered the canopy. From some reflex action he had done the wrong thing again—he'd rolled the canopy open and the flames had been sucked into the cockpit, into his face. He had already unlatched his safety belt in order to jump, and in dodging the flames he was thrown about in the pilot's compartment, though he must evidently have got the canopy closed again, for the flames were held out by the glass.

Couch went through long seconds of torture as he was thrown about in the bottom of the spinning plane—the rudder pedals struck his burned face, and sharp projections hurt his shoulders and back. He struggled to his feet again, rolled the hatch back and was thrown out and away from the burning ship.

For Couch, however, the peril was only beginning. He told me that his chute opened with a "crack," and at the same time he heard his P-40 strike the top of a mountain, just under him. He was so close to the wreck that he was burned again as his chute drifted over the burning plane. He struck the ground heavily, just down-wind of the fire. As he fought back to consciousness, he could hear the roaring of the flames in the underbrush; the wind was blowing them towards his position. With a desperate effort, for the force with which he'd hit the ground had almost paralyzed his legs and arms, he somehow wrapped the opened chute about him. In the memory of half-consciousness, he knew that the fire had burned up to him and had destroyed part of his chute. He remembered that he felt fear when he heard the explosions of the pistol bullets that he carried as extra ammunition for his Army 45 in the seat-pack of his parachute, which was partly under him as he lay there. But the silk tightly wrapped about him must have kept him from breathing the flames, for his lungs were unharmed, and his burns were going to be all right.

Couch had been brought in by Chinese villagers who had

climbed the mountain and had worked all night to carry him in to the little Chinese hospital. I congratulated him on the good job he had done in his attack, and we took him down to be carried to our hospital in Kunming in the same transport that was to take Mooney's body. Tex Carleton was just landing on the field.

We tried the same defense to hold the advantage over the Japs if they should come again. During the first hours of the morning I flew low over the surrounding hills and saw the forest-fires set by the burning of the enemy planes that we had shot down the day before. From over one village West of Yeching, I could see the wreckage of the two ships that had flown together; the natives were standing about looking at what had come out of the skies. As I took my formation into the air and followed out the instructions the General had given me, I realized that for all practical purposes he was in the fighter with me; I was merely privileged to press the trigger and send the enemy into the ground and destruction. Yes, the General rode with me on those flights in more ways than one. If we kept following out his tactics we'd hold our ratio of twelve-to-one over the Japs as we battled them in China.

None of us in China was fooling himself—we knew that what little we had accomplished against the enemy would have very small bearing on the outcome of the conflict. But under General Chennault we had made the most of what we had. We had developed fighters with an urge for combat and the aggressive spirit of battle. We had bases in China from which to attack other bases in China, that were Japanese. With more equipment we could hold our bases and we could take the bases farther East, from which we could bomb the heart of Japan. And from them we could flank the enemy supply lines to the Solomons and Australia, and to Saigon—through which travelled the supplies to Burma. There was a supply problem, yes—but that problem, just like any other problem that developed in this war that had to be won, was a "must."

I expect I wouldn't have been much good in combat that day if it had come, for I was doing too much thinking, and fighter pilots can do only one thing at a time. Even when I landed and walked about among the Chinese dead from the Christmas Day bombing, I just kept on thinking.

That afternoon at two o'clock I got all our ships in the sky again. I rode on Holloway's wing over the top of them all, and we watched and waited for our interceptors on the Mekong to yell, "Here they come." Nothing happened—I guess General Chennault was right again. "You destroyed their group yesterday," he had said that morning. "We've got them worried, and they'll have to wait for their long supply line around to Burma to send some more planes."

When the sun got low on the blue hills of Yunnan, I began my thinking again. There was no use fooling ourselves—the situation in China was bad. All of China that was developed at all was in the hands of the Japanese. The Jap had worked with extreme foresight in preparing for this war, and the "heart of the octopus" was going to be hard to get at. But it could be done more easily from China—and it had to be done. These people, who with their stoical bravery had seen their cities bombed for over six years, deserved more help. We must equip their land armies, help train them—and give them air support.

I got to thinking about something that had occurred a few days before, when the Christmas season was approaching. I had just had my twelfth little Jap flag painted on the fuselage of my P-40K. Each of these represented a confirmed victory over the enemy, and my crew chief was as proud as I was. But I learned that day that some one else was sharing in that pride too.

On my way to work that day, driving from the General's house to the operations shack, I had seen a crowd of Chinese around my ship. They were sitting there silently and waiting, and I wondered at them. But the old American answer came to me—"We never can figure them out"—and I went on. As I passed by during the morning the Chinese people were still standing around my plane in the drizzling rain.

Finally I called for my crew chief and asked the meaning of the crowd. With a puzzled look, he replied that he didn't know: they had told him through an interpreter that they just wanted to sit there and wait for the pilot of the ship. I sent one of my interpreters to investigate and learned that they were really waiting for me; they had received permission from the Chinese Commandant to enter the field.

Some time later I walked over to where they were still standing in the slow rain. As I approached my ship they bowed as the Chinese do, by standing at what we would call "Attention" and nodding the head in respect. As I smiled at them—ragged children, old men and women, coolies from the fields, and several who I thought were school teachers—they raised their thumbs high towards me and yelled, "Ding-hao, ding-hao!" And they pointed with pride to my twelve flags.

They were cheering me, a foreigner, for my fights over

their homeland. I realized then, as tears mixed with the raindrops on my face, that they had bestowed on me an honor that exceeded in importance any medal that their country could have awarded me officially. I realized too that though the coast-lines of this country were in the hands of the enemy, though the lands to almost every side were hostile, the hearts of this people were free and would be free forever.

Later I learned that the group had walked all through the night before from a village twenty-odd kilometers away. Now they were on their way home again. I believe that if I had thought about a tribute like that in combat, I would have gone head-on into a Japanese fighter or closed to point-blank range with a bomber with a smile on my face.

The sun was going down now, even from our vantage point up there at twenty-five thousand, where Holloway and I were patrolling. We called to the other ships to land, and as we saw them go into the Lufbery circle and the rat-race that fighter pilots like to land from, Holloway rolled over and dove straight for the ground. I started to roll with him—then I turned back for one more look at the setting sun. Down on the earth, to those earthbound creatures, the sun was down. There the shadows of the approaching night covered the ground, but up here I could see above the mountains, and the sun still shone on my fighter. I pulled almost straight up in the steep climb that I like to make before diving home, and looked into the vivid blue of the Yunnan skies. Some verses were running through my thoughts. Against the drumming of the engine I heard my own voice repeating the words of another fighter pilot, John Magee, who had died with the RAF in the battle of Britain.

"Up, up the long delirious burning blue
I've topped the wind-swept heights with easy grace
Where never lark, or even eagle, flew,
And while with silent, lifting mind I've trod
The high untrespassed sanctity of space,
Put out my hand, and touched the face of God."

Enrichment for the spirit...

These books? Fiction.
Keep telling yourself that as you read.